FOOD, CONSUMPTION AND THE BODY IN CONTEMPORARY WOMEN'S FICTION

This study explores the subtle and complex significance of food and eating in contemporary women's fiction. Sarah Sceats reveals how preoccupations with food, its consumption and the body are central to the work of writers such as Doris Lessing, Angela Carter, Margaret Atwood and others. Through close analysis of their fiction, Sceats examines the multiple metaphors associated with these themes, making powerful connections between food and love, motherhood, sexual desire, self-identity and social behaviour. The activities surrounding food and its consumption (or non-consumption) embrace both the most intimate and the most thoroughly public aspects of our lives. The book draws on psychoanalytical, feminist and sociological theory to engage with a diverse range of issues, including chapters on cannibalism and eating disorders. This lively and accessible study demonstrates that feeding and eating are not simply fundamental to life but are inseparable from questions of gender, power and control.

SARAH SCEATS is Senior Lecturer in English at Kingston University, specialising in twentieth-century literature and women's writing.

FOOD, CONSUMPTION AND THE BODY IN CONTEMPORARY WOMEN'S FICTION

SARAH SCEATS

CAMBRIDGE
UNIVERSITY PRESS

PUBLISHED BY THE PRESS SYNDICATE OF THE UNIVERSITY OF CAMBRIDGE
The Pitt Building, Trumpington Street, Cambridge, United Kingdom

CAMBRIDGE UNIVERSITY PRESS
The Edinburgh Building, Cambridge CB2 2RU, UK   http://www.cup.cam.ac.uk
40 West 20th Street, New York, NY 10011–4211, USA   http://www.cup.org
10 Stamford Road, Oakleigh, Melbourne 3166, Australia
Ruiz de Alarcón 13, 28014 Madrid, Spain

First published 2000

Printed in the United Kingdom at the University Press, Cambridge

Typeface Baskerville MT 11/12½   *System* QuarkXPress™   [SE]

A catalogue record for this book is available from the British Library

Library of Congress Cataloguing in Publication data

Sceats, Sarah.
Food, consumption and the body in contemporary women's fiction/Sarah Sceats.
p.   cm.
Includes bibliographical references (p.) and index.
ISBN 0 521 66153 6
1. English fiction – Women authors – History and criticism.   2. Food in literature.
3. Women and literature – Great Britain – History – 20th century.
4. English fiction – 20th century – History and criticism.
5. Consumption (Economics) in literature.   6. Eating disorders in literature.
7. Body, Human, in literature.   8. Food habits in literature.   1. Title.

PR888.F65 S34 2000
823′.91409355 21 – dc21   99–042109

ISBN 0 521 66153 6 hardback

For my food-loving family

Contents

Acknowledgements

I am grateful for having had the opportunity to give papers on food and eating in fiction at the ESSE Conferences of 1993 (Bordeaux), 1995 (Glasgow) and 1997 (Debrecen) and at the Angela Carter *Fireworks* conference at York in 1996. Articles on food and power, Carter and appetite, and Lessing's writing of food and the body, on which parts of this book are based, were published as chapters in *Image and Power: Women in Fiction in the Twentieth Century*, eds. Sarah Sceats and Gail Cunningham (London and New York, NY: Longman, 1996); *The Infernal Desires of Angela Carter: Fiction, Femininity, Feminism*, eds. Joseph Bristow and Trev Lynn Broughton (London and New York, NY: Longman, 1997); and *Theme Parks, Rainforests and Sprouting Wastelands: European Essays on Theory and Performance in Contemporary British Fiction*, eds. Richard Todd and Luisa Flora (Amsterdam: Rodopi, 1999).

I wish to express my gratitude to Kingston University for research leave and to students of 'Consuming Passions' and 'Fictions of Appetite' for their enthusiasm and relish for the subject. I would like to thank my colleagues, friends and family for encouragement, advice and titbits of subject matter. Special mention goes to John Mepham and Elizabeth Maslen for reading early drafts and their helpful comments. Thanks above all to Doron Swade, to whom I owe so much.

Introduction

Eating is a fundamental activity. It is more or less the first thing we do, the primary source of pleasure and frustration, the arena of our earliest education and enculturation. Food is our centre, necessary for survival and inextricably connected with social function. What people eat, how and with whom, what they feel about food and why – even who they eat – are of crucial significance to an understanding of human society. The major significances of eating, however, are not biological but symbolic. According to psychoanalytic theory, formative feeding experiences are inscribed in the psyche; food and eating are essential to self-identity and are instrumental in the definition of family, class, ethnicity. These are not vague associations, for eating practices are highly specific: encoded in appetite, taste, ritual and ingestive etiquettes are unwritten rules and meanings, through which people communicate and are categorised within particular cultural contexts. The essential and necessary qualities of eating invest its surrounding activities with value, whether psychological, moral or affective.

The central role and multiple significances of food and eating entail a link with epistemological and ontological concerns. The prevalence of eating disorders in western culture indicates at least an insecurity about embodiment, the nature of being and the boundaries between the self and the world. Physical boundaries are clearly crucial to food and eating activities as substances pass into, and out of, the body. Uneaten food is 'other', part of the world outside, but its status changes as it is taken in to the mouth, is chewed, swallowed, digested. At what point does it become part of us? How do we locate activities such as tasting and regurgitation, and liminal substances such as spit and vomit? We live in a state of uncertainty about how much the self is influenced, changed, nourished or poisoned by what is taken in of the world, the extent to which people are defined by what they eat, or are affected by whoever provides their food. These questions are gendered, for both bodily and ego boundaries are

I

subject to varieties of influence and pressure, from the internalised patterns of tradition and custom to the physical disruptions of puberty and old age.

In interpersonal and social arenas, too, an enormous amount of uncertainty centres around food. Eating is an act of absolute trust, for how can we know what is in the food we are given? We cannot even be sure of the qualities of the food we provide, especially in the modern world of additives and modification. What food and its surrounding activities signify socially is equally problematic. The symbolic significances of specific foods and eating rituals in particular circumstances are established by various traditions and rituals, but even so, since these are often largely 'understood' rather than articulated, there is scope for error and confusion. As a means of exchange, whether prescribed or informal, eating and drinking may be saturated with meanings that are not at all necessarily apparent.

Women write about food and eating. Why should this be so? Women's bodies have the capacity to manufacture food for their infants which categorises them as feeders, and in western culture women have traditionally borne most of the burden of cooking for and nourishing others, with all that this implies of power and service. The caring, providing roles and their malign counterparts certainly contribute much mimetic content to women's writing. But women eat as well as cook, starve as well as serve, and contemporary fiction is as much concerned with women's appetites as their nurturing capacities. Some psychoanalytic theories suggest that because of girls' long period of attachment to the maternal figure, women have compelling boundary concerns as eaters. Cultural pressures in recent years have certainly made women particularly conscious of their body boundaries in relation to food and eating (or not eating). As this book illustrates, though, women's writing manifests far more diverse areas of engagement than such basic explanations suggest, ranging from explorations of female culinary sensuousness, creativity and authority in cooking, to the exercise of power or political responsibility through food and acts of eating, to the revisiting of earlier depictions of women's sexuality through appetite and eating, from Genesis onwards.

Although the specifics of food and eating are clearly defined by their cultural context, there is a temptation, especially in the light of psychoanalytic theories, to consider the functions of food as essential to all human beings and therefore somehow 'universal' or outside of cultural difference. Contemporary women's writing does not, in general, do this;

indeed it demonstrates both historical and cultural influences. When, in *The Sadeian Woman*, Angela Carter writes, 'flesh comes to us out of history; so does the repression and taboo that governs our experience of flesh' [*sic*], her referent is sexuality, but her remarks are equally relevant to food.[1] The significances of food and eating, like those of sexuality, are psychologically, socially and politically constructed, and symbolisms, customs and behaviours are indicators and results of cultural conditioning. An obvious if paradoxical contemporary example is bingeing and self-starvation, which occur in a cultural context of rampant consumerism in which consumption (literal or metaphorical) is promoted as wholly desirable, while overweight women are stigmatised and often portrayed as joke figures, as coarse, stupid or sexually promiscuous.[2] Even where eating practices are less obviously culture-specific, however, it is still only possible to consider their general political significance in relation to specific historical and cultural contexts.

The writers considered in this volume have in part been selected precisely because of their evident concern with contemporary history, society and politics (in its broadest sense), especially women's roles and experience. This interest manifests itself very differently in each writer, both formally and in terms of philosophical or political emphases and how these are coded through food, appetite, eating and female bodies. The major focus of attention is on Doris Lessing, Angela Carter and Margaret Atwood, and to a lesser extent Michèle Roberts and Alice Thomas Ellis, all of whose writing of food and eating is inextricably linked to explorations of what it means to be a woman in the latter part of the twentieth century.

Doris Lessing confronts the matter of twentieth-century life over an extended period, most obviously in her realist novels such as the 'Children of Violence' sequence or *The Golden Notebook*. Lessing's scope is comprehensive, and food and eating in her writing act as central vehicles for the expression and working through of problems and questions of value. Her novels (realist and fabular alike) are solidly grounded in contemporary history and culture, highlighting, among other things, the difficulties of establishing self-identity and meaning in the modern world, the dangers of excessive mentalism and concomitant importance of psycho-physical integration and, most importantly, how individuals relate to the greater social body. These questions and other issues are explored in close relation to female bodies, food and its associated activities.

Angela Carter is, typically, more perversely ambitious:

I would like, I would really like, to have had the guts and the energy and so on to be able to write about, you know, people having battles with the DHSS. But I haven't. I've done other things. I mean I'm an arty person. OK, I write over-blown purple, self-indulgent prose. So fucking what![3]

Carter's fiction is not social realism, notwithstanding its 'entertaining surface' of characterisation, physical detail and the prevalence of food, eating and desire.[4] Her writing is nevertheless political, as her non-fiction with its sardonic voice and iconoclastic tendency makes quite clear. Styling herself 'the pure product of an advanced, industrialised, post-imperialist country in decline', Carter does not seek to distance herself from the world she anatomises; while she deconstructs the models and conventions by which we live, she recognises their potency and the complexities of human involvement.[5] Fiction is part of that involvement; Carter insists that the novel is part of 'social practice' and this is evident in her detailed, dramatic and often outlandish fictional exploration of issues surrounding power, sexuality and the construction of gender. The play of appetites is a constant in her complicated repre-sentations of power and desire and the challenging of the *status quo*; not surprisingly, perhaps, her writing of food and eating is acutely self-aware and often ironised.

Margaret Atwood's political and artistic position is not dissimilar: 'For me, it's axiomatic that art has its roots in social realities.'[6] Food, eating and hunger feature substantially and in detail in Atwood's fiction, both as part of the 'social realities' with which her characters must contend, and as a series of compelling metaphors and symbols that run right through her work, and through which she focuses majors issues. Though her novels are often taken to be realist, with their central, psychologically and socially convincing focus on women, Atwood incorporates elements of genre fiction (Gothic, thriller, fairy tale, historical romance) that connect with her extensive symbolic use of food and eating to highlight themes such as the commodification of women, the duplicity of sexual predation or the negative power of the victim. Atwood's writing con-fronts a number of pressing issues in this way, but food and eating are especially used in relation to the politics of oppression and individual freedom and responsibility.

Two further writers in whose work food and eating assume a large importance are Michèle Roberts and Alice Thomas Ellis. Michèle Roberts tends to address contemporary issues obliquely or historically, but always with a strong focus on women's lives and experience. She is much concerned with ontological anxiety and the relation of this to both gender and religion, but located in a highly material context, and her novels combine an acute sense of physical being with explorations of the historical and cultural definition and regulation of femininity. Food and eating suffuse the novels. Poetic and often lyrical, her writing is both deeply sensuous and perspicacious; characters are often literally hungry, but also psychologically, affectively, spiritually.

Alice Thomas Ellis's writing gives a good deal of attention to the functions and pleasures of food, most specifically to the secular role and power of the cook. Like Roberts, Ellis has a Catholic background, but she is less ambivalent about it; Ellis's fiction suggests a desire to face away from contemporary society and towards spiritual or religious contemplation. Her characters are nevertheless *in* and *of* the contemporary world, grappling with what Ellis represents as its baseness and folly. They are often frankly contemptuous of 'fashionable' ideas, including feminism, though feminist issues abound in the complicated interactions and power struggles played out through cooking and eating.

The modern world manifests an overwhelming human yearning for wholeness, oneness or integrity, a yearning apparent in oral appetites, sexual desire, religious fervour, physical hunger, 'back to the womb' impulses, death wishes. Even Doris Lessing's explorations of realism itself, explicitly in *The Golden Notebook*, suggest how strong is the human desire for a unifying vision. Some such yearning underpins the writing of food and eating in all these writers' work. Its most literal manifestation, perhaps, is in deep, often unacknowledged longing to be reunited with the maternal figure, a fantasised return to the status of wholly fulfilled infant at the breast, or even *in utero*. This might almost be said to be the ur-longing, a desire to be reunited with the block off which we are a chip. Such a sense of yearning is partly what powers Lessing's Alice Mellings in *The Good Terrorist*, and it is present throughout Michèle Roberts's writing, as her female protagonists struggle with all that might separate them from the maternal bond: men, social convention, betrayal, external controls, their own ambition, their mothers themselves. It is as part of that struggle that they sometimes revisit attachments to the maternal, discovering their own independent physicality through sensuous relationships with food and its preparation, as well as in relation to religion, culture, men and, above all, with other women past and present.

If a yearning for the mother is evident in Roberts's work, elsewhere the desire for oneness is more subterranean and more coded. It is discernable, for example, in love relationships sought by hopeful romantics such as Atwood's Joan Foster (*Lady Oracle*), in sexual desire and in the wider play of appetites that pervade the fiction of Angela Carter. Eros, the libidinal drive, powers Carter's nurturing mother-substitutes (Aunt Margaret in *The Magic Toyshop*, Uncle Peregrine in *Wise Children*), her life-enhancing eaters, such as Fevvers in *Nights at the Circus* and her various sexual initiates. Indeed, the erotic appetite almost irresistibly demands completion. But the connection of food with sex, in Carter's fiction at least, can assume an insatiable and sometimes malignant eroticism, and both the predatory quality and the unappeasable nature of the appetite suggest not only Eros but something more deathly. The longing for consummation by negation is manifest in motifs and figures of cannibalism and vampirism in both Carter's and Atwood's novels and short stories. The monstrous appetites of these figures suggest an inner emptiness, fantasies of omnipotence or unfulfillable yearning for an impossible state of wholeness – a condition that may suggest deathly appetites in the modern sensibility.

A desire for oneness does not have to be either negative or regressive, however. It may indeed fuel the passage to enlightenment, as occurs to some extent with Carter's Desiderio and Walser (*The Infernal Appetites of Dr Hoffman* and *Nights at the Circus*) and Roberts's Thérèse and Léonie in *Daughters of the House*. Several of Doris Lessing's protagonists (Martha Quest and the protagonists of *The Golden Notebook*, *The Marriages of Zones Two, Three and Four* and *The Making of the Representative for Planet 8*) achieve a kind of wholeness through personal and spiritual growth. Lessing sets up this path to growth through a paradoxical *lack* of desire, as if to suggest we do not understand what we yearn for; in order to gain integrity and a sense of human connection her characters are put through breakdown and *dis*integration. This is brought about, in part at least, through self-starvation, the antithesis of Roberts's women's sensuous engagement. Elsewhere in Lessing's writing, characters such as Jane Somers are powered by a desire for more immediately human association, even attachment, and become materially involved in feeding and physical care for others, confronting in the process what is most disturbing about the body.

The spiritual growth Lessing focuses on is associated with striving for human or super-human connection and, even when this moves into a metaphysical realm in her writing, the desire and its fulfilment have a somewhat secular, and certainly anti-messianic, flavour. Religious impulses seek a similar sort of metaphysical completion, but through the divine, and this can be seen in Alice Thomas Ellis's novels, which have a manifestly religious undercurrent of longing that is directly contrasted to the entanglements of food, sex and power that dominate her fiction. Each of Ellis's novels has a non-participant or semi-detached character whose longings are focused quite elsewhere, usually on death or divine immanence. This is thrown into relief by contrast with the most worldly of desires: the central characters' longing is for power, not for political but for personal reasons. This desire for power is an appetite, its gratification therefore fleeting and ultimately unsatisfying, and especially so by implied comparison with the numinous. Unlike the other writers considered here, Ellis's interest is moral rather than political: her self-aware, theatrical cooks use their cooking for delight, parody, social comment or even vicious satire; power is strenuously if wittily fought for and dubiously coupled with responsibility.

Emphasis on the need for responsibility and autonomy suggests a less egocentric interpretion of yearning for wholeness or integrity, and one which is implicit in all these writers, if most evident in Lessing and Atwood. Atwood, like Carter, explores the general and particular construction of victims (the eaten, the over-eaters, the self-consumers). Against the forces of oppression – in which she includes cultural constraints, political necessity, marital and familial pressures, the coercion of friends and self-created persecutions – she sets the need for women to resist the victim position. This resistance is effected through political engagement of the most basic (and food-related) kind. It suggests a connectedness that opposes social fragmentation and allays both individual and cultural yearnings for completion. Integrity has a similar ambiguity in Lessing's and Carter's writings, in both of which is discernible a socially focused, public agenda in which the desire for integrity takes the shape of political ideals and concomitant disillusion. Here we see both what is longed for and that it remains an ideal; community – the mutuality of, for example, shared cooking and eating – is punctured by individual isolation, and resisted by that in humans which cannot or will not join the feast.

Such hungers are the stuff of psychoanalytic theory, and much of the discussion in the following chapters consequently draws on Freud, Klein, Kristeva and others. This book is not restricted to psychoanalytic accounts of food and eating in literature, however, and its arguments draw on a number of disciplines, including literary criticism, cultural studies and sociology. The central focus is on literary texts, illuminated by insights and ideas from a variety of perspectives. The resulting inter-disciplinary approach is intended to reflect the complexity and importance of the subject, to allow a productive overview and to mirror the contradictory, integrative and associative functions of eating itself.

The book as a whole argues for the centrality and versatility of food and eating in women's writing. Not only does the action of the novels examined often occur through food preparation and eating, or through oral and alimentary preoccupation of one sort or another, food and eating themselves convey much of the meanings of the novels. This results from diverse factors such as the longings or hungers outlined above, deep associations between food and the psyche, specific socio-cultural pressures, especially on women's bodies, cultural and artistic inscriptions, and from the fact that food and its activities offer multiple possibilities for expression and action. Indeed, if anything could function as a universal signifier, it would surely be food.

The book is organised into chapters centred on specific food-related topics. The first chapter, 'The food of love: mothering, feeding, eating and desire', concerns the powerful relationship between food, love and sex across a range of writers. It examines maternal and pseudo-maternal nurturing, its responsibilities and failures, and the satisfactions and (dis)empowerment of the mothering role in a number of texts, Nancy Chodorow's seminal work *The Reproduction of Mothering* providing an analysis of this role and its perpetuation. The chapter moves on to an examination of the connection of food with sexuality, with the focus on Angela Carter's frequently erotic writing and Freud's linking of genital, anal and oral desire in 'Three Essays on the Theory of Sexuality'.

Chapter 2, 'Cannibalism and Carter: fantasies of omnipotence', considers both the 'positive' desire for union with another expressed through cannibalism, and the more usual brutal and predatory cannibalism of myth and monster. Carter's cannibal motifs are considered briefly as figures of oppression and colonialism, but the chapter concentrates on interpretations in the light of psychoanalytic theory, especially Melanie Klein's theory of the oral stage and Freud's theory of life and death drives.

Despite their differences of focus and content, the perspective of these first two chapters is generally personal or individual. The third and fourth chapters provide a hinge between this and the more thoroughly social focus of the final two chapters. Chapter 3, 'Eating, starving and the body: Doris Lessing and others', examines eating and not eating in relation to a culturally constructed 'ideal' female body image and in the light of anxieties about bodily functions and boundaries. Theory about the body and eating disorders, together with Julia Kristeva's writing of abjection, provides a perspective on self-starvation and related questions of control, empowerment and enlightenment, especially in Doris Lessing's fiction. The chapter concludes with a brief examination of the complicated relationship between the fat body and pleasure in eating, and argues for the disruptive, if equivocal, potential of the big woman.

Chapter 4, 'Sharp appetites: Margaret Atwood's consuming politics', takes as its focus a single writer whose writing encompasses virtually all the aspects of food, eating and appetite discussed in the book as a whole. The sheer variety of cultural and political issues focused through food and eating by a single writer testifies both to the importance of the activities themselves and to the richness and mutability of the subject as an adaptable metaphor or symbol. The central argument of the chapter concerns Atwood's overall emphasis, through food and eating, on women and responsibility.

The last two chapters discuss social eating. Chapter 5, 'Food and manners: Roberts and Ellis', is concerned with signifiers, tracing in Michèle Roberts's fiction the ways in which the connotations and significances of both food itself and the conventions surrounding it may be used to convey a wealth of subsidiary meanings. The argument draws on both sociological and anthropological research and broaches the question of control through social training. The chapter moves on to examine customs, manners and their significance in the context of Foucault's theory of 'micro powers', investigating the play of power relations through the activities surrounding cooking and eating in the novels of Alice Thomas Ellis.

'Social eating: identity, communion and difference', the final chapter of this book, is an attempt to formulate how we might truly speak of social eating, how the activities surrounding food might connect through food and eating. Factors examined in earlier chapters inform the discussion of fiction by Doris Lessing and Angela Carter, as do Anthony Giddens's analysis of the disconnections of modernity and Bakhtin's theory of carnival, and the complexity and difficulties of human interaction figure significantly. Indeed, the difficulties of any kind of community or communion are probably more firmly established than any ideal of collectivity, though none of the writers discussed extols an alimentary individualism. If Carter stresses disruption and Lessing and Atwood emphasise both difficulty and responsibility, their fiction – like that of many other contemporary women writers – nevertheless repeatedly examines the social significances of all the activities connected with food.

CHAPTER I

The food of love: mothering, feeding, eating and desire

Food is a currency of love and desire, a medium of expression and communication. The crucial centrepiece of Christian worship is a simulated meal – the giving of symbolic bread and wine as a token of love and trust – and in most religions ritual communicative eating of some sort is prominent. From infants' sticky offerings to anniversary chocolates, from shared school lunch boxes to hospital grapes, the giving of food is a way of announcing connection, goodwill, love. For friends, food may be an expression of support or an invitation to celebrate; for lovers there is an intimate, sexual subtext, appetite incorporated into sexuality. In the all-important sphere of mothering, food-giving is a matter of routine; nurturing depends on repeated and regular care and feeding rather than the occasional spontaneous act and is, in theory at least, essentially altruistic.

For many people the connection of food with love centres on the mother, as a rule the most important figure in an infant's world, able to give or withhold everything that sustains, nourishes, fulfils, completes. It is this person who shapes or socialises a child's appetite and expectations of the world, by feeding on demand or adhering to a rigid schedule, by the cultivation of 'table manners', through the provision of fish fingers or porridge, raw fish or curry.[1] Along with nutrition she feeds her child love, resentment, encouragement or fear. Maternity provides a figure of limitless, irresistible authority, as the ancient matriarchal archetypes suggest. Yet the maternal role in western society is ambiguous, if not ambivalent; mothers are overwhelmingly powerful but at the same time are socially and domestically disempowered by their nurturing, serving role.

This ambiguity is reflected in representations of mothers and mother figures both as enslaved and as powerful providers of food. Actual mothers in literature, from Shakespeare to Carter (not to mention the nineteenth-century novel), are also frequently absent. Non-biological mothering is widespread in literature, used both as an indicator of love and nurturing (or its lack), and to suggest burdens and disempowerment. Where nurturing mothers are featured, the experience evoked is most often that of the child, the grateful or resentful recipient, rather than that of the nourishing provider. Even in the plethora of 1970s' feminist novels and autobiographies featuring mothers, the mother–daughter relationship is almost invariably written from the daughter's perspective. This is partially accounted for in commonsense terms by the fact that we have all been children with wants and hungers, and that even women writers have not all been mothers. But occupying the child position also arguably has something to do with a prevailing culture of egocentricity, a clamour for gratification and a contemporary tendency to constantly re-examine our pasts. There are, of course, exceptions.

The writers who largely form the subject of this book between them explore and portray many of the complexities of maternal nurturing, from desperate infantile hungers and difficulties of relationship to the contradictory demands of the mothering role itself. The question of whether women's association with nurturing is biologically prompted or a social construction underlies the whole subject and will be seen to recur; it is notable how often these writers transpose female nurturing onto non-biological, substitute mothers. The importance of good mothering, its requirement of responsibility and individual mothers' failures through personal inadequacy, wickedness or the impossible and contradictory demands of the role itself are equally evident in these writers' work.

But first to return to the undeniably potent infantile extreme of the experience. Michèle Roberts's two earliest novels both retrace a young woman's almost ecstatic hunger for her mother, which is only in the end pacified by some sort of revisiting of the mother–child attachment. In *A Piece of the Night* Julie Fanchot rehearses in memory her sense of loss at being separated from and distanced by her mother ('The child is joined to the mother, the woman is joined to the man,' says her mother, 'That is what being a woman means'[2]), as she is trying to create adult bonds with her, and with her own women friends and lover. In *The Visitation* the protagonist Helen, aided by her closest friend Beth, accomplishes a symbolic revisiting of the pre-Oedipal, through which she achieves release. (Though Roberts herself does not specify the pre-Oedipal, the suggestion is of such an early bond, corresponding with Freud's view of the primary relationship between little girls and their mothers as being longer, more significant and more complex than that of boys.[3])

In the following passage from *The Visitation*, the frantic, angry quality of Helen's hunger leaps out, almost drowning the mother's own difficulties and conflicts in handling her baby:

The first word that she utters is *more*. It's a demand, a despairing plea, a shout of rage and frustration. Her mother has twin babies to feed. It's a lot of work, having two. Helen is all mouth, a gaping hole crying out to be filled. Her mother consults the words of doctors on the printed page. Fifteen minutes per baby, per breast, at specific intervals. No demand feeding in between. They'll have to learn, just like their mother does. If only I'd been able, she shyly tells Helen years later: to trust my own feeling rather than the books, I'd have fed you at night when you cried. I used to walk with you up and down the room, and I knew you were hungry and I didn't dare to feed you, because the doctor in the book said it was wrong. Instead, her own daughter later vilifies her. Helen's all impatience, hunger turning to a greed that's never known satisfaction, the pleasure of lying back, full and content. She strains for the forbidden breast, crying and red-faced, she gulps eagerly, too fast, and chokes. She distrusts this food, this thin, short-lived love given too abruptly and taken away too soon. She knows pleasure only by its absence. Instead of sweet milk, she is full of bilious hate: wind and emptiness. Oh, she's bad, a bad baby, there's no doubt of that. The baby book cracks like a whip.[4]

The narrative encompasses both maternal and filial experiences, but the primary focus is with the daughter; the descriptions of her are vivid and urgent, and the crying baby's emotions are named and written in a partially internal mode. It is hunger and frustration that Roberts emphasises, not nourishment. The upshot of mother's and daughter's mutual frustration is a prickly and unsatisfying relationship, and it falls to the significantly named grandmother, Mrs Home, to provide the food and endorsement that Helen craves. It is only with the grandmother's death that a rapprochement can begin between Helen and her mother, aptly enough encoded in food: 'Catherine has ransacked her larder and kitchen, now that her daughter proves willing to accept her gifts; they are suddenly pleased with one another, the items of food expressing all that remains unsaid' (119). The roots of adult dissatisfaction, Roberts suggests, lie with the earliest of eating experiences, a view quite in keeping with that of many psychologists (as will be seen in chapter 2).

Although she portrays relations as difficult for particular daughters and mothers, Roberts seems to endorse the idea of women-as-mothers-as-nurturers. This is expressed in its most general form in her fictional autobiography of Mary Magdalene, *The Wild Girl*, which proposes a female principle that would complete a Blakean unity, combining Father, Son and Holy (Mother) Spirit.[5] Female nurturing is equally evident in a handful of caring mothers (*The Book of Mrs Noah, A Piece of the Night, In the Red Kitchen*) and in displaced mothering, by grandmothers (Mrs Horne), by nuns – such as those who teach Hattie to cook in *In the Red Kitchen* – by friends or simply by women in the grip of maternal impulses, like Hattie when she finds and comforts the ghostly Flora Milk shut in the cupboard for not eating her porridge, a time-leaping nurturing rendered literally and emotionally persuasive by its attention to detail: the remnants of bread, cheese and cold porridge, the child's crusted snot and smell of urine, her tears and shuddering and the comforting physical contact.[6]

Margaret Atwood's mothers, by contrast, are (with a few young exceptions) almost invariably portrayed through their daughters' eyes as monstrous or absent or ineffectual. Certainly most of them cause damage one way or another, profoundly affecting their daughters' appetites and capacity for future nurturing, though Atwood does use the device to varying effects, and whereas some of the daughters can become locked into reactive strategies, others develop a high level of independence.

The mothers come in different guises. They may be over-intrusive, controlling and competitive, driving their progeny to guilt and over-eating (Joan in *Lady Oracle*). They may be kind but unaware or unable to help, like the self-consuming Elaine's unconventional mother in *Cat's Eye*. They may die, like Grace's poor young mother in *Alias Grace*, or they may disappear, like Tony's runaway mother in *The Robber Bride* and the alcoholic mother who 'sells' Elizabeth and her sister to an unnurturing aunt in *Life Before Man*. Worst of all is the hopeless abusive mother of Charis in *The Robber Bride*, who cannot cope with being a single mother and yet does not understand the brusque, earthy nurturing her own mother provides. This slightly witchy grandmother is a positive if eccentric mother-substitute. She provides Charis with hearty unfussy food, country solace, psychic endorsement and a robust dismissal of conventional rules of hygiene and behaviour:

For dessert there was applesauce, and after that strong tea with milk in it. The grandmother passed a cup to Karen, and Karen's mother said, 'Oh, Mother, she doesn't drink tea,' and the grandmother said, 'She does now.' Karen thought there might be an argument, but her grandmother added, 'If you're leaving her with me, you're leaving her with *me*. 'Course, you can always take her with you.' Karen's mother clamped her mouth shut.

When Karen's grandmother had finished eating she scooped the chicken bones off the dinner plates, back into the stewpot, and set the plates down on the floor. The animals crowded around them, licking and slurping.

'Not from the dishes,' said Karen's mother faintly.

'Less germs on their tongues than on a human's,' said the grandmother.[7]

There is a pleasurable confuting of the unnurturing mother in these exchanges, as well as indications of the beginnings of a significant relationship between Charis and her grandmother. *Lady Oracle*'s Aunt Lou, seen by Joan Foster as a magical antidote to her angry, controlling and inadequate mother, provides an urban variation of this idiosyncratic nourishing.

The transposing of the nurturing, feeding aspects of motherhood onto substitute figures is a way of avoiding a biologically determined essentialism, and Angela Carter's writing does just that. Natural mothers, as Nicole Ward Jouve points out, hardly feature in Carter's work but non-biological mothers are allowed to behave – and be constricted – maternally.[8] *The Magic Toyshop*'s Aunt Margaret is able, despite her subjugation at the hands of the patriarch Uncle Philip, to find solace and eloquent expression through her cooking. She welcomes Melanie and her siblings with food described in comforting, almost nursery terms: a 'steaming and savoury' pie, 'white bread and brown bread, yellow curls of the best butter, two kinds of jam (strawberry and apricot) . . . and currant cake'.[9] She pours tea from a huge brown teapot and 'presides' over the table with evident satisfaction. The bright, homely picture evoked goes some way to sketching a maternal archetype, but it is an equivocal one. The giving of food and love are inseparable in the scene, but when the girls go to bed, Aunt Margaret gazes broodily at Victoria, and writes on her notepad, 'What a fine, plump little girl!'(48) – a fairy-tale flavoured reminder of the maternal capacity to devour.

The nearest Carter comes to providing an unequivocally nurturing maternal figure is with Grandma Chance in *Wise Children*. Encouraging and protective, Grandma Chance is a positive non-mother. Her strict vegetarianism provides the girls with vitamins, love and a code of empathetically moral behaviour, setting her in polar opposition to the twins' predatory, carnivorous cousin Saskia. Grandma Chance's attitude to food, though cabbage-ridden, is not joyless and she embraces treats, from theatre trips with cucumber sandwiches to lavish birthday cake and – her own favourites – Guinness and crème de menthe. Her nurturing is distanced by her being (ostensibly) grandmother rather than mother; it is vigorous, colourful, life-enhancing and fiercely loving, but never smothering.

The question of maternal responsibility is a theme Doris Lessing makes explicit in more than one novel. *The Memoirs of a Survivor*, in particular, is in part a review of nurturing and its lack in both personal and public contexts. Early in the novel the narrator accepts what is in effect a maternal responsibility for a young girl called Emily who is left with her (thereby becoming a surrogate mother figure). Her care is quietly expressed through food: she goes out to find something for a 'welcoming meal' for Emily and her cat-dog Hugo; she provides for them both and encourages Emily in her cooking and foraging; she monitors Emily's adolescent eating phase and subsequent starving phase; she provides a refuge (with food) to which Emily can return from the stresses of living with the young leader Gerald and his household. Like any mother, she becomes anxious for her charge: 'how dark a foreboding it was, how I had come to watch and grieve over her, how sharp was my anxiety when she was out in empty buildings and waste lots'.[10] Such anxiety has partly to do with control: how can a person exercise a duty of care over an absent charge? The parental dilemma of when and how to let go is clearly signalled, as is concern, not only about personal safety, but about influence, for once a child goes out into the world the parent's or guardian's power to mould and influence becomes diluted; as the narrator recognises, in a telling eating metaphor: 'people develop for good or for bad by swallowing whole other people, atmospheres, events, places' (50).

As the narrator's understanding progresses in the outer world, so her visits to a 'personal', dreamlike realm through the wall reflect, illuminate and expand upon her perceptions. Scenes from a composite early infancy (suggesting the narrator's, Emily's and her mother's childhoods[11]) indicate general truths. The narrator witnesses a frenzied baby desperate for food and attention, portrayed just as frantically as Michèle Roberts's babies:

The baby was desperate with hunger. Need clawed in her belly, she was being eaten alive by the need for food. She yelled inside the thick smothering warmth; sweat scattered off her scarlet little face; she twisted her head to find a breast, a bottle, anything: she wanted liquid, warmth, food, comfort. (129)

She observes an uncomfortable hot child confined in a cot, in a white nursery with no visual stimulation or affectionate attention; she sees a sick child yearning to be cuddled by her mother; she watches helplessly while a little girl is 'tickled' remorselessly by her uneasy father; she sees the child listening to her mother complain endlessly about the burden of caring for her. Of all the scenes of deprivation and repression, the most immediately shocking is the disgusted mother's reaction to this infant's naturally curious exploration and tasting of her own excrement, the physical cruelty of the child's subsequent fierce cleaning, and the long lingering of her desolate sobs.

These scenes together add up to a representation of feeding without nurturing, providing a psychological aetiology for Emily's and the narrator's sense of duty and Emily's desire for fulfilment by Gerald. They suggest, too, grounds for the disintegration of the society at large. Though reader sympathy is initially engaged by the narrator's intense feeling for the miserable child, the infant's transmutation from Emily into her mother makes it clear that this woman too is helpless, doomed to repeat patterns of mothering within a socially constructed role of motherhood.

Lessing stresses the need for fundamentally different models of caring and responsibility. The possibility of achieving these is utopian, however, for the concept of an irresistible repetition of certain patterns of mothering is a powerful one. We know from the empirical evidence that has surfaced over the last few years that people who abuse children tend themselves to have been abused. Nancy Chodorow claims more radically that mothering *itself* is a repeating pattern; mothers produce daughters with definite 'mothering capacities' and evident 'desire to mother'.[12] She stresses that in nuclear families the narrow focusing of responsibility for 'mothering' on mothers alone, and consequent intensification of the mother–child relationship, becomes a vicious circle and is therefore self-perpetuating. Chodorow's 1978 study is obviously of its era, but her discussion is relevant to most of the fiction discussed here. In any case, her argument relies on ahistorical psychoanalysis: because of the disparity in the length of the pre-Oedipal phase between boys and girls, girls (with their extended attachment to the mother) are more imprinted with parental modes than boys and are thus more likely to subsequently place themselves in primary parent–child relationships.[13]

The danger posed by an extended mother–daughter attachment is of insufficient separateness. The ability to know when and how to relinquish control is as important as the initial provision of total care, and Chodorow outlines some of the dangers of a too-close bond: over-control, guilt feelings, lack of autonomy, mother–daughter hostility and even loss of self for the mother.[14] One might add over-feeding, literally or metaphorically. The difficulty of recognising over-closeness, even where the bond is neither biological nor excessive, is apparent in the narrator's retrospective self-castigation in *Memoirs* in a comment which is simultaneously enlightened, judgemental and rueful in tone: 'Now I judge myself to have been stupid: the elderly tend not to see – they have forgotten! – that hidden person in the young creature, the strongest and most powerful member among the cast of characters inhabiting an

adolescent body, the self which instructs, chooses experience – and protects' (52).

To return to the reproduction of specific patterns of mothering,
which I take to be more or less implicit in Chodorow's general argument:
in the 'Children of Violence' novels, Lessing specifically names a 'nightmare of repetition', as Martha Quest struggles not to repeat her
mother's pattern of upbringing. Both May Quest, who narcissistically
cannot let go of the daughter she nevertheless fails to nurture, and
Martha, who finds herself engaged in debilitating and frustrating
feeding battles with her own little girl, find themselves failing to provide
the mothering that they feel they should – and want to. Martha extri-
cates herself from the situation to avoid repeating May Quest's failure
to 'mirror' her child, to see her as separate and then reflect her back to
herself as independent being – an essential developmental stage for both
mother and child. But the cost of Martha's escape is to deprive her
daughter of herself, and another fictional infant must thus be brought
up by a surrogate mother.

It is not surprising that discussion of negative mothering should
return to examples of biological mothers, for actual mothers frequently
come under attack for failure to nurture. As suggested earlier, this may
have to do with the portrayal of mothers from the perspective of the
indignant infant (of whatever age). Even Martha Quest manages to pass
on to her mother much of the blame for her own difficulties. Maternal
failures may be variously categorised: as intrusiveness or excessive distance, for example, as force-feeding or denial, smothering or neglect.
Sometimes writers exaggerate such failings into grotesque caricatures
(Dickens, *par excellence*) and it is true that their symbolic value is great.
Repressed or repressive, distant or unnurturing mothers are a particular
feature of the literature of upper-middle-class English life. The mother
in *Good Behaviour* (discussed in chapter 3) is a particularly unlikeable spec-
imen: she treats her children with a vague and chilly disregard, prefer-
ring her painting, her gardening and her husband (in about that order);
she neither supervises the abominable nursery food nor intervenes in
times of illness or unhappiness, and her relief at being spared her children's company is almost palpable.

Failures of nurturing don't have to be associated with malignity, and
may on the contrary reflect a mother's own insecurities and inadequa-
cies (or, like Atwood's mothers, combine the two). Alice Thomas Ellis,
who focuses acutely on maternal shortcomings, portrays a number of
mothers whose nurturing of their offspring is problematic. Rose, in *The*

Sin Eater, feeds her adored twins on beguiling, magical food but she is too busy playing power games to protect them from mortal danger. The older Mrs Marsh in *The Birds of the Air* is benign; she is just hopelessly unable to reconcile her regard for conventions and appearances with affection for her troubled family.

In the novels collected as the 'Summerhouse Trilogy', which centre on the projected marriage of Margaret and Syl, Ellis portrays three separate mothers who fail, one way or another, to nurture.[15] Most appealing of these is the elderly Mrs Munro, who is distanced from her unspeakable middle-aged son Syl by her own aging and by the fact that she does not in any case much like him. Margaret's estranged father's new young wife is condemned because she feeds her children pickled red cabbage and exists in a miasma of nursery incompetence. Finally Monica, Margaret's mother, is like Mrs Marsh without the affection. She bears some resemblance to Lessing's complaining maternal figure in the realm behind the wall in *The Memoirs of a Survivor*, seeing only her daughter's failure to conform to what she desires her to be. Crushed and disappointed, Monica's nurturing consists of attempts to mould Margaret into the (perfectly bourgeois) wife she feels she herself could – and should – have been. Her cooking is at once dull and fussy, her caring unimaginative and intrusive. Her actions are hopelessly contradictory; she both tries to hustle Margaret into middle age, in marriage to one of her own contemporaries, and infantilises her by trying to control what she wears and eats and trying to limit her intake of alcohol.

Apart from their failures of nurturing, what these fictional women share is a sense of embattlement, and their shortcomings are indeed at least in part attributable to the ambiguities inherent in their roles as mothers. In a child's eyes, the mother is immeasurably powerful, yet, especially before a child is 'socialised' into cooperativeness or obedience, the mother may, like Martha Quest with Caroline, find herself confronted by a small being with a powerful will. Anyone who has had charge of a baby or toddler will recognise the frustration of having to deal with clamped-shut lips and spat-out food. The experience of combined omnipotence, responsibility and powerlessness is deeply disturbing. It is difficult, to say the least, to handle concurrent tyranny and disempowerment.

The role of mother is equivocal, both in terms of ambivalent power relations with her children and because motherhood is associated in western culture with social and political powerlessness – that is to say a lack of legitimate and recognised power, not the manipulative and covert influence traditionally associated with women. Angela Carter places *The Magic Toyshop*'s Aunt Margaret in a maternal role precisely to emphasise her disempowerment. But the situation is neither straightforward nor static, and relative status can shift about considerably. The nurturing aspects of mothering and the pleasures to be gained from feeding people are apparent in the pleasure Aunt Margaret manifests in watching her brothers and the children eat. Such satisfactions are empowering. Aunt Margaret is the beneficent creator of nourishing and well-appreciated food, and in her husband's absence presides at the table. When Uncle Philip returns, however, her serving function is accentuated and her manner becomes entirely propitiatory. Patriarchy, Carter suggests, likes its mother figures benign, but impotent.

Given the thanklessness of the maternal role, surprisingly few novels dwell on the difficulties – or delights – of combining motherhood with something else, though there are literary landmarks, such as Lessing's *The Golden Notebook* or Margaret Drabble's *The Millstone*. Michèle Roberts's *The Book of Mrs Noah* touches on the rewards and stresses of motherhood in its explorations of women's subjectivity, and her *A Piece of the Night* suggests an emotional juggling act for its protagonist Julie, if she is to nurture, love and feed both her child and the relationship with her lover Jenny. Roberts opposes a model of relaxed communal mothering (of several children by several mothers) to the pressure-cooker nuclear family of Julie's own background, but she does not gloss over the difficulties of cooperation, injecting Julie with a sudden jealousy that her daughter should be happy with other carers.

Implicit in scenes of positive maternal nurturing, particularly when seen from the mother's perspective, is the congruence of food and love. At the initial stages of an infant's life, indeed, they are almost inseparable, especially for mothers who breastfeed, and women almost invariably express love for their children through food. In a fulsomely hortatory article exploring some of the physical, emotional and spiritual resonances of breastfeeding, Stephanie Demetrakopoulos suggests that a danger of over-feeding flows directly from this congruence: 'Women who force their children to eat, who stuff them with food/love, may be extending their lactation powers and own fulfilment, forcing the child to act as the replete and filled vessel of her gift of nourishment.'[16] The satisfactions are, it seems, as great for the giver of nourishment as for the recipient, characterised here as surprisingly passive. This is not only the case where children are concerned, the old adage 'the way to a man's heart is through his stomach' sardonically suggesting both the potency of food and how it may be manipulated. Women sometimes infantalise husbands by replicating childhood experiences of indulgent feeding (love) by their mothers, or may, like Martha Quest, be resented for refusing to do so. Reference to childhood experiences is one of the sources of women's power as cooks; not only do they have control over the food, and thus its associations, but through something like the 'nightmare of repetition' they are able to take advantage of men's subordination to the powerful maternal figures of their childhoods.

Considering the giving of food as an expression of love demands reference not only to the power relations of maternity but to the gender politics of sexual entanglement, though it is worth noting that the work of the main writers considered in this book has examples of disinterested or loving food provision that is neither maternal nor sexual. Friendship, sisterhood, sibling love, altruistic caring, responsibility, religious communion: all use the well-established vehicle of food-as-love. But so, too, does romantic or sexual love, and fiction – like life – is filled with occasions on which courting, seduction or even the simple affirmation of love are accompanied by food or drink in one way or another.

Simply from a mimetic point of view, examples are legion. In Angela Carter's first novel, *Shadow Dance*, the temporarily besotted Emily cooks for Honeybuzzard, feeding Morris too, but ablaze with love when Honeybuzzard is her object. In Carter's last novel, *Wise Children*, twin Nora mixes sex, love and learning to cook with her Italian husband-to-be, graduating from passionate lovemaking and cooking cannoli, canneloni and ravioli, to the wedding-day debacle in which Tony's mother showers her with marinara sauce.[17] Margaret Atwood suggests an understood *quid pro quo* in the food relations of lovers and potential partners. In *Lady Oracle* young Joan is gastronomically wooed by the chef in the restaurant where she works; he plies her with forbidden treats, piling her plate with shrimps and gazing at her from the griddle, sighing and pleading as her appetite diminishes. The reticent Nate in *Life Before Man* first takes Lesje to a cheap sandwich lunch, but in his embarrassment spends most of the time holding forth about the forthcoming election in Quebec. Lesje is certain she is being asked for something but is unclear what this will be; although she agrees to show Nate's children around the museum – which might be deemed a fair exchange for a grilled cheese sandwich and a glass of milk – the highly charged atmosphere indicates that this food has a higher tariff. Michèle Roberts's heroines too have a tendency to meet or negotiate with their lovers over food: Julie and Ben, Julie and Jenny (and friends) in *A Piece of the Night*; Helen and George (negatively), Helen and Robert (nourishingly) in *The Visitation*; Hattie and the lover who so much enjoys her appetite in *In The Red Kitchen*.

Alice Thomas Ellis's novels are filled with food, including love-food and food fantasies. In *The Birds of the Air* Mrs Marsh's unhappy daughter Barbara concocts a seduction fantasy around her husband's editor, Hunter (highly misguided, given his homosexuality), which centres on the cooking of a surprise hotpot for him, and in *The Other Side of the Fire*, Claudia buys a game pie from Harrods for the stepson of whom she is enamoured, spending the entire train journey home planning the rest of the meal, fruitlessly, it transpires, as Philip has gone out to dinner.[18] Doris Lessing similarly includes the food–love–sex nexus in the realist detail of her fiction, in the sundowner culture of drinking, dancing and eating that surrounds the sexual relationships and marriage of Martha Quest, in the meals Anna Wulf lovingly and sensuously prepares for her lovers in *The Golden Notebook*, and in the meals and drinks that Richard and Janna share in place of sexual consummation in *The Diaries of Jane Somers*.

The connection of food with sex is complicated, for there is an intertwining of two drives or appetites that are not easy to disentangle or identify as distinct. The link is constantly reinforced in western culture, from images insinuating the fellatio of chocolate bars, sausages and asparagus to the almost routine comparison of breasts with fruits or the attribution of aphrodisiac qualities to oysters and other genitally suggestive foodstuffs. Even the term sexual *appetite* makes the connection, somehow conflating food and sex. The link is made linguistically, so that what is subject-specific language moves freely between the two areas of food and sexuality, people being described as 'tasty', a 'dish' or a 'tart', or people being said to 'feast their eyes' on the object of desire, to be 'hungry for love'. It works the other way round too, with 'sinful' puddings or cream cakes which are 'naughty but nice'.

Ella Freeman Sharpe, in an essay on metaphor, claims that metaphorical speech springs inevitably from psycho-physical experience. She maintains that speech is itself a metaphor, the discharge of ideas in place of bodily substances. 'Metaphor,' she says, 'evolves alongside the control of the bodily orifices. Emotions which originally accompanied bodily discharge find substitute channels and materials.'[19] Drawing on a large body of clinical material, Sharpe categorises metaphors into those relating to suckling experiences ('When I wander off the point bring me back to it'), the anal and urethral ('I've a fear of letting myself go altogether') and some miscellaneous ones ('His desperation grows; as it grows, he grows more and more pompous. I have a desire then to prick the balloon, but I don't see him becoming less.').[20] The implication of Sharpe's essay is that language in common use is much more certainly rooted in early experience than we are consciously aware of, and that these experiences relate specifically to eating, defecation and Oedipal transition. The examples above are, in this light, simply the most obvious.

Linguistic connections are not accidental; if we put this conclusion together with Chodorow's emphasis on the importance of the pre-Oedipal stage for girls, it seems inevitable that women's writing of food and eating will connect with an oral sexuality. But what of overt depictions of food in connection with sex? Explicit examples of sexual activity in which food is involved seem to occur more frequently or more nakedly in men's writing (and films) than in women's. In Michèle Roberts's *In the Red Kitchen*, for example, Flora and her husband George feast in bed on cold chicken, gherkins, champagne and each other, a veiled consummation suggesting the wholesale satisfactions of pre-Oedipal devotion. Philip Roth's young narcissist Alexander Portnoy, by contrast, famously and fetishistically takes a piece of liver for a sexual object (liver that is subsequently cooked for the family's supper).[21] His activities are explicit but solitary; the 1986 Japanese food film *Tampopo* goes further, incorporating food directly into heterosexual play: there are carnal games with cream and honey, a live crayfish and the ultimately orgasmic passing back and forth of an egg yolk between the mouths of the lovers.[22]

The use of food and eating as a deliberate sexual metonymy or metaphor is a long-established tradition, especially for suggesting human flesh and sexual intercourse. Is this simply what is going on with the scenes described above, only with metaphors that are more extreme, their depiction more self-conscious and more playful? Or is there, actually, an underlying connection, a concurrence or dissonance between sexual appetite and a hunger for food? Does desire necessarily manifest itself indeed through one appetite rather than the other? Or is the connection perhaps not so much a link between food and sex in themselves as a linguistic short circuit, between the language of food and the language of sex, producing the incidental manifestation: food/sex ?

This last idea has some appeal because all three focus to an extent on the mouth, but it comes under pressure from what it leaves out of account, namely the physical body. At an evolutionary level the connection must surely be explained by the necessity to sustain life: both food and sexual congress are sought in response to the sharpness of appetite;

both are primarily concerned with the body's needs, acting on the body and affecting attitudes towards it. Through the connecting medium of the body, food and sex certainly interweave, and it is important for survival that both appetites be stimulated and satisfied, but this deterministic explanation hardly accounts for what is a cultural phenomenon and in any case does not justify a linking of the two appetites, since they might just as easily be satisfied in parallel.

Perhaps the psyche provides a more convincing provenance than the body for the interconnection of these two powerful appetites. Quite early in his work, in his 'Three Essays on the Theory of Sexuality', Freud puts forward the thesis that the sexual instinct is generated out of the infant's earliest experiences of eating. From taking nourishment at the mother's breast, the infant graduates to a proto-sexual satisfaction in sucking (as Melanie Klein so forcefully conveys later on in her conception of the breast as a love object).[23] The activity of sucking and the flow of milk stimulate the mucous membrane of the mouth, giving a sexual pleasure, so that, in Freud's view, the lips 'behave like an erotogenic zone':

The satisfaction of the erotogenic zone is associated, in the first instance, with the satisfaction of the need for nourishment. To begin with, sexual activity attaches itself to functions serving the purpose of self-preservation and does not become independent of them until later. No one who has seen a baby sinking back satiated from the breast and falling asleep with flushed cheeks and a blissful smile can escape the reflection that this picture persists as a prototype of the expression of sexual satisfaction in later life. The need for repeating the sexual satisfaction now becomes detached from the need for taking nourishment.[24]

Expressed in this way the connection may seem tenuous but, psychically speaking, according to Freud, sexual desire has its roots in, and grows directly out of, the satisfaction of hunger for food.

Maud Ellmann, who deals with some of this material from a somewhat different perspective, claims polemically that, despite his focus on sex, Freud's fundamental preoccupation is food, that eating represents the 'primal violation of the ego'.[25] She argues that food is the repressed in Freud, and that his 'vast encyclopedia of sexual malaise was constructed to evade the everyday catastrophe of eating'. Food as the repressed is a fascinating and disturbing idea, though it begs the question of why Freud should see a need to 'evade' eating.[26] What it certainly suggests is an inextricable connection between food and sexuality.

At the end of the essay on infantile sexuality, Freud asserts that the

connecting pathways between sexuality and other functions are travers-
able in both directions:

> If, for instance, the common possession of the labial zone by the two functions
> is the reason why sexual satisfaction arises during the taking of nourishment,
> then the same factor also enables us to understand why there should be disor-
> ders of nutrition if the erotogenic functions of the common zone are disturbed.
> (*SE*, vol. VII, 205–6)

The claim that, 'sexual satisfaction arises during the taking of nourishment' suggests a cross-over that is entirely normal, routine and non-
pathological (the reference to nutritional disorders and disturbance to
erotogenic functions suggesting a disruption that manifests itself *through*
the cross-over rather than as a result of it). Theoretical analysis and
'commonsense' view coincide.

Food and eating in Angela Carter's writing are thoroughly enmeshed
with sex and power. Her writing suggests the inevitability of exchange
between food and sex, that there is a profound if ambiguous interconnection; indeed, in a 1985 book review she approvingly quotes Lévi-
Strauss's claim that 'to eat is to fuck'. In this review, Carter uses the term
'gastroporn' which itself suggests a confusion of appetites.[27] Carter's
fiction manifests something of this ambiguity of appetite as a lascivious-
ness of the gut: eating as erotic activity. This is not quite the same as the
eating-as-foreplay or metonymic eating referred to earlier, but it is a
question of food itself being presented as the focus of desire, and eating
as the central act. In this way food preparation or the activity of eating
may involve arousal, satiety, narcissistic self-contemplation, degradation,
sado-masochism and so on (seen with the Count in *The Infernal Desires of
Dr Hoffman* or Zero in *The Passion of New Eve*).

The manifestation of sexual behaviour in relation to food is hinted at
in seduction meals, and also where there is no likelihood of imminent
sexual congress. Helen Simpson plays on the connection in a short story
about a middle-aged gourmet roué who deliberately blends the two, sal-
ivating 'wolfishly' (and pretentiously) over both 'some delicate noisette of
milk-fed lamb' and his prospective conquest. Simpson emphasises the
character's narcissism in his contemplation of the spectacle of himself
beating egg whites: 'The expressionless face, slight breathlessness and
controlled energy of the rhythmically moving arm is nothing short of an
erotic spectacle.'[28] Angela Carter sketches the connection in reverse; in
Heroes and Villains, the 'half-witted,' and therefore socially uninhibited,
son of Dr Donally falls on his food with 'grunts of pleasure,' but when

he asks for wedding cake and is told there will be none, sighs heavily and begins to masturbate.

More often, food and sex are mutually saturated in a way that is more difficult to disentangle. An unforced interpenetration of food with sex, gastronomy with eroticism, is typified in Carter's short story 'The Kitchen Child'.[29] This tells the tale of a Yorkshire cook in the house of a very wealthy upper class couple who is in despair at being restricted to providing only minimal food for her employers and endless sandwiches for the guests on the yearly Great Grouse Shoot. When, to her delight, a visiting French *duc* requests lobster soufflé, her painstaking preparations are interrupted by an amorous valet; surprised, she shakes too much cayenne pepper into the mixture, pushing the soufflé quickly into the oven the more readily to succumb to her seduction. A child is duly born, and becomes a kitchen prodigy, learning the trade and witnessing his mother's forlorn annual cooking of a lobster soufflé that no-one eats, until he is sixteen and the *duc* arrives once more. The boy goes to see him and relates the tale; it transpires that the valet is now dead, but the *duc* remembers relishing the soufflé and he determines to visit the cook. All is set for a reprise, but the cook, this time sure about her priorities, swats the *duc* with a wooden spoon. The result is a perfect (and splendidly rising) soufflé: sexual satisfaction, reward, victory. Needless to say, she marries the *duc*.

I relate this story at length since its detail best illustrates the point. Food and sexuality both form the manifest content of the story, and it would be inappropriate to suggest that it is *either* the food or the sex that is titillating. The cook bending over the range to stir flour into the butter is enticing and the pair of hands that appear and clasp themselves around her waist make her more so; the combination of the twitch she gives to her 'ample hips', the sliding of egg yolks into the roux, and the mixing in of the lobster meat tickles both salacious and gastronomic appetites. The post-coital soufflé is rampant, going up 'like a montgolfier' and knocking its 'golden head . . . imperiously against the oven door' (92), and the second soufflé transcends this almost to the point of blasphemy. The food's lusciousness is presented in sexual terms; the cook's sexuality is inseparable from her gastronomic function, her bulk and humour testifying to the quality of her cooking and lusty approach to life. What is interesting and distinctive here is that it is not possible to disentangle the food from the sexuality; they are presented jointly. Unusually, perhaps, the one does not in some way stand for the other.

The model outlined earlier for a psychically healthy interconnection between eating and sexuality ('sanctioned', as it were, by Freud) is nicely illustrated by 'The Kitchen Child'. But this is not the end of the story where Freud is concerned, for he classes (completed) sexual satisfaction other than that achieved through the penetration of a vagina by a penis as aberrant or perverse. Any sexual satisfaction associated with food – if it takes the place of intercourse – might to a Freudian be coloured by this judgement. It should be emphasised that Freud ascribes perversion descriptively, not judgementally, but nevertheless it does seem that deviations from what he sees as normal (i.e. heterosexual, genitally penetrative) intercourse are, by definition in his view, some sort of malfunction. Interestingly, he again invokes eating:

The normal sexual aim is regarded as being the union of the genitals in the act known as copulation, which leads to a release of the sexual tension and a temporary extinction of the sexual instinct – *a satisfaction analogous to the sating of hunger*. But even in the most normal sexual process we may detect rudiments which, if they had developed, would have led to the deviations described as 'perversions'. For there are certain intermediate relations to the sexual object, such as touching and looking at it, which lie on the road towards copulation and are recognised as being preliminary sexual aims. On the one hand these activities are themselves accompanied by pleasure, and on the other hand they intensify the excitation, which should persist until the final sexual aim is attained. Moreover, *the kiss, one particular contact of this kind, between the mucous membrane of the lips of the two people concerned, is held in high sexual esteem among many nations (including the most highly civilized ones), in spite of the fact that the parts of the body involved do not form part of the sexual apparatus but constitute the entrance to the digestive tract.*[30] (my italics)

The first italicised phrase recalls the passage about the baby at the breast. The comparison is not accidental, since in both cases appetite is being satisfied, and indeed stimulated, if we liken 'touching and looking' to smelling and tasting. However, it is not an equation but 'a satisfaction *analogous* to the sating of hunger' (my italics).

In the longer italicised section Freud considers the curious coincidence of digestive and sexual pleasure centred on the mouth. When he describes deviations or perversions as either the extension of interest to inappropriate areas of the body, or the arrest of interest at some point which 'should normally be traversed rapidly on the path towards the final sexual aim' (150), oral and anal sexuality (at the two ends of the digestive tract) are particularly in focus – though it is worth noting that he stresses that the condemnation of such practises as perversions arises from conventional or hysterical disgust and is quite irrational. Indeed he states categorically that a disposition to 'perversions of every kind', though he does not specify these, is a 'general and fundamental human characteristic'.[31]

For the very young Freud acknowledges, in what seems a rather coy manner, that the anal part of the digestive tract normally affords great sexual pleasure: 'The contents of the bowels, which act as a stimulating Mass upon a sexually sensitive portion of mucous membrane, behave like forerunners of another organ, which is destined to come into action after the phase of childhood' (186). Defecation has come to feature in recent writing on the body, and there is a vivid evocation of its pleasures in Michèle Roberts's *Daughters of the House*, in a passage that suggests pleasure in evacuation is far from being confined to the infantile. It is a highly sensual, indeed sexual pleasure, so the pre-pubescent Léonie ruminates:

Pissing was a tremendous pleasure. Voluptuously abandoning control. Relief as the bursting bladder emptied itself, easing discomfort. Shitting was an equal delight. It was, to begin with, so varied. Some days knobs of shit as hard and beadlike as rabbit droppings fell away from her. Some days slugs or pellets. On others she watched a thick brown snake dive down between her legs. Letting it out felt so good. Shiver as the shit took over, nudged her open, swelled, dropped softly out.[32]

This childish delight is part of the generalised receptivity to sexual pleasure that Freud refers to as 'polymorphous perversity', an innate aptitude for 'sexual irregularities' before 'the mental dams against sexual excesses – shame, disgust and morality' are constructed. At the time of her speculation (above) Léonie is pre-pubescent, her pleasures focusing intensely on her body, the satisfactions of eating and of digestive processes and gentle sexual explorations with her cousin Thérèse. Though the adult Léonie does not manifest such all-body pleasures, her (hetero)sexuality being genitally focused, she is throughout the novel characterised by an active, sensuous enjoyment of her body, and of food and eating in particular. The physical, sensuous, sensual pleasures of eating continue to be indulged, but never so easily nor so sexually; the 'mental dams', it seems, slide into place almost unnoticed, only breached by a rare and involuntary physical memory, such as the fleeting sensation of having been suckled by the bountiful Rose Taillé. Whether such a change is innate, part of psycho-sexual maturation as Freud would have it, or a result of social and cultural training, is open to question.

The foundations of an easy transfer between sexual pleasures and alimentary appetites seem to sit happily in their temporary identity during infancy and childhood. It is only when it comes to adult connections between the two that there is a gulf, or obstacles suggesting perversion. Some writers are drawn to focus precisely on the gulfs and obstacles, on the 'mental dams' themselves, and the proliferation of 'sexual excesses' and 'irregularities' in Angela Carter's writing suggests that polymorphous perversity is not merely implied, nor confined to childhood, but is actively manifest. *The Infernal Desires of Dr Hoffman* deals explicitly in all manner of 'perversions', but even if we look only at examples that focus on the digestive tract, there are numerous suggested instances of polymorphous desire throughout Carter's work. In *Nights at the Circus*, for example, the combination of champagne, sweet tea, the prospect of bacon sandwiches and Fevvers's vast and energetic yawn produces in Walser a 'seismic erotic disturbance' (52); Mignon's response to chocolates betokens an 'infantine voluptuousness' (128); as Fevvers identifies Walser's face as 'the face of desire' she bites absentmindedly into a chunk of bread so that he feels her 'hungry' eyes (204); and when he is lost she goes off her food altogether.

At the other end of the digestive tract Carter's writing embraces occasional buggery, from the throwaway pre-experience of Jack Walser in *Nights at the Circus* ('a sharp dose of buggery in a bedouin tent beside the Damascus road') to the ritual humiliation of Eve by Zero (who also enjoys making his wives miss their breakfast) in *The Passion of New Eve*.[33] The nine deconstructing acrobats of desire who sexually assault Desiderio, the picaresque hero of *Dr Hoffman*, seem to enjoy themselves, but Desiderio complains of feeling as though he had been penetrated by an arsenal [*sic*] of swords. The incident is framed by the drinking of Turkish coffee, the post-coital cup accompanied by arak. Since Desiderio goes on almost to boast of 'the most comprehensive anatomy lesson a man ever suffered, in which I learned every possible modulation of the male apparatus and some I would have thought impossible' (117), the whole incident – like many in this novel – may be read as a projection of Desiderio's own desires.

In a novel so concerned with the release and sublimation of desire, it is hardly surprising that the protagonist's sexual, gustatory and alimentary appetites should be intertwined and that his sexuality (in his intercourse with Mama, for example) be stimulated through his palate. One possible reading of the novel, emphasising psychoanalytic parallels, would be to see Desiderio as passing through particular psychic stages, including the exploration of polymorphous perversity with its pauses and deviations. There is certainly a sense of goals deferred (also a narrative device of the romance, of course): in his life with the river people,

Desiderio never gets to copulate with his child bride, despite a good deal of manipulation and fellatio and plenty of kitchen dalliance with the grandmother; at the castle of desire, he describes the exquisite meal he eats with the Doctor and Albertina as disappointing, and wonders whether congress with her will prove to be the ultimate disillusionment.

Hunger, it seems, is preferable to consummation, and the greatest satisfactions are somehow only obtained for this polymorph, 'on the road towards'. David Punter even associates Desiderio's holding back with a failure of political consummation, reading the text as 'a series of figures for the defeat of the political aspirations of the 1960s, and in particular of the father-figures of liberation, Reich and Marcuse'.[34] Notwithstanding the defeat of Dr Hoffman, however, desire is ultimately victorious in this novel, for Desiderio, having awakened and failed to satisfy his appetite, continues to yearn for Albertina for fifty years after her death.

Desire and sexuality are fundamental concerns in Carter's writing, but so is power, and especially sexual power. This is obviously one of the reasons for her attraction to Sade; in *The Sadeian Woman* she writes that Sade 'urges women to fuck as actively as they are able, so that powered by their enormous and hitherto untapped sexual energy they will then be able to fuck their way into history and, in doing so, change it'.[35] The repetition of the active 'fuck', the use of 'power' as a verb and the hyperbolic 'enormous and hitherto untapped' evoke irresistible force. Women of appetite are the really powerful women in Carter's work, and the stronger the appetite the more they prevail.

Fevvers, in *Nights at the Circus*, is the prime example of largeness of appetite, suited in more ways than one for the 'woman on top' position, but it is in Carter's last novel, *Wise Children*, that appetite is most robustly celebrated and the life instincts taken to Rabelaisian extreme in the Chance twins, Dora and Nora, who retain their defining libido (and even – by proxy – their fertility) into their seventies. Their lifelong robust and no-nonsense dedication to show-business is reflected both in their sexual conquests and their relish for the greasy succulence of fried bacon, the strength of well-brewed tea, the power of gin. The figure of Saskia, their half-sister rival and the focus of their disapproval, is the twins' dark opposite, combining food and sex to confound the maternal and nurturing role in favour of her own appetites and lust for vengeance. This she achieves through a naked and potent manipulation of (male) appetite and greed.

Saskia begins her career early; her childhood pleasures include putting frogspawn in the porridge (a foretaste of oral sex, perhaps). For her and her twin's twenty-first birthday she cooks a suspect lunch ('very bitter' nettle soup, duck vampirically 'swimming in blood' and a 'disgusting syllabub' according to Dora), prompting Dora to speculate: '"Has she done it on purpose?" A poison meat!'[36] While Dora struggles with jealousy and indigestion, the two putative fathers engage in an unspoken eating competition, vying with each other in appreciation. The sexuality may be Oedipal and it may be subliminal, but it is unmistakably intestinal.

Saskia's power is evident both in the food that upsets people's stomachs and in her incestuous hold over her putative half-brother, Tristram, who is weakly unable to break their sexual tie even though he is in love with Tiffany. Dora's claim that Saskia ensnared Tristram by means of some substance added to his food, and her account of how Tiffany had been stricken with an upset stomach during their stay at Saskia's villa in Tuscany attributes much of her power to ingested substances. Dora also admits, however, that Saskia is dramatically good-looking and sexually provocative:

She had a lovely nape, on which that knot of scarlet hair sat like a Rhode Island red on a clutch and her nape was on display in all she did, intimate, exposed and sexy as she bent over the stove to poke around with a spoon suggestively in a pot or stick a prong into a drumstick with quite sadistic glee. (180)

The combination of exposed neck (passive, sacrificial) and poking with spoon or 'prong' (about as phallic as you can get) suggest a comprehensively sado-masochistic sexuality.

Saskia's particular exploitation of food, sexuality and cruelty is vividly encapsulated in Dora's description of a television cooking programme in which Saskia jugs a hare:

She cut the thing up with slow, voluptuous strokes. 'Make sure your blade is up to it!' she husked, running her finger up and down the edge, although the spectacle of Saskia with a cleaver couldn't help but remind me and Nora of how she'd run amok with the cake knife on her twenty-first. Next, she lovingly prepared a bath for the hare, she minced up shallots, garlic, onions, added a bouquet garni and a pint of claret and sat the poor dismembered beast in that for a day and a half. Then she condescended to sauté the parts briskly in a hot pan over a high flame until they singed. Then it all went into the oven for the best part of another day. She sealed the lid of the pot with a flour-and-water paste. 'Don't be a naughty thing and peek!' she warned with a teasing wink. Time to decant at last! The hare had been half-rotted, then cremated, then consumed. If there is a god and she is of the rabbit family, then Saskia will be in

deep doodoo on Judgment Day. 'Delicious,' she moaned, dipping her finger in
the juice and sucking. She licked her lips, letting her pink tongue-tip linger.
'Mmmm . . .' (180–1)

From the first 'slow, voluptuous strokes' through to the moaning and lip-
licking, the whole scene suggests a displaced copulation, to which the
teasing winks and coy exclamations are invitations. Reminders of
Saskia's sadistic potential are included, in the (also sexual) running of her
finger up and down the knife, in the recalling of her 'run[ning] amok'
with the cake knife at her twenty-first birthday lunch and in the singeing
of the hare flesh. But the overwhelming impression is of the sensuality
of cooking, and Saskia's tasting of the resulting juice recalls the satisfactions of breastfeeding as well as promising both mouthwatering tastes
and brute sexual pleasures.

Saskia promises gratification of the combined lusts for food and sex.
She wields a power that may not be denied and which is by no means
benign: she 'jugged a hare for Tristram, once,' we are reminded by Dora,
and 'that cooked his goose' (181). Three times she tries to poison
Melchior. What clouds her apparently irresistible combination of food
with sex is that she is motivated primarily by revenge: against her
(assumed) father, against the schoolfriend who becomes his third wife,
against anyone who arouses her jealousy. These negative aspects might
be seen as the complementary energies of Eros, the dark powerhouse of
its blazing appetite. But not only is Saskia's sexuality devouring and illegitimate in its objects, it is associated repeatedly with toxic intention, and
her business, as the 'half-rotted' hare suggests, is that of greed and corruption. In some respects, indeed, it would be fair to see her as a meeting
place – or battleground – between the ebullient appetites of the libido
and the controlling, vengeful and destructive impulses of the death
instincts. These powerful, negating appetites of Thanatos are at the
centre of chapter 2.

Cannibalism and Carter: fantasies of omnipotence

The connotations of 'cannibalism' imply a cultural archetype, conjuring up irredeemably savage, most primitive and distant tribes, or the pathological disintegration of personality and social order. Such archetypal images of cannibalism are propagated, teased and tested in periodic macabre prosecutions that hit the headlines and account for something of people's horrified fascination with the subject, fuelled in popular novels and films such as *Alive!*; *The Silence of the Lambs*; *The Cook, the Thief, his Wife and her Lover* and *Delicatessen*. Notwithstanding the publicity, cannibalism in this culture remains, as Margaret Atwood puts it 'the taboo of taboos'.[1] However much sexual prohibitions are eroded – bestiality, sado-masochism and incest becoming admissible, if not approved – cannibalism remains firmly outside the pale. It may be joked about, rendered harmless by humorous packaging or speculated about in the most abstract way ('If *you* were shipwrecked, would you . . . ?') but it is not permissible. Eating people, it seems, is simply and absolutely wrong.

Yet cannibalism is close to being a primary image: the suckling child connotes consumption by the flesh of our flesh, devouring a bodily substance emanating from the breast that psychoanalytic theory tells us is not yet known to be separate from the self. The simple urge to consume is an unknowing beginning point from which we develop to a condition of more or less discrimination in our appetites as we meet, eat and incorporate the world, both literally and metaphorically. Images of cannibalistic consumption are everywhere: children eat jelly babies and bake gingerbread men; ethnic groups are swallowed up (assimilated) by host societies; sharp business practice is described as 'dog eat dog' in a competitive world of 'eat or be eaten'; lovers are invited to oral congress, 'Eat me.'

As a metaphor cannibalism is rife. A secondary definition as 'savage and inhuman cruelty' no doubt lies behind its colloquial use as an insult.

The word also has associations of dismemberment in the verb 'to cannibalise'.[2] Most potent, though, are the images of ingestion that cannibalism evokes, figuring an extreme desire to devour a person, to incorporate someone into oneself, a lust for total possession or a rage for obliteration and supremacy. The suggestion of rapacious dealings and profound yearning for union together indicate the conflicting motivations of power and love. Indeed, my argument in part maintains that these conflicting feelings are not mutually exclusive, and that cannibalism, whether actual, fantasised or metaphorical, is a self-contradictory, complex phenomenon.

If for this reason alone, the idea of cannibalism is of immense attraction to writers of fiction, and particularly so for Angela Carter, drawn as she is to subterranean conflict and contradiction in society and culture. Cannibalism – both in Carter's writing and in literature in general – usually appears in one of two forms: the depiction of the literal eating of human flesh, and the use of cannibalistic desire or behaviour as a metaphor. Many texts employ figurative cannibalism; indeed it may be argued that any writing about eating (or assimilation and possession) is at some level dealing with impulses which are broadly cannibalistic, much of it far more obvious than the instances Ella Freeman Sharpe cites in her discussion of metaphor.[3] In the light of psychoanalytic theory, cannibalism can be seen to relate to almost every aspect of eating other than that of merely feeding the body to stay alive. And *in extremis* that too.

It is important to distinguish between survival cannibalism, such as that detailed in Piers Paul Read's *Alive!*, which chronicles the events following a plane crash in the Andes, and the kind of cannibalistic desire appropriated by the psychoanalysts.[4] There is any amount of difference between an unconscious yearning to consume a loved one in nostalgic pursuit of a mythical state of oneness, and the ingestion of strips of frozen or rotting corpse to postpone the hour of death. Somewhere between the two lies the often highly formalised or ritualised cannibalism of so-called primitive tribes. Without going into anthropological detail, it can be said that cannibalistic societies tend to fall into two groups: those who consume their enemies as an act of destruction, and those who consume friends (or enemies) by way of homage.[5] While the first of these takes no account of the effect on the eater (other than the satisfying rage of annihilation), the second group apparently seeks to keep alive something of the person consumed, or even to achieve a transformation, for if you are what you eat then you become a different individual once you absorb another. The symbolism is not unlike that of the Christian Eucharist or Mass.

But tribal and survival cannibalism are both remote from the bulk of contemporary cannibalistic reference, and they tend not to reveal the peculiar quality of appetite evident in what might be called western cannibalism (in both its tabloid newspaper and literary manifestations). More than the recurrence of a regular hunger, this appetite is characterised by its sheer insatiability. It is this insatiability which suggests a psychological drive or compulsion.

Freud does offer a possible generalised explanation for cannibalistic desire in his claim that, because sexual intercourse is a fleeting and less than absolute form of union, it is ultimately unsatisfying in comparison with the fantasy of cannibalism. The idea of total fusion is potent, though unrealisable (in Freud's view its unrealisability has the beneficial upshot that the ensuing disappointment, duly sublimated, leads to culture and civilization).[6] Benign or idealistic cannibalism, as we might call it, is certainly in evidence in passionate lovers' fantasies or visceral responses to babies, and in some fiction, such as Italo Calvino's *Under the Jaguar Sun* which explores passion in terms of mutual cannibalism.[7] Michèle Roberts, too, in *Impossible Saints* writes a passionate, quasi-spiritual cannibalism bordering on the erotic, as the uncorrupted body of Josephine is progressively nibbled at by pilgrims: 'The fingernails of the left hand, the toenails of both feet, the eyebrows, the eyelashes, the end of the nose. Someone had torn open the habit and bitten off the nipples. Someone else had nibbled the earlobes.'[8] Later on Sister Maria, by way of conservation, covertly prepares a heavy 'pork' stew, to be pack into earthenware jars and sealed with fat: potted Josephine.

Though neither is a *necessary* characteristic, however, threat and fear are predominant elements in popular conceptions of cannibalism in fiction and film. The writing of Angela Carter embraces both aspects, but there's no doubt she finds the predatory more beguiling and more useful to her purposes. Leaving aside the vampiric characters of her first novel *Shadow Dance*, Carter's first rapacious eater is the puppet-maker Uncle Philip in *The Magic Toyshop*, to whose bleak domain Melanie and her two siblings are transplanted from their roots in rural middle-class comfort. They find the toyshop a place of contradictory appetites, though from their arrival they eat well. Francie's strange grace, 'flesh to flesh', while offering a simple recognition of the literal process, suggests something carnivorously sinister. Any appetite for life, whether expressed by Aunt Margaret and her brothers or by the children, is snuffed out by the presence of Uncle Philip, by his tyrannical restrictions and control of the household budget (economic dependence is an important factor in Carter's analysis of gender roles and sexuality, since the financially disempowered rarely have much in the way of choice). Slippage between the desire to eat and sexual desire, generally characteristic of Carter's writing, is in this novel strongly coloured with cannibalism.

The satisfaction of sexual appetite is far from mutual in Uncle Philip's toyshop; his appetites are grimly satisfied with no hint of sharing. Aunt Margaret and her brothers, Francie and Finn, embody a spirit of passionate and anarchic zest (proclaimed by their wild blazing hair) but this is released only in Uncle Philip's absence. Their covert appetite for life is revealed in Aunt Margaret's and Francie's incestuous hunger for each other, a Romantic dimension to this family group's nostalgic desire. Finn has an erotic appetite, but it initially proves too much for Melanie's nascent sexuality; she has first to escape from the devouring patriarch, Uncle Philip, whom she privately labels Bluebeard (hallucinating a severed hand in the knife and fork drawer) and who enacts a symbolic and artistic rape upon her through the medium of his puppet theatre in which she must play Leda to his lovingly created man-size swan.

Uncle Philip's bullying is inseparable from his relationship to food and its provision. He is a domestic tyrant, beating Finn for being late for breakfast and generally abusing members of the household. He controls the family finances not just meanly, but in order to be in control. The food is bought on credit and he alone pays the bills monthly; nobody may have any of 'his' money to spend for themselves. His very presence is controlling; he is memorably described as somehow even draining the flavour from the food and making the dining-room 'as cold and cheerless as a room in a commercial traveller's guesthouse' (124). Yet he gives every appearance of enjoying his food, dominating the table and eating hugely. Melanie can barely recognise him as the same man she saw in the photograph of her parents' wedding, so enormous has he grown from eating and (we may conclude) feeding off his wife and her brothers.

The satisfaction Uncle Philip takes in food is not merely from eating it. On Sunday afternoons, he obliges Aunt Margaret to wear her 'best' (threadbare grey) dress and to don his wedding present: a silver choker which prevents her eating and restricts her breathing. She takes on a 'tragic' beauty, wearing this, and at teatime is able just to sip at a cup of tea and nibble a few stalks of mustard and cress. Uncle Philip meanwhile tucks in relentlessly:

[he] broke the armour off a pink battalion of shrimps and ate them steadily, chewed through a loaf of bread spread with half a pound of butter and helped himself to the lion's share of the cake while gazing at her with expressionless satisfaction, apparently deriving a certain pleasure from her discomfort, or even finding that the sight of it improved his appetite. (113)

The description suggests the calmly relentless exercise of power of the tyrant; it is on Sunday nights, after this tea, that Uncle Philip exercises his conjugal rights. The implication is clear: his appetites are well sharpened by the denial of his wife's appetite and the exhibition of her imprisonment in the roles he chooses.

Degradation is a major tool of Uncle Philip's tyranny and his war against (or fear of) exuberant life outside his control. The one person immune to his wrath is Melanie's younger brother Jonathon who poses no threat, eating with a polite but absent-minded enthusiasm and spending most of his time, like an embryonic Uncle Philip, in a fantasy world of crafted models. The cheeky and defiant Finn in particular attracts Uncle Philip's blows and abuse which, together with the denial of physical comforts in the house, exacerbates the atmosphere of tension and resentment. All this is grist to Uncle Philip's mill; in addition to ruling by brute force, he attempts to manipulate the defloration, and hence degradation, of Melanie by instructing Finn to rehearse the rape of Leda with her before the performance.

Brutality is Uncle Philip's hallmark, though not where his puppets are concerned; to these he exhibits the most sentimental tenderness, unthreatening and controllable as they are. With humans he is capable of murder, the culminating act of control and brutality. His capacity for this, too, is revealed in the context of eating, such as when he carves the Christmas goose:

He attacked the defenceless goose so savagely he seemed to want to kill it all over again, perhaps feeling the butcher had been incompetent in the first place. . . .The reeking knife in his hand, he gazed reflectively at Finn . . . (160)

He does not yet translate his thoughts into action, merely serving Finn a 'mean portion of skin and bone' while himself giving a hearty imitation of Henry VIII. It is when he discovers his wife and her brother *in flagrente delicto* that he moves to kill, beginning his rampaging where else but in the kitchen.

What motivates this monster? His meanness is clearly not simple cupidity. He is neither a mere miser, nor, despite his posturing, is he a self-righteous puritan such as Carter portrays in the Andrew Borden of

'The Fall River Axe Murders'.[9] Uncle Philip is in every respect a greedy man. He eats heartily for the same reason he bullies and controls the household: his appetite is omnivorous, he wants to eat the world. Significantly, Melanie describes him not only as Bluebeard but as 'heavy as Saturn' (168), Saturn being the god who castrated his father and ate his children for fear they would supplant him, becoming in the process a symbol of antagonism between the generations.[10] Just such a conflict might be said to be played out in *The Magic Toyshop*, Uncle Philip representing an overblown and abusive patriarchy and the rest of the family a younger, anarchic and perhaps feminine principle.

This interpretation can be taken further, for there is a contradiction between the apparent and external power of an Uncle Philip and the driving emptiness that lies inside, whether this is seen as a psychic, moral or political lack of substance. The seemingly irresistible external force is subverted both by an insatiability in the monster/cannibal's hunger (whether hunger for sexual satisfaction, food, affirmation, control and domination or all of these), and by his wholly self-referential attempts at resolution; Uncle Philip's love for his puppets suggests both the emptiness and the solipsism.

Psychoanalytic theory provides some illuminating insights. What underlies insatiability of appetite (and what Uncle Philip's behaviour enacts) is an impetus towards incorporation. Cannibalistic appetite invokes incorporation inasmuch as it expresses a desire to swallow or subsume something that cannot otherwise be dealt with in some way. Nicolas Abraham and Maria Torok explain it like this: the fantasy incorporation of an object (a person or part of a person) is used to avoid the introjection or acceptance of loss.[11] Since loss of all kinds is an inevitable and perpetual part of human life, such avoidance suggests a dysfunctional or arrested psychic condition.

The point at which Uncle Philip is psychically 'stuck' is plainly somewhere in the early Oedipal stage, initially characterised by Freud and later elaborated by Abraham and then by Melanie Klein into the theory of the 'oral-sadistic' (Abraham) or 'oral' stage (Klein). The oral stage, conceived as the first stage of libidinal development when nutrition is inseparable from the love relationship with the mother, is saturated with the resonances of eating and being eaten.[12] According to the theory, during the earliest stage the infant is unaware of anything outside itself; indeed it takes everything it experiences to *be* itself. Once the infant discovers difference, he or she may be said to have entered the 'oral-sadistic' or 'cannibalistic' stage, which is characterised by ambivalence; the infant experiences a conflict of love and aggression towards the love object or person (or part object, in the case of the breast) which is now perceived as external and unfamiliar, and a potential source of fear.

According to Klein, as a defence against anxiety the object becomes split into 'good' and 'bad' according to whether it gratifies or frustrates (the 'good breast' gratifying desire and the 'bad breast' causing frustration by its withdrawal); the infant or subject also projects libidinal or destructive instincts onto the object, through, for example, the desire to incorporate it (but thereby destroy it) or the destructive aim of sucking the breast dry. The subject's ambivalence is further complicated by a fear that these destructive impulses will be reciprocated by the parent, a fantasy of being eaten that is a projection of, and reaction against, the infant's own desire to assimilate and possess what is external to the self.[13]

An adult urge for incorporation thus reflects both nostalgia for a (mythical) state of union and a degree of ambivalence. Such a union, like the incorporation featured in the oral-stage theory (which provides the model for more mature introjection and identification) might provide pleasure through the penetration of the self by the object, give satisfaction by the destruction of the object, or keep the object within the self specifically in order to appropriate its qualities. The parallel with the satisfactions of literal cannibalism is quite startling here: eating someone through love, as the ultimate act of union or possession; eating through hate, to destroy someone by superimposing oneself; or eating a brave enemy as a token of respect and to achieve bravery. To (re)achieve the desired union would involve introjecting or ingesting what has become separate, 'other', both loved and threatening, whether this is the love object or something less differentiated, some representative of the whole world. One who desires incorporation seeks pleasure; in Freudian terms, 'the original pleasure-ego wants to introject into itself everything that is good and to eject from itself everything that is bad'.[14] The pleasure is distorted, however, because incorporation is an avoidance mechanism, and because it embraces destructive impulses, for the object is destroyed by being incorporated.

The process outlined here is not limited to individual psyches, but provides a social or cultural mechanism. In her account of western culture, *From Communion to Cannibalism*, Maggie Kilgour explains what she sees as major attempts to construct 'transcendental' explanatory systems in western thought as stemming directly from 'nostalgia for a state of total incorporation'.[15] The terms she uses are directly psychoanalytic,

suggesting that movement to resolve differences by assimilation or incorporation is similarly prompted. By this token, lovers yearning for despotic possession of the love object are fuelled by the same basic drive as
societies with an assimilating impetus which invent xenophobic accusa-
tions against resistant minorities (such as Jews in the Middle Ages,
accused – ironically enough – of cannibalism).

   Nostalgia for union, the desire to incorporate and its psychophysical
underpinning are, according to this explanation, common to literal and
metaphorical acts of cannibalism. Kilgour's comment contains a caveat:
such an analysis itself runs the risk of courting an inappropriate wholeness, by offering a reductive analysis of all human activity in terms of
cannibalistic desire. Considering oral nostalgia on a wider canvas is
useful, however, and allows us to see how individual or small-scale cannibalistic acts may be representative. This is especially true of Carter's
writing, since by her own admission all her characters bear a heavy
weight of signification.[16] On large or small scale, incorporation involves
a form of colonialism; if the object is taken in, then everything about it
may be appropriated by a form of digestion. Like a society or state that
seeks to destroy opposition by the assimilation of its minority groups,
Uncle Philip moves to bring the children into the same condition of seedy
enslavement as the rest of the household. If Uncle Philip is taken as a
figure for patriarchy, then 'cannibalism' – subjugation by assimilation
and degradation – may be seen as one of its main weapons in exerting
power over women, young people, the Irish, and spontaneity of all kinds.
Uncle Philip's likeness to a Victorian mill owner and his all-round greed
(for food, power and money) extend what Foucault calls the 'the limitless
presumption of the appetite' into the realm of western capitalism itself.[17]

   The idea of a monstrous appetite for absolute power is something
Carter returns to several times. Doctor Donally in *Heroes and Villains* is
another brutal and skilful man, a cross between shaman and mad scien-
tist, whose rationality, taken to excess, will end in the logical conclusion
of apocalypse, and who uses every means at his disposal, from snake
religion to poison, to subdue the people. In *The Sadeian Woman* Carter
suggests that Sade, via the Romantics, is responsible for, 'shaping aspects
of the modern sensibility; its paranoia, its despair, its sexual terrors, its
omnivorous egocentricity, its tolerance of massacre, holocaust, annihilation'
(my italics).[18] Since Carter is presumably not simply portraying two isolated megalomaniac individuals, she is shaping her narratives to
comment upon precisely this 'modern sensibility', a sensibility she
clearly represents as cannibalistic in its indications.

Self-perpetuating appetite and monstrous egocentricity go hand in hand, the insatiability of the appetite itself being the product of a relentless and unsupported ego. Framed slightly differently, self-perpetuating appetite (consumer desire for goods and services perhaps) and a potentially monstrous self-serving group (or corporation or market) easily become a metaphor for political cannibalism, the unsupported ego representing an absence of worth or value. It is not, I think, straining Carter too far to infer that her use of the cannibal mimics attempts in the latter half of the twentieth century to cut loose from the restraints of the superego, attempts which, while exhilarating, breed a sense of separation from what is or was sustaining. With a wholly rejected parent there is no primary love object, no breast, good or bad, and therefore no conceivable sense of union, wholeness and satisfaction; the self has to be recreated in a psychic vacuum, with, it seems, variously cannibalistic results.

Carter's short novel *Love* deals with a trio of just such narcissistic, alienated and dependent egos: Annabel, her husband Lee and his brother Buzz, all of whom engage in a complicated dance of mutual and self-damage.[19] Lorna Sage crisply identifies the process: 'They construct their selves, cannibalistically, out of each other, and inscribe their meanings on each other's flesh' – quite literally inscribe in one instance, when Annabel makes Lee have her name tattooed on his breast.[20] Ordinary appetite for food is not much in evidence in this novel, except, tellingly, when Lee first wakes up after a party and finds Annabel lying with him for warmth. The hunger in her face touches him so deeply that he takes her home and gives her breakfast, thereby initiating a pattern of caring. But her hunger is not for food, and is suspiciously predatory:

Annabel ate a little, drank her tea and covered her face with her hands so he could not watch her any more. Her movements were spiky, angular and graceful; how was he to know, since he was so young, that he would become a Spartan boy and she the fox under his jacket, eating his heart out. (15)

These characters are part of the 'love generation' of the late 1960s, Carter herself describing them as 'pure perfect products of those days of social mobility and sexual licence'.[21] Sexual appetite is definitive, yet their hunger for sexual adventure and fulfilment is highly suspect. Lee has a premarital affair with the wife of his philosophy tutor and, when married, an affair with a girl called Carolyn, both of whom mean little to him other than as food for his narcissism. After Annabel's first suicide attempt, her breakdown, relationship with Lee's brother Buzz – and in fact while she is killing herself – Lee, 'ravenous for the commonplace', takes refuge in the bed of a pupil, Joanne, who is astonished by his drowning desperation.

Annabel and Buzz become alarmingly close, dangerously blurring boundaries in their fantasies, but their attempt at sexual union is disastrous. Buzz, tormented with fears about women's sexuality, can only bring himself to enter her from behind, having first inspected her for evidence of a *vagina dentata* and handling her 'as unceremoniously as a fish on a slab, reduced only to anonymous flesh' (94). They try to behave like libertines, but Carter punctures their style in tellingly carnivorous, even cannibalistic terms: 'connoisseurs of unreality as they were, they could not bear the crude weight, the rank smell and the ripe taste of real flesh' (95).

Annabel's sexual hunger is the most self-deceptive; with Buzz she effectively seeks union with herself. If all three characters are profoundly narcissistic (and the novel contains a good deal of play about the cult of appearances), Annabel is the most thoroughly solipsistic: 'she had the capacity for changing the appearance of the real world which is the price paid by those who take too subjective a view of it' (3). She sees Lee in terms of certain paradoxical images – a herbivorous lion, a flesh-eating unicorn, ultimately a unicorn castrated of its horn – but has no sense of him as a real and separate person. Indeed, when she sees him on the balcony with Carolyn, she can barely bring herself to absorb his 'absolute otherness' and understands the act only in symbolic terms. Her puzzlement is that of the all-devouring infant, her jealousy the barely formed awareness of something beyond the self.

Her idea of having Lee's children relates only to 'certain explicit fantasies she had of totally engulfing him' (35) – an incorporating if not overtly cannibalistic image. Her most pleasurable, because unfamiliar, experience in their sexual relationship is the sensation of intimacy she experiences in bed with him, which she says she had only previously read about. She is a desolate child. When she returns from the disastrous encounter with Buzz she is desperately determined to seduce and possess her husband and attacks him with vampiric fervour. Although this confirms a sexual connection between all three characters, it is not a completion, but a 'mutual rape'; Lee can only experience Annabel as a sexually predatory diablesse or succubus, wearily wishing her dead so that he can be released from caring.

While in the mental hospital Annabel tells the psychiatrist that she has eaten her wedding ring, Lee tells the Fool in the park that she also tried to eat him alive. Sexual desire in much of Carter's writing masks a struggle analogous to that of cut-throat business and colonising cannibalism: 'eat or be eaten'. The struggle is not inevitably deathly. It is explicit and quite without the cruelty evident in *Love*, for example, in a dream sequence in the slightly earlier novel *Several Perceptions*. The distinction between food and sex is elided in typically jokey Carter fashion in the anonymous figure of a client of the high-class prostitute Mrs Boulder, who sits with her in the cafe, 'buttering his crumpet with the air of a man of the world'.[22] The fact that he will eat his crumpet does not necessarily indicate the balance of power in this particular relationship. Mrs Boulder is a woman who will not be exploited sexually, since she puts a price on her body, a role that, according to Carter, allows her both sexual licence and power:

The whore has made of herself her own capital investment . . . In an area of human relations where fraud is regular practice between the sexes, her honesty is regarded with a mocking wonder. She sells herself; but she is a fair tradesman and her explicit acceptance of contractual obligation implicit in all sexual relations mocks the fraud of the 'honest' woman who will give nothing at all in return for goods and money except the intangible and hence unassessable perfume of her presence.[23]

Carter does acknowledge the social reality of Mrs Boulder's situation and its problems, however, by turning her to alcohol. The mother of his friend Viv, Mrs Boulder becomes the focus of Joseph's fantasies, featuring in a dream whose importance is underlined by being recalled several times through the narrative.

Joseph, who like the characters in *Love* is also an alienated and self-regarding protagonist, teases Viv about his mother, and yet he (Joseph) sinks with utter content into the security of banal conversation and her motherly care, speculating momentarily about Viv suckling at her once splendid breasts. At the same time, he is startlingly aware of her alarmingly open gaze, the expression in her eyes some thirty years younger than she is. When he sees her in the café he has the sensation of falling through her eyes into the country of an uncomprehending virgin. It is immediately after this that he dreams of her as an ice cream, the first indication of his ambivalent, gently cannibalistic desire for her.

She is, unsurprisingly, delicious, and in the dream Joseph tucks in with gusto. No problem so far: suckling at her breast and eating her as ice cream are not so very different. Joseph can indulge, fantastically, in both sexual and oral appetite, be actor and recipient at the same time. However, the bowl and its contents begin to grow, increasing in proportion as he eats. He can, it seems, incorporate her without destroying her.

He sets to with a will, but the more he eats the larger she grows, his eating efforts are inadequate and soon he jettisons his spoon and climbs into the bowl, scooping Mrs Boulder into his mouth by the handful. Eventually, alas, Joseph is submerged by an untimely avalanche and he is extinguished by the grotesque 'polar night of Mrs Boulder's belly'; it is she who in the end engulfs or incorporates him (76).

The dream functions as wish-fulfilment, expression of fear, explanation and, obliquely, as a prefiguring. Joseph is excited by the idea of penetrating Mrs Boulder at the same time as he wants to be nurtured, but he is fearful and suspicious. He wants to be mothered and fears being smothered. Carter draws on an archetypal fear of the enveloping woman complementing the *vagina dentata* fantasy of which Buzz in *Love* is victim, and which Dr Donally uses to manipulate the fears of the Barbarians in *Heroes and Villains*. The dread of being eaten refers again to the oral stage; Joseph's ambivalence, his simultaneous fear and desire correspond precisely with the loving and destructive responses to the breast in Klein's theory. The apprehension is purely Joseph's; when later, after an initial failure, he achieves sexual union with Mrs Boulder and tells her about his dream, she is merely touched that he should dream about her at all. It is the reality of her ageing (and maternal) body that reconnects him with life (like Annabel, he had been an attempted suicide) and fills him with tenderness; in moving towards orgasm his desire is described in terms that suggest a yearning to regress even further, to return to an incorporated condition inside the womb:

the uncreated country of fountain and forest deep inside her, deep as the serene Beulah Land where Viv once slept fleecily clad in lanugo down, under blue trees shedding fruit of light. (114–15) [24]

In *The Sadeian Woman*, Carter identifies Sade's refusal in *Philosophy in the Boudoir* to allow the mother of Eugenie to reach orgasm as his sticking point, and she considers that this results in the failure of his woman to fully subvert her society. In Freudian terms, she argues, no matter what size the phallus, Sade cannot satisfy his mother, for that is the father's function. The mother remains guardian of a fearful and secret place that he must seal up before it devours him, a cannibalistic place for which he has powerful negative feelings. Carter, with no such patriarchal hang-ups, affirms, in richly phrased accordance with Klein, that the body of the mother is the 'great, good place, the concretisation of the earthly paradise' (134), enriched by infant fantasies of the good breast, 'the place where love and hunger meet' (134).

Through Joseph, Carter portrays the enrichment of the primal object; his symbolic or fantasised return to the paradisal mother's body allows a symbolic rebirth into 'trust, hope and a belief in the existence of good' (*SW* 134), an extraordinarily naked affirmation. The mutual satisfaction of Joseph and Mrs Boulder, his substitute mother, represents a release, a rebirth, following which Mrs Boulder is able to find again her wonderful black lover from the war, and Joseph is freed to a normally healthy hunger for tea and boiled eggs. The narrative is resolved with a Christmas Eve party, the novel ending on an upbeat, optimistic note, the town a clean page covered with snow and the cat producing six pure white kittens.

If *Several Perceptions* does much to confound love and hunger, sex and maternity, *Heroes and Villains*, with its post-catastrophe emphasis on chaos, pushes cannibalism right back to its predatory, vampiric paradigm. The 'heroine' Marianne escapes from her white steel and concrete tower to run away with the Barbarians in a world of dystopian pastoral, which has at least a passing resemblance to the hippy movement. The principle of 'eat or be eaten' is central to this novel, both literally, in terms of survival, and figuratively, in the sexual struggle between Marianne and the Barbarian Jewel, the power struggle with the shaman patriarch Donally and in the general strife amongst Jewel's family and tribe.

The primitive conditions that Carter creates in this novel provide an opportunity to suggest human nature at a fairly elemental level. Ignorance and superstition are sketched in, though despite this and the setting the characters are in many ways not unlike those in any other Carter novel; their superstitions are simply more literal. The imagery suggests a reversionary *Wuthering Heights*, dark and foul, full of fire, meat, animals and brooding passions. Cannibalism is outlined as a plausible and realistic fear, and is used as a threat or bogey by the villagers. Marianne's nurse warns her that if she is not good the Barbarians will eat her, wrapped in clay, baked in the fire and seasoned with salt. In a well-signalled parallel, the Barbarian child Jen tells Marianne about her father's disappearance: 'He dressed up and went away and he didn't come back and the Professors had killed him and baked him and eaten him with salt' (35).[25] Cannibalism is a vivid emblem of the primitive, always lurking in Marianne's imagination, so that it leaps to mind as a possibility during the semiotic wedding ceremony she is forced to undergo: 'I thought he was going to kill me,' she says of Donally's blood-mixing ritual, 'cut me up, fry me and distribute me in ritual gobbets to the tribe' (76).

A more figurative, cultural or colonial cannibalism (comparable to Uncle Philip's in *The Magic Toyshop*) is invoked in the purpose of the marriage, as Jewel explains to Marianne after he has raped her: 'I've got to marry you, haven't I? . . . Swallow you up and incorporate you, see. Dr Donally says. Social psychology.' (56) The outsider Marianne must be incorporated so that she will no longer be perceived as a threat, the same mechanism as is invoked in *The Infernal Desire Machines of Dr Hoffman*, when the centaurs seek a means of 'digesting' Desiderio and Albertina.

The dilemma faced by Marianne is how to interact with the Barbarians – and specifically Jewel – without being completely subsumed. To begin with, she behaves rather as Annabel does in *Love*, denying Jewel an existence independent of their relationship and seeing him as two-dimensional. The difference is in the quality of their sexual contact, which between Jewel and Marianne is described as a 'third thing':

this erotic beast . . . eyeless, formless and equipped with one single mouth. It was amphibious and swam in black, brackish waters, subsisting only upon night and silence; she closed her eyes in case she glimpsed it by moonlight and there were no words of endearment in common, anyway, nor any reason to use them. The beast had teeth and claws. It was sometimes an instrument solely of vengefulness, though often its own impetus carried it beyond this function. When it separated out to themselves, again, they woke to the mutual distrust of the morning. (88–9)

Eros is not kindly. The language evokes Dionysian passion and violence, and a deadly struggle for supremacy. Jewel intimates a link with butchery, daubing Marianne's face one evening with blood from the slaughtered animal carcasses. It is a conspicuous connection, sharply in evidence in the big butchering scene earlier in the novel, a scene full of noise, movement, animals, children and excitement, a 'whirling conflict of black and red' (46) in which the brothers, with violation in mind, manoeuvre Marianne towards the table where the carcasses were so recently cut up. Only the arrival of Dr Donally prevents a pack rape. These scenes perform a brutal sexual exploitation, marking women as meat for men's consumption.

Carter associates meat and living flesh again in *The Sadeian Woman*, but here in order to make a distinction. The butcherly delights of meat, she says, are not sensual but analytical, and any pleasure to be gained can only be technical (in addition to the pleasure knowing oneself to be the cutter or the eater and not the victim). Hence the shock value when the boundary is breached, as in Alina Reyes' erotic tale *The Butcher*, in which the butcher's sexuality and the meat he handles in his work are so closely linked that descriptions of butchery and of intercourse are frequently almost interchangeable: 'I saw the knife enter the firm dead flesh, opening it like a shining wound.'[26] When the narrator glimpses the butcher copulating with his woman it is in the freezer, as though she is one of the animal carcasses. According to Carter, when flesh is treated as meat – she has Sade in mind – then sensuality and ambiguity are banished, and sexual relations become utterly distorted.

Carter herself plays with these elements in the short-story reworking of Bluebeard, 'The Bloody Chamber'.[27] In this story the Marquis's hunger for his new wife is overlaid with vampiric suggestion (from the Marquis's wet red lips to the Transylvanian postcard from Carmilla) and hints of cannibalism. Intimations of possession, objectification and fragmentation, specifically of women, pervade the story. Consider, for example, the heroine's description of the Marquis's behaviour at the opera, the night before their wedding:

I saw him watching me in the gilded mirrors with the assessing eye of a connoisseur inspecting horseflesh, or even of a housewife in the market, inspecting cuts on the slab. (11)

This recalls the photographs in pornographic magazines of parts of women: the outsize breasts, the cheekily inviting buttocks, or the genital close-up chillingly referred to in the trade as 'split beaver'.

The Marquis is a consumer; the exquisite cruelty of the ruby choker he gives the narrator for a wedding present ('like an extraordinarily precious slit throat'(11)) and his 'sheer carnal avarice' suggest he is one of arcane tastes. The imprisoning and stifling qualities of Aunt Margaret's choker are here given an additional and suitably Gothic twist. The new bride's choker prefigures the end the Marquis has in store for her, but also, like a dog collar, signifies total mastery (a mastery underlined, incidentally, by the difference in their ages, wealth and status). He sees her as his to do with as he pleases. Since what pleases is the satisfaction of appetites and his appetites are unchecked and perverse, the Marquis indulges in an ambiguous carnality. The narrator describes his approach as as blasé epicurean:

He stripped me, gourmand that he was, as if he were stripping the leaves off an artichoke – but do not imagine much finesse about it; this artichoke was no particular treat for the diner nor was he yet in any greedy haste. He approached his familiar treat with a weary appetite . . .

and likens herself to the girl in a pornographic etching, 'bare as a lamb chop' (15).

Everything about the Marquis suggests cannibalism. The stems of his lilies in water are like severed limbs; his cigar is as 'fat as a baby's arm' (12). They eat an erotically gastronomic lunch including pheasant with hazelnuts and chocolate and a white, 'voluptuous' cheese; the food is libidinous and sexuality carnivorous. In the end, the distinction between lusts all but disappears as the Marquis's unsatisfied (and unsatisfiable?) appetite is monstrously quickened by his bride's delayed approach to the execution:

Don't loiter, girl! Do you think I shall lose appetite for the meal if you are so long about serving it? No; I shall grow hungrier, more ravenous with each moment, more cruel . . . Run to me, run! I have a place prepared for your exquisite corpse in my display of flesh! (39)

Yet he is not solely a monster, or at least he is one who also appears to suffer. His delight in his wife's virginity and his appalling despair when it becomes apparent that she has visited his torture chamber suggest redeemable potential. Like the bored countess in *Vampirella* and 'The Lady of the House of Love' he is impaled upon his desire while longing to be free of it, a freedom that demands innocence, not complicity.[28] Satisfaction is ephemeral and desire self-perpetuating; the eaten may only temporarily assuage tormenting appetite and the sole release for the Marquis is negation, which effectively means death. This dilemma is played out more fully, and with greater emphasis on negation, in the figures of the Count in *The Infernal Desire Machines of Doctor Hoffman* and the Clowns in *Nights at the Circus*, which are discussed later in the chapter.

Murder, and still more so cannibalism, in Carter's view demonstrates the 'meatiness' of human flesh; it is a fundamental exploitation, in which one person is seen by the other in absolutely primitive terms and the abyss between what she calls 'master' and victim is at its greatest. This view has to do with what she identifies as the Sadeian libertines' 'economic' theory of sexual pleasure: that pleasure shared is pleasure diminished. This measure of exploitation cannot take account of the victim as an equal person in any real sense at all. The 'economic' theory also reflects the libertines' almost puritan sense that flesh as a means of production must be owned, and, like any resource, be made to pay for itself. Hence the importance of coprophagy: even excrement is not allowed to go to waste. In controlling the means of this particular production (by way of diets and timetables), the libertines strike at the primary and most fundamental autonomy of their victims, for faeces are supposedly a child's first gift, and the production or withholding of them (to the delight or distress of his or her parents) becomes the first expression of independence. To be deprived of this primary autonomy is the ultimate enslavement. In this context, cannibalism, both politically and psychically, is nothing short of dehumanisation.

Sawney Beane, the Scots cannibal with a walk-on part in *Vampirella*, describes cannibalism as a curse, the 'most insatiable hunger in the world' (96), but here Carter gives the curse strong political overtones. The Beanes have fourteen children and times are hard. When Beane suggests cannibalism to his wife as a solution, she replies 'aye, Sawney, let's eat them up the way they've eaten us', an allusion, perhaps, to Swift's *Modest Proposal*. True to their words, they dine on the aristocracy. Political revenge for oppression suffered, like the longing to achieve union with another, casts cannibalism in a less than heinous light.

Its common insatiability does suggest a psychic (mal)function, however, and incorporation fantasy may become obsessive, as Abraham and Torok suggest.[29] The hunger can be seen as regressive, expressing unrealisable longings for that idealised state of wholeness in which the world is not other, and the eater is undifferentiated from the eaten. What such hunger obsessively focuses on is the (real or imagined) point of transition, a realisation of separation, the loss of arcadia. The area in which much of Carter's writing seems to me to hover is precisely where the individual becomes conscious of difference, of self and other. The angry and frightened ambivalence and the mixture of love and aggression that accompany this discovery are what power many of her voracious characters, for Carter focuses on boundaries, margins, what is overlooked, repressed or suppressed, in both psyche and society.

Carter's novels and stories reverberate with psychological, political and cultural ideas. Her view that a narrative is 'an argument stated in fictional terms', her scathing comments about writers who claim that their characters 'take over' a novel and her assertion that her characters 'have always got a tendency to be telling you something' emphasise her control and sense of purpose.[30] David Punter asserts that this purpose is in part to chart 'the unconscious processes of Western society', processes which include the making of identity.[31] Though Carter takes a socio-political view as much as a psychoanalytic one – in her later novels especially, identity is shown to be socially constructed (or reconstructed, in the case of New Eve) – she is undoubtedly fascinated by the hidden drives and motivations of psyche and society. The charting of 'unconscious processes' is evident to some extent in her earlier novels, but it becomes overt in *The Infernal Desire Machines of Doctor Hoffman* and *The*

Passion of New Eve. Underpinning the processes of the unconscious in Freud's final instinct theory are the two great opposing classes of instincts: the life instincts, or Eros, and the death instincts, or Thanatos.[32] Carter's writing vividly displays the operation of these instincts in cannibalistic desire which may be seen as an emanation from one or other, and sometimes from a conflicting mixture of the two.

The Infernal Desire Machines of Doctor Hoffman postulates a war between reason and desire: between the establishment, embodied in the supremely rational Minister, and Dr Hoffman, the apostle of desire; between restraint and imagination; between 'an encyclopedist and a poet'.[33] The conflict begins with the Doctor bombarding the city with illusions. The Minister in his struggle against libertarianism attempts to give everything a 'reality rating', an effort that bears a more than passing resemblance to Kilgour's 'transcendental system . . . that could contain all meaning'.[34] It is the very lack of such a system that is promulgated by Dr Hoffman, the anarchic effects of whose efforts the Minister experiences as chaos. What is 'real' becomes impossible to disentangle from what is perceived and what is desired; 'reality' is elusive and inconstant, a conception gnomically endorsed by the proprietor of the peep-show: 'Nothing . . . is ever completed; it only changes,' there is no 'hidden unity' (99).

This is not to say unity is not itself desired. The phrase 'persistence of vision' that recurs in the novel applies not only to Dr Hoffman's own vision but to the sustaining of human longings and illusions concerning continuity and coherence.[35] Psychic tenacity has no dealings with empirical evidence, and humans continue to strive for coherence and order against all evidence of separation and fragmentation – or to put it another way, they pursue an ideal of unity. The contradiction between, on the one hand, Hoffman's move towards the fulfilment of desire and, on the other, the impossibility of realising any desire for a coherent unity (ironically embodied in Hoffman's own continuing relationship with his embalmed wife) creates a tension that supplies one of the dynamics of the novel.

Desire – Eros and Thanatos – is the energy source in this novel. It is manifest in the emblematic images of the peep show, the narcissistic eyes, edible breasts, penis candle, perpetual congress, mutilated flesh and *in utero* landscape, all of which suggest a potently masculine appeal to the voyeur. Desire powers the illusions Dr Hoffman projects onto the city and is responsible for much of what appears or happens to the protagonist Desiderio in his picaresque quest, since the force of desires in this novel leads to their apparent embodiments. The 'transmutations' that afflict the city are both literal and metaphorical projections; since psychological projection is a mechanism whereby hidden desires and impulses are externalised, despite a few lyrical ones most of the 'transmutations' are bestial and bloodthirsty.

The contents of the peep-show confront the most inadmissible of ideas. One of the samples Desiderio looks at in his futile attempts to catalogue them is a 'typical' scene of a nursemaid toasting and eating her small charge. Since this follows not long after Desiderio's escape from the jaws of the river people, it obviously reflects his experience there; the discovery that you are to be the main dish at your own wedding feast is disturbing to say the least, and responses might well be projected, particularly given the surreal possibilities in this world for realisation. But the scene also looks forward (to the cooking of the Count), and, like the other samples, sketches archetypal fears and desires. The samples ambiguously represent 'everything it was possible to believe' (108), either through direct simulation or Freudian symbolism, and it is Freudian symbolism that connects this scene with the intertwining of cannibalism and desire running through the novel.

Cannibalistic desire operates in two directions here. Desiderio's longing to belong represents a desire for absorption that is only repudiated when his actual survival is threatened. He wants, really, to be incorporated, and the family of boat people represent his ideal of 'belonging'. This is no simple family substitution, however. Not only is Desiderio a stranger to the tribe, but the Indians themselves are marginalised, turned in on themselves, rejecting outsiders for fear of assimilation. They are immune to Dr Hoffman's manifestations because of their logical self-sufficiency; when an elder says something is so, it *is* so, and desire is repressed by tradition and ritual. For a while Desiderio is enchanted by this communal solipsism and delighted to look indistinguishable from the others. He learns their chirruping language, which, with no abstract nouns, complex tenses or verb 'to be', suggests a society only on the brink of language and the symbolic. The density, complexity and skill of Carter's narrative are evident here; this little society, its members 'frozen in themselves' (87), represents an arrested pre-conceptual, pre-symbolic stage in the development of subjectivity.

The snag with the family, as with the stage, is that it is all-devouring. Desiderio wants to be incorporated, but not, ultimately, to be destroyed. However, he is not only desirous but 'the desired one', and as much the focus of the river people's fantasies as they of his. The anthropological narrative of the episode is that Desiderio possesses the ability to read and write that the people want and they plan to obtain this quality through literal incorporation, so that by eating pieces of him they will each effortlessly receive his knowledge. Primal fantasies are also suggested: Desiderio's wish for (re)incorporation indicates a longing to return to the womb; his sexual relationship with 'Mama' represents half the Oedipus Complex (his mission to kill Dr Hoffman providing the other half); the doll-fish nursed by Aoi, his child-bride-to-be, is a Freudian symbol for desire and the phallus which, when it is replaced by a knife, sharply suggests the castration complex.

Desiderio's experience with these people becomes a symbolic rebirth; into consciousness and language and out of the regressive desire whose fulfilment can only lead to a self-perpetuating and incestuous circle of ignorance and obliteration. He discovers the impossibility of unity, and indeed of stasis, the major flaw in the nostalgic myth of wholeness being the fantasy that a sense of completion in the moment can be developed into an existential state. As the peep-show proprietor confirms, 'Nothing . . . is ever completed; it only changes' (99). Desiderio's visit to Hoffman's castle, a second symbolic return to the womb, leads him finally to confront the powerhouse of desire. Here he embraces not Eros so much as Thanatos, thereby negating both the consummation of his own desire and the possibility of fantasy emerging into the world. This, at least, is how David Punter sees it, though as suggested in chapter 1, Eros seems to me to have the last word, given that Desiderio is doomed to live the rest of his days in insatiable desire for his lost love.

Desiderio's unrealisable yearning for incorporation by the family is, in classic Freudian terms, sublimated into a wider social activity. The impossibility of achieving his desire comments on the inadequacy – or failure to prevail – of passive desire in general. Desiderio's position renders him unequal almost to the point of death; the one advantage he has, that of education, is the very factor that will seal his sacrificial fate. It is interesting to note – especially given the fact that female passivity unfailingly excited her derision – how far Carter pushes Desiderio's submissiveness. His enforced passivity is increasingly apparent as the wedding night approaches, as he is excluded from jokes, feels like a 'love slave', is already 'eaten' in pre-nuptial fellatio, and senses a veiled hostility on the part of his putative father-in-law. It is only at the final moment of revelation that he feels constrained to act, or react. The same is true of his later behaviour with the cannibal chief; not until the Count is cooking does Desiderio do anything to try to rescue Albertina and himself. This passive, reactive posture, halfway to compliance, reveals Desiderio to be as much object as subject, and (quite apart from giving a male character a taste of female experience) reinforces the negative or deathly aspect of both the character and his society.[36]

The death instinct is manifest in the second major cannibalistic episode of the novel, involving the Count and the cannibal chief. The Count makes the grandiose claim of living to negate the world. His obliterating egocentricity is evident in the picnic on which he feasts so heartily as to leave almost nothing for Desiderio and Lafleur, in his voracious and bestial sexual appetite, and in his habit of never answering questions (since he rarely notices the questioner). With his Sadeian superiority and fantasies of omnipotence, the Count has strong cannibal tendencies. At the 'House of Anonymity' he chooses a prostitute creature with a whipped back whom he slaveringly describes in terms of meat, fire and cannibal feasting, proceeding to ravish her with gusto. Their revels are cut short by the arrival of the Count's alter ego, the black pimp, 'my retribution . . . my twin . . . my shadow' (139), whom the Count most desires and fears and whose presence is described as 'baleful', 'appalling', like 'a depth of water': pure negation. What is represented in the Count is the *reductio ad absurdum* of Desiderio's negating impulse; if Hoffman's daughter Albertina is an embodiment of Eros, the Count is three quarters Thanatos. His thanatic tendencies are in turn projected onto his alter ego, the black pimp, who becomes, in accordance with the Count's desire, the cannibal chief in Africa.

In this chief's small but perfectly brutal society cannibalism is not an aberration nor a rite of passage but a way of life, given the same physiological rationalisation as Sawney Beane asserts in *Vampirella*: that it produces strong, healthy, virile and libidinous children. The political motivation is diametrically opposed to Beane's egalitarian sentiments, however; here (as for the Sadeian libertine) cannibalism's function is one of total social control, maintained through the ever-present threat to dissidents of being shipped off to the kitchens. The cannibal chief's rule is despotic and deathly; his women soldiers are encouraged to negate human feelings and eat their firstborn children, and disfigured wives and concubines bear witness to the depredations of Sadeian libertinism.

The relation of cannibalism to desire here is one of power not of love (to recall the distinction made at the beginning of the chapter). Desire is for negation; indeed the whole scene and its cast of characters may have been called up by the Count's powerfully negative impulses. The Count is said to live on closer terms with his own unconscious than others, a closeness which explains the strength of his desires, the punning ship-board anachronisms and his palpable rage and fear when thwarted; he responds like the infant to 'good breast' and 'bad breast'. His anguish in chains on the ship is the terror of the disempowered monster, but it is also the infant's fantasy that the love object he so desires to incorporate and demolish will, in fact, consume and destroy him.

The overwhelming nature of his desire, an exaggerated version of Uncle Philip's mania in *The Magic Toyshop*, again demonstrates omnivo-rous egocentricity. The Count might also be said to be desperate for a sense of wholeness, but here the similarity ends, for while Uncle Philip longs for love, the Count craves obliteration; one strives furiously towards Eros, the other surrenders wholeheartedly to Thanatos. As with Annabel (in *Love*) the union the Count seeks is with himself; uroboros-like, he will complete his own circle. The cannibal chief, his alter ego, voices the desire in gustatory terms: 'I wish to see if I can suffer, like any other man. And then I want to learn the savour of my flesh. I wish to taste myself' (162). The Count's triumph comes as he begins to boil and learns at the moment of death to feel ordinary pain, to be (re)unified with himself, completed as both subject and object. It is also the moment that spurs Desiderio once again to reject annihilation; in killing the can-nibal chief he rejects incorporation and negation in pursuit of an equally illusive and ultimately unsatisfiable goal of erotic completion. The irony is that his behaviour parallels that of the Count; the Albertina he desires is, as he narcissistically admits, the reflection of himself: 'I was entirely Albertina in the male aspect. That is why I know I was beauti-ful when I was a young man. Because I know I looked like Albertina' (199).

This apprehension of another in terms of one's own desire and self-image, a process analogous to cannibalism, is a theme that runs through Carter's fiction. It is what Eve retrospectively perceives to have been the case in her relationship (as Evelyn) with Leilah in *The Passion of New Eve*; she muses regretfully that Leilah had mirrored Evelyn only too well, including the incapacity to love. Like the cannibal chief, all Evelyn can taste is himself. The callous and stereotypically 'masculine' way in which he treats Leilah, and the condition in which he leaves her (pregnant, aborted, sterile) provide the narrative dynamic of this novel. Captured in the desert by the angry women of Beulah, Evelyn is transformed by Mother's surgery into a pornographic pin-up, a luscious blonde who escapes prior to projected impregnation with sperm from her previous male self. Her capture by Zero, a self-styled Nietzschean superman somewhat in the mould of the *Dr Hoffman*'s Count, subjects her to an experience of total female subjugation and humiliation before she escapes again, into the arms of transsexual Tristessa and an ultimate symbolic rebirth into womanhood.

There is little about eating in this novel, and still less reference to cannibalism. Nevertheless it does pick up some of the cannibalistic issues from *Dr Hoffman* and relate them more specifically to questions of gender. The conflict between order and chaos in a (just) futuristic America might itself be read as a conflict between the genders as well as between the 'haves' and the 'have-nots', continuance and negation, myth and history. The opposition of Eros and Thanatos in *Dr Hoffman* here becomes a gendered struggle: Zero, associated with negation and masculinity, represents an urge towards destruction, entropy and sterile control whereas Mother, 'Our Lady of the Cannibals', is associated with change, revolution and a potentially fertile chaos. The cannibalistic allusion relates to Mother as proto-goddess; in a parallel to Desiderio's absorption by the river people, Mother literally engulfs Evelyn, so giving birth to Eve.

The figure of Tristessa is more ambiguous. Although in reality a man, s/he appears to embody the 'essence' of femininity, the point being – as Carter is at pains to point out in *The Sadeian Woman* – that there is no such essence; femininity is constructed by history, ideology and the other social forces that go to shape subjectivity. Tristessa's 'femininity' is fixed, just as her glass sculptures are fixed by being dropped into the pool; her image is frozen onto celluloid where she remains unchanging, like Desiderio's frozen tribe of river people. In the same way as Garbo and Eve herself, she is too perfectly female (and indeed too static) to be a credible woman.[37]

There is some gender play: Tristessa is really a man masquerading as a woman; Eve is a woman who used to be a man; they are forced into a cross-dressing marriage. There is a fleeting complementary completion, whichever way they are put together. The one overtly cannibalistic image of the novel occurs when they are alone without water in the desert. Looking down, Eve sees her sandy, 'delicious' limbs; aroused by her resemblance to a gingerbread woman she mutters, 'Eat me. Consume me.' She is racked with desire that has never been fulfilled (despite the 'unqualified success' of her clitoris), because this desire is the insatiable ache for unification with another. Her coming together with Tristessa is like the 'great Platonic hermaphrodite':

The erotic clock halts all clocks.
Eat me.
Consume me, annihilate me. (148)

But, like all such couplings, even when phrased in an erotic cannibal language that would grant them permanence, the congress cannot last, and the memory of Tristessa is relegated to an emotional cul de sac: 'his cock stuck in his asshole so that he himself formed the uroborus, the perfect circle, the vicious circle, the dead end' (173).

Like Desiderio, and Joseph in *Several Perceptions*, Eve makes a return to the womb, but the idea here is taken through several stages. Evelyn (involuntarily) first goes through such an experience in Beulah when he is turned into a woman. This 'rebirth', like Desiderio's, is rich in psychoanalytic symbolism: in this 'place of transgression' Evelyn is urged to kill his father, copulates with his 'Mother' (with heavy significance now called Jocasta) and is castrated, thus literally enacting Freud's metaphorical stages of psychic development. (Carter rewrites some of Freud though: the newly created Eve shows no sign of penis envy; indeed when offered the return of Evelyn's penis, she laughs and refuses, and Lilith throws it into the sea.) But rebirth as a woman is not in itself a solution and Eve is left with a sense of incompletion, of division and doubleness. At the symbolic heart of the novel lies the mirror – Leilah recreating herself in the mirror, Eve first meeting herself in the looking-glass at Beulah and Tristessa providing both a partial reflection of Eve and an image of femininity through Hollywood. This trope of the mirror irresistibly suggests Lacan's 'mirror phase', during which the infant begins to imagine a self separate from the mother, a conceptual development related to literal or metaphorical reflection, or projection. Both the narcissistic and fantastic quality of the desired, ideal self and the conflict between this and what the world feeds back resonate in the representations of Leilah, Tristessa and Eve. These 'women' are involved in the process of conceptualising the self, juggling actual and imagined images with their own experiences of lack.[38]

The plethora of reflected (or constructed) images offers a whole range of possibilities for do-it-yourself identity and this may, in the end, provide an active antidote to unrealisable urges for completion, and consequent stasis. Congress, as we have seen, is bound to be fleeting and, as Freud suggests, ultimately insufficient. Desires to stop the clock, longing for unity, for the healing of self-division and a sense of wholeness, are reflected in both active 'cannibalistic' urges and passive desires to be consumed, to return to the womb. Eve's attempted symbolic return at the end of the novel yields among other things a cracked and fissured mirror which reflects nothing – a symbol that may allow her to remake herself. Her search reveals that Mother is absent, a 'figure of speech' who fails to respond to her cry. Returning to the womb does not answer and Eve must give birth to herself, a solution that keeps alive the possibility of fluidity and change. Even symbolically, it seems, the doubly unappeasable hunger of being human and female cannot be satisfied by external agency.

A burgeoning female assertiveness in Carter's last novels does suggest, though, that alternatives may be found. In *Nights at the Circus* the winged heroine Fevvers twice resists being associated with cannibalistic behaviour. When describing to Walser the dinner she is offered at the house of Mr Rosencreutz she reflects fastidiously that given the option she will not eat fowl and 'play the cannibal'. Later, on the train in Russia when the appetite of the circus proprietor, the Colonel, is sharpened by rhapsodising about the omnivorousness of pigs and the similarity in taste of human flesh to pork, she responds by giving her 'nasty' veal cutlet to the pig. Though she has an appetite to match her size, it is not a predatory one; her appetite is for life, experience and change, an antidote to the 'frozen' and hopeless appetite of the cannibal.

The Colonel, by contrast, does manifest an oblique cannibalistic tendency, in the shape of an omnivorous business appetite. Like Uncle Philip in *The Magic Toyshop* he exerts control, but he is an attenuated monster in comparison. He is largely good tempered and much less solitary than Uncle Philip, and his intelligent (female) piggy sidekick and the performers in his show are living creatures rather than a product of craft and imagination. The Colonel's empire-building is less pathological than Uncle Philip's, though still alarming in its effects (it is, after all, his fake publicity about Fevvers's relationship to the prince of Wales that leads to their train being dynamited). Despite his status and power as the proprietor of the circus, he is both comic and pitiful. He falls asleep when trying to seduce Fevvers, is outfoxed by the chimpanzee Professor's assiduity, weeps when he learns of the elephants' death, melodramatically and sentimentally demands that he should be eaten before Sybil the pig, and keeps bunting flags in his flies. It is only with the aid of Sybil, whose loyalties are in any case divided, that he can hope to succeed.

The circus itself – that metaphor for life and the public presentation of the self – has an omnivorous and autonomous quality of its own that suggests the Colonel is truly in *its* service. The circus ring echoes the self-completion of the uroboros, reflecting both outwards, to life, and inwards, to the desire for completion:

What a cheap, convenient, expressionist device, this sawdust ring, this little O! Round like an eye, with a still vortex in the centre; but give it a little rub as if it were Aladdin's wishing lamp and, instantly, the circus ring turns into that durably metaphoric, uroboric snake with its tail in its mouth, wheel that turns full circle, the wheel whose end is its beginning, the wheel of fortune, the potter's wheel on which our clay is formed, the wheel of life on which we are all broken. O! of wonder; O! of grief. (107)

Carter has used the uroboros in earlier novels to represent solipsism and sterility; here, with a more social than personal flavour it suggests inclusiveness and flexibility, with even the potential to absorb mayhem and still continue.

The show – as life – must go on. But there is no sense that either is easy or unproblematic, even though this is a comic novel. The bitter underside of comedy is revealed in the figures of the clowns, especially Buffo, the one truly cannibalistic character in the desperate sense used earlier. Buffo's hunger for the world is insatiable because it is powered by despair. He has a 'tremendous and perpetual thirst', but his prodigious drinking is always unsatisfactory: 'as if alcohol were an inadequate substitute for some headier or more substantial intoxicant, as though he would have liked, if he could, to bottle the whole world, tip it down his throat, then piss it against the wall' (118). In psychoanalytic terms this recalls a destructive oral-cannibalistic desire to suck the breast dry, but goes beyond it in desiring not to retain the world but to annihilate it.

Buffo's hunger is a cruel hunger and this makes his comedy cruel, playing out his cannibalistic and ultimately murderous impulses at the expense of the hapless Walser. The Clowns' 'Christmas Dinner' act – conceived as a slapstick reversal in which the dinner takes control from the diners – becomes, as he pursues Walser the Human Chicken with a carving knife, Buffo's Last Supper, at the end of which the Clown is symbolically crucified in a straightjacket. Yet there is no Ascension; clowns are 'doomed to stay down below, nailed on the endless cross of the humiliations of this world' (120). This suffering Christ offers no redemption; the world is all bad breast; it gives him nothing and he desires to make it nothing. Buffo is a figure of negation, a creature of Thanatos: '*Nothing* will come of nothing. That's the glory of it,' he says in a positive celebration of Lear's threat (123). The requiem the clowns dance for Buffo – a repetitive, incantatory surrender to the forces of entropy and negation – invites disintegration and regression:

They danced the perturbed spirit of their master, who came with a great wind and blew cold as death into the marrow of the bones. They danced the whirling apart of everything, the end of love, the end of hope; they danced tomorrows into yesterdays; they danced the exhaustion of the implacable present; they danced the deadly dance of the *past* perfect which fixes everything fast so it can't move again; they danced the dance of Old Adam who destroys the world because we believe he lives forever. (243)

Buffo and the clowns represent the death instinct in its extreme form, unalloyed by the admixture of libido that transforms it into the will to power seen in the Count in *Dr Hoffman*. It is not surprising that Fevvers, the incarnation of Eros, should tell Walser emphatically that she hates clowns and regards them as an assault on humanity.

Of course Fevvers herself is not exempt from helpless longings and nostalgia. As her substitute mother Lizzie suggests, all wise children want to stay in the womb, to remain whole and undifferentiated, but she goes on to say that 'nature' will prevail, and nature is what Fevvers embraces, in all its changeableness and ambiguity. Carter uses Fevvers to reject the use of women to embody abstract notions (such as Justice or Virtue), such representation being a dangerous, constraining and denaturing practice: Fevvers is seized by shivers whenever she senses someone intending to appropriate her and she progressively frees herself from labelling and entrapment through the course of the novel. She will not be confined and reduced into some category of 'woman', a resistance encapsulated in the recurring question 'Is she fact or is she fiction?'(7). Insisting instead on plurality and potential, she escapes from her fate as spectacle (in the brothel, in Mme Shreck's gallery of freaks and even in the circus itself) and – like the wings confined in her bodice – breaks the bounds and 'spreads'.

New Eve's dilemma is here given an alternative slant: Fevvers's ambiguity offers the continuing possibility of creating an identity that does not have to stem from a return to the breast or womb (or egg). What is suggested is self-creation, an alternative to what Carter describes herself in typically acerbic terms 'as having discovered to be the 'social fiction of my "femininity" . . . created, by means outside my control, and palmed off on me as the real thing'.[39] Fevvers is not in the end the victim of a male-created ideology, though she is often enough the object and victim of male gaze. What the mirror holds for her is femininity in the aspect of the tiger, and though she is quite capable of playing the nurse she likes to take an active role. Walser luxuriates as the object of her gaze in the imagined impression that 'her teeth closed on his flesh with the most voluptuous lack of harm' (204). This is 'positive' cannibalism, though for Walser only in its passive form, for although Fevvers is as much an object of desire as Desiderio, she is an active subject and never a potential cannibal feast. Even mutual eating is only hinted in Walser's rueful contemplation, 'Am I biting off more than I can chew?' (293).

What Walser's experiences teach him is to feel, to be feminised, to be a 'serious person':

now he knew the meaning of fear as it defines itself in its most violent form, that is, fear of the death of the beloved, of the loss of the beloved, of the loss of love. It was the beginning of an anxiety that would never end, except with the deaths of either or both; and anxiety is the beginning of conscience, which is the parent of the soul but is not compatible with innocence. (292–3)[40]

Fevvers remains superior, equipped by ambiguous 'nature' for the 'woman on top' position. The coming together of these two, unequal but reconstructed, suggests a healing reciprocity in which both taste but neither gets eaten. The ending of the novel is truly comic inasmuch as it stresses fertility, continuance and the restorative power of laughter; the spirit Fevvers embodies is none other than that of libido, evoked by Carter herself in that last *Omnibus* interview: 'the inextinguishable, the unappeasable nature of the world, of appetite, of desire . . .'

CHAPTER 3

Eating, starving and the body: Doris Lessing and others

Literary representations of the handling, cooking and consumption (or indeed non-consumption) of food and its effects embrace widely differing degrees of physicality. Compare, for example, Magwitch's pie, Mrs Ramsay's *bœuf en daube* and Proust's madeleine, which might crudely be characterised, respectively, as gut food, heart food and food in the head.[1] To focus on the body as an eating, digesting, excreting organism draws attention to fundamental questions of survival, the nature of nourishment, and – more obliquely – subjectivity, autonomy and empowerment. It also evokes all manner of conflicting and contradictory cultural reverberations. This chapter will attempt to map some of these, exploring ideas and perceptions about the consuming and non-consuming body and the literary significance and function of eating in relation to embodiment. The discussion will cover a variety of novels, but the major part of the chapter is devoted to the writing of Doris Lessing.

To give a physical context to the discussion, it is worth beginning with a brief consideration of the body in western culture. Attitudes towards the body are complex and contradictory; in religion, education and the criminal justice system, for example, a guiding principle seems to have been the subjugation of the body as a means of disciplining the spirit. In a talk at the South Bank, Roy Porter, medical historian at the Wellcome Institute, outlined how western society has traditionally taken a punitive attitude towards the body, being ever ready to mortify or torment the flesh, particularly in the name of religion or justice.[2] Kim Chernin draws a feminist inference, claiming that a struggle to dominate the body is endemic to British culture, and is perhaps a central feature of any patriarchy.[3]

Yet in the Judaeo-Christian tradition the body is held to be sacred, a concept exemplified in the doctrines of individual life after death, the incarnation of the son of God, transubstantiation, the bodily resurrection of Christ and so on. (Religion is rather less comfortable with women's bodies, the Jewish *mikva* or ritual bath and the 'churching' of women after childbirth to cleanse them suggesting a repugnance for the messy and contingent aspects of womanhood.) For the body to be subjected to crushing oppression and yet also to be revered suggests that it is the source of considerable, frightening and perhaps unknown potential. It is not difficult to identify this apprehension in literature; from Shakespeare to *Paradise Lost*, Gothic fiction to fantasy, there is a sense of unknown and unknowable physical – as well as extra-physical – power.

The body has been extensively theorised in recent years. One of its appeals to postmodern culture is precisely its powerful potential, which is seen as oppositional and liberating. Resurgent interest in Sade is indicative: the body as locus of desire, irrationality, passion and subversive appetite is the focus of a romantic rebellion against what Bryan S. Turner describes as 'capitalist rationality' and 'bureaucratic regulation'.[4] Since it is in opposition to reason, the body is also seen by some as the object of colonization *by* reason (particularly perhaps in its gendered form, in reproductive practices, for example), even when this does not take the violent forms catalogued by Porter. Indeed, according to Foucault, regimes of surveillance lead to the production of useful and disciplined bodies both externally and through internalised restraints 'inscribed' upon the body.[5] The parallels Foucault draws between the micro-politics of body regulation and the macro-politics of population surveillance are especially pertinent to the question of body *image* (and thus dieting), which, given its wide scale, is arguably a means of social control.[6] The body is thus subject to external and internalised constraints, is itself a constraint or limitation and in addition is a source of immeasurable potential. Being palpably and organically whole, moreover (notwithstanding the modifications of implant surgery), the body is invoked as a material antidote to deconstructive theory.

There are, however, different conceptions of body according to context; as Foucault might put it, bodies are produced within specific discursive practices. The body in military practices, for example, will hardly be the same as the maternal body. Arthur W. Frank outlines four categories of body usage that throw some light on eating practices. First there is the 'Disciplined body', of which Foucault is the great theorist and which is characterised by dissociation, predictability and desired subordination within a hierarchy. The 'Mirroring body' reflects what is around it through a kind of consumer assimilation, a continual surface play to prevent the entrance of pain. The 'Dominating body', almost invariably male, acts through a sense of lack, seeks 'subhuman enemies' to fight, is incapable of relating, is without self-knowledge and is threatened (by contingency) as much as threatening. Finally, there is the 'Communicative body', an ideal exemplified in dance, performance and the caring practices of medicine.[7] This is a body in the process of creating itself and for which contingency therefore offers possibility rather than problems. Women's embodiment, incorporating contingency in the processes of the reproductive cycle, may according to this formulation be predisposed towards the communicative.

Gender is an issue; bodies are not only biologically determined, but socially, culturally and politically so. It is here that feminism asks such questions as how have cultural perceptions allowed men to so dominate women, for it is generally accepted, both historically and currently, that women's bodies occupy – to put it in Foucauldian terms – a particular locus of social control. This presumably has something to do with the very contingent and communicative characteristics outlined above. If reason is seen as colonising, disciplined (and male), its opposite is necessarily other and the body identified with desire, irrationality, helpless passion and subversive appetite becomes a colonised, contingent and probably female one. It is surely no coincidence that late twentieth-century reclamations of the body ride the wave of feminism.

Polar oppositions cannot be simply overturned, however, and attempts to reclaim and reconstruct the despised or subjugated female body can run into difficulties, as Jacqueline Rose points out:

> When feminism takes up, and valorises for women, the much-denigrated image of a hysterical outpouring of the body, it has often found itself doing so, understandably, at the cost of idealising the body itself . . . In a classic feminist move, [the] argument inverts a traditional devalorisation of women. But in the very process of this inversion, what is most discomforting about the body disappears. The body must be positive, it must figure as pure (aesthetic and moral) value if its low-grade ideological colouring is to be removed. Thus uplifted, this body often seems remote from sex and substance, strangely incorporeal, suspended in pure fluidity or cosmic time.[8]

The problem Rose identifies is this: how to reclaim, validate, empower what the body, and especially the female body, represents, without either on the one hand removing what is most characteristically body-like or on the other simply reproducing a polarisation that will serve to reinforce old prejudices (the view that women are irrational and emotional and therefore inferior, for example).

Part of the problem may be inadequate recognition of gender differences in psychic development, as identified by Nancy Chodorow and discussed in chapter 1.[9] Mythical, traditional and psychoanalytic traditions all largely focus on the male, on the separated son striving to surpass his father. Kim Chernin points out that, while this is neither adequate nor appropriate for women, there are no mythic guides, nor any rule about girls surpassing their mothers.[10] Eating disorders, she claims, in allowing daughters to evade the whole problem of 'normal' development and separation, provide a clue to the understanding and theorising of female development.

The self-destructiveness of eating problems, says Chernin, suggests an archaic mechanism: the anorectic bears an unconscious 'Kleinian memory', desiring to incorporate and destroy at the same time as believing and fearing that she has done so. As seen in previous chapters, Freud's and Klein's theories of human development devote considerable attention to the significance of feeding, and others go further. Chernin herself, for example, disagrees with Freud's view that the move from mouth to bowels leads to autonomy, suggesting, on the contrary, that struggles over food continue, and prefigure those of toilet training. She goes so far as to claim that all issues involved in development appear first in relation to food and feeding.[11] As cited earlier, Maud Ellmann makes a similar if more sweeping point, in the extravagant claim that food and not sex is the repressed in Freud.[12] Eating, claims Ellmann, is a fundamental violation of the ego, an 'everyday catastrophe', since 'all eating is force-feeding', for the simple reason that our first experiences of eating are of being fed by others, 'ravished by the food they thrust into our jaws' (35). Thus, she suggests, is hunger constructed (note the flavour of the language Ellmann uses: the emotive language of anorexia).

Is it the case, we might ask, that female infants, who do not have to experience a dramatic separation from the primary love object through identification with the father, must somehow effect their separation through the battleground of food? It is temptingly simple to appoint Freud for men and Klein for women, and to see eating disorders as evidence of failure to achieve autonomy. Though crude, this tactic has some validity: psychically speaking, male separation relieves boys of responsibility for their mother (which may explain the relative scarcity of male anorectics); male rage against the mother may be enacted in verbal or physical domination, but female rage, simultaneously protecting and rejecting the mother, is more problematically expressed, in the symbolic (self-) destructiveness of eating disorders.

There is a wider context, though, and my aim here is to examine the relationship between women, eating and their bodies not just in individual psychoanalytic terms but in relation to late twentieth-century western society as represented in literature. One thing is certain: there is a culturally (and commercially) endorsed ideal slim (even thin) female body. The provenance of the slim body ideal is not easy to establish, but it is a potent and seemingly increasing influence. Susie Orbach points out, for example, that the 'right' size for women has decreased every year since 1965, a claim substantiated in the figure of a 'supermodel' 5 ft 11 in. tall weighing just 7 st 7 lb.[13] (Things have changed a bit since Marilyn Monroe's fabled vital statistics.) Susan Bordo makes a direct link between the existence of the thin ideal and such disorders, arguing that eating disorders are not anomalous but entirely in keeping with ordinary experience in western culture, resulting from hunger, desire and fat being culturally saturated with negative associations.[14]

Eating disorders are well represented in non-literary texts, especially theoretical and soft-scientific studies (and magazines), but there are also some novels *about* eating disorders, as well as numerous more oblique treatments of the subject. One such 'eating disorder' novel is *Life-Size* by Jenefer Shute, which portrays and offers some explanation of the phenomenon of anorexia. The novel is a slim text, witty, elliptical and caustic but, like its lean and bony heroine, capable of binges; the first-person narrator occasionally breaks out bulimically into luxuriant eloquence or rant.

Shute's novel traces the slow and unwilling path towards recovery of a fiercely expert anorectic, incorporating on the way almost every characteristic attributed to sufferers of anorexia by Hilde Bruch in her seminal work, *The Golden Cage: the Enigma of Anorexia Nervosa*.[15] Symptoms include the need to do something outstanding, frantic preoccupation with self, a sense of enslavement, rejection of anything the parents offer, severe disturbances in body image, fear of loss of control, bulimic fits, exhausting exercise; obsession with food, manipulative and intimidating behaviour towards therapists and many more. Shute acknowledges various first-person accounts, and the work of Bruch, Kim Chernin and Susie Orbach amongst others. The novel suggests, in keeping with the thesis of Joan Jacobs Brumberg, that her protagonist Josie's condition is 'multidetermined', its origins interweaving biological, psychological and cultural factors.[16] As at least one reviewer has noted, anorexia nervosa is a complex phenomenon and Shute's comprehensive depiction, acknowledging this, offers no easy response.[17]

Life-Size presents a portrait of the anorectic as punitive, selfish and rude, full of arrogance, rage and hate. Josie translates her fears and

misery into a self-loathing that results in a punishing battle to deny
herself which must logically end in death. The novel provides a gradual
revelation of her fears until a terrible underlying hunger becomes apparent. Josie's pursuit of the slim body ideal is revealed as pathological,
which (leaving aside for the moment the question of individual psychological cause) is a danger courted by a society that makes a cult of the
body predicated on both narcissistic indulgence and rigorous self-discipline. There is a profound contradiction driving Josie as a character and
western capitalistic society as a whole. What in the third world betokens
poverty and starvation has in the West replaced plumpness as a sign of
affluence; 'you can never be too rich or too slim,' the Duchess of
Windsor is reputed to have said, and the anorexic body is perversely
prevalent among the privileged middle and upper classes of affluent
societies. Along with transforming the shape of the body goes a whole
industry devoted to its surfaces, enumerated in *Life-Size* as: 'painting,
plucking, powdering, steaming, soaking, shaving, spraying, scenting,
smoothing, straightening, oiling, creaming, curling, coloring, conditioning, toning, tanning, bleaching, blackening, moisturizing, abrading,
exfoliating . . . '[18] The female image that emerges here is lean, taut,
smooth and hairless, something like a mobile, androgynous statue.

What is going on here is commodification of the body. Both John
Berger and Susie Orbach have identified how our bodies are, as it were,
taken from us, reconstructed and then offered back to us through advertising, conjoined to consumer goods.[19] The implication of such advertising (for its purpose is to foster discontent and a sense of lack) is that our
bodies are deficient, requiring the intervention of whatever is being
offered, be it dietary aids, fast cars or the comfort of chocolate. Needless
to say the bodies that are offered back with the goods are slim, firm,
young, et cetera, et cetera, et cetera. We are constantly bombarded with
images urging consumption and promising instant gratification; advertising panders to the child, to the id, to the insatiable appetite. We are
simultaneously exhorted to be thin and to consume, to be hedonistic and
virtuous, to worship the body and punish the body; the difficulty, even
impossibility, of achieving a homeostasis in this culture is reflected in
anxiety, guilt, anger and obsession.

Advertising alone does not, however, explain the desirability of thin
female bodies. Western culture as a whole is racked with confusions and
contradictions about materiality, fear of uncontrolled impulses, of processes spilling over, of disorder and riot. If, as suggested earlier, female
bodies are seen as more contingent, abundant and undisciplined, and

have historically been more subject to control than their male counterparts, then fears of disorder may well be focused directly onto female
bodies. It is surely no coincidence that the more women are empowered
the more culturally desirable the thin body has become. Fears of engulfment by femaleness translate into the cultivation of hard outlines; anorectics simply take this to its logical conclusion. Far from being a
gender-bending liberation, what we are seeing is a renewed and obses-
sional adherence to bodily oppression. If as a society we can no longer
work to *pro*duce as a sign of grace, then at least we can work to *re*duce.
The process has generated an evangelical zeal. As Joan Brumberg suggests, it is a pseudo-religious quest; anorexia nervosa represents a perfec-
tionism that links personal salvation to body shape.[20]

The narcissism, obsessiveness and competitive conformity of this per-
fectionism are illustrated in *Life-Size*, as Josie ritualistically examines her
contours:

Every morning the same ritual, the same inventory, the same naming of parts
before rising, for fear of what I may have become overnight . . . the first thing I
do is feel my hipbones, piercingly concave, two naked arcs of bone around an
emptiness. Next I feel the wrists, encircling each with the opposite hand, checking that they're still frail and pitiful, like the legs of little birds. There's a deep
hollow on the inside of each wrist, suspending delicately striated hands, stringy
with tendon and bone. On the outside of the wrist, I follow the bone all the way
up to the elbow, where it joins another, winglike, in a sharp point. (9–10)

And so it goes on, the knee hollows, hardened thighs, bony buttocks,
coathanger collarbone, corrugated ribs and vertebrae like 'a row of
perfect little buttons', the poetic language conveying a perverse delight
in fragility. Josie is as near as possible to being a skeleton. Significantly,
she avoids taking note of her breasts, remaining indicators of some femininity. Not only is she typically amenorrhoeic, but she has a real horror
of menstruation, with its reminder of the body's dark and 'rotten' interior: 'Who, given the choice, would really opt to menstruate, invite the
monthly hemorrhage – a reminder that the body is nothing but a bag of
blood, liable to seep or spatter at any moment?' (5). This suggests not
only an aversion to femaleness but resonates with alarm about the very
condition of embodiment. With her self regard and chilly distance from
sexual excitement, the autonomous, androgynous, idealised, ethereal-
material girl of the advertisements is realised: 'Be Some Body'; '*The secret
word is* body' (66–7); 'It all seemed so simple, at sixteen. If I could lose
enough flesh, I could have any body I wanted, look like anything,
anyone' (140). Unlike the ideal creature, however, Josie is almost fatally

unsure of her outlines, of her place in the world. She frets about how she can justify taking up so much space, a direct reference to Susie Orbach's claim that anorexia is precisely an expression of female uncertainty about the space women are allowed to occupy in the world.[21]

Taking space is directly related to a person's sense of (bodily) boundaries. In a fascinating book, *Freaks: Myths and Images of the Secret Self,* Leslie Fiedler writes of the challenge 'freaks' pose to the fragile boundaries of self-identity, between male and female, animal and human, sexed and sexless, large and small, self and other. He argues that we have a psychic need for freaks precisely because of uncertainty about the limits of our bodies and our egos, suggesting that if freaks did not exist we should have to invent them (as of course we do, in fiction and film, myth and legend). He points out how stories not only play with scale (*Alice* and *Gulliver's Travels*) but blur boundaries, between animal and human for example (fables and fairy tales), playing with perplexities and anxieties about sexuality and embodiment. Women (and men) who make themselves very thin or very fat are acting out profound and common anxieties about body limits.

Julia Kristeva's writing on abjection also focuses on bodily boundaries. Arguably at the core of anorexia, the concept of abjection illuminates Josie's embattled subjectivity. Kristeva opposes 'violent, dark revolts of being' (associated with feelings of revulsion, disgust, shame) to the 'clean and proper' body, a sense of whose limits is necessary for the functioning of the symbolic order and the acquisition of personal identity within it.[22] In a parallel with Freud's post-polymorphous ideal of straightforward genital sexuality, the 'proper' subjectivity she identifies relies upon the expulsion of what is improper and unclean, disorderly or polluting (Kristeva draws a parallel here with the dietary laws in Leviticus, which are based upon the concept of not transgressing clear categories).

The abject – literally what is thrown away – comprises all that is grotesque, unspeakable, disgusting, yet which, being part of the self, and specifically the body, cannot be fully rejected or obliterated. The recognition that total expulsion is impossible provokes abjection, a necessary condition, but one which creates a sort of black hole, an abyss both alluring and repugnant, at the borders of identity. The unstable nature of abjection (removed and not removed, self and not-self, attraction and repulsion) threatens disruption, giving rise to self-disgust, guilt, a sense of impurity, and insecurity lest the abject break back in. Elizabeth Gross encapsulates perfectly both the instability and contradiction: 'The abject defines a pre-oedipal space and self-conception: it is the space between subject and object, both repulsive and attractive, which threatens to draw the subject and its objects towards it, a space of simultaneous pleasure and danger.'[23]

Abjection focuses on bodily processes and substances – such as food (notably slimy or glutinous stuff or milk with a skin), vomit, faeces, urine, pus, semen and mucus – which cause disgust. Kristeva identifies three categories: oral disgust, which enacts a rejection of the mother and thus a refusal of life ('I abject *myself* '(3)); repugnance towards bodily waste, which suggests an inability to accept the body's materiality, its rhythms and mortality (the corpse itself being the ultimate example of bodily waste); and revulsion from signs of sexual difference, encompassing the taboo against incest and horror at menstrual blood.

What is interesting about this theory from the point of view of eating disorders is the combination of visceral disgust at the body's processes and insecurity about boundaries. The boundary between the 'clean and proper' body and the abject is at once highly demarcated and non-existent (because subject to incursion). The boundaries between the inside and outside of the body are insecure, both inasmuch as they are indefinite (are the vagina, the mouth, the nostrils truly inside?) and in view of the fact that they are constantly breached, or at least traversed. Even the margins of self-identity are highly precarious, vulnerable to abjection. It is the transgression, or potential transgression, of boundaries that is so threatening: the tainting of the 'clean and proper' body, the reirruption of the abject, the passage of substances through the body's boundaries. The more ambiguous the substance or process or relation to the body's boundaries, the stronger and more troubling the abjection, and Kristeva emphasises ambiguity: 'It is . . . not lack of cleanliness or health that causes abjection but what disturbs identity, system, order. What does not respect borders, positions, rules. The in-between, the ambiguous, the composite.'[24]

The applicability of this theory to Josie is unmistakable, all three of Kristeva's categories (oral disgust, horror at bodily waste, repulsion from menstrual blood) being evident. Josie's project to achieve the ultimate in 'clean and proper bodies' requires abjection of all that is oral, messy, material, disorderly, female. At the same time, she is threatened by an intense and shameful desire for precisely what she denies: 'How could I appear among people as the ravening monster I truly was – huge, with a crammed, bloated maw, hands full of food, half-chewed matter drooling from a never-empty mouth, lumbering insatiably towards everything, everyone, in my path?' (175). The self-disgust and revulsion seen here preclude any harnessing of the repressed to positive ends (artistic creativity or sexual fulfilment, for example); for her, abjection results in the most serious sense of threat from all that she imagines to have consigned beyond the fragile borders of her self. Which is why her strategy fails to work; Kristeva's delineation of abjection offers a model of the self whose borders are neither complete nor secure: 'we may call it a border: abjection is above all ambiguity' (9).

Josie's limits are both very clearly defined – by her wilful determination, her boniness and her 'naming of parts' – and tenuous, since she feels threatened by her repressed desire, invaded by physical contact, food or medical care. Her ambiguous boundaries are portrayed as very alarming to her. Her one ambition is to shrink the limits further. But her desired body shape and self-negation are achieved only at the expense of massive struggle, a mind-numbingly oppressive regime of starvation and punishing exercise, devised according to self-imposed rules of mathematical precision and obsessive scheduling. The obsessiveness lies in the detail. Every rejected mouthful, every hundred sit-ups represents a 'victory of the will', an 'exercise of power'. Josie's control is represented as a response to a sense of oppression; interpreting all expressions of concern, affection, love as attempts to impose control and to force(-feed) her, she aligns herself with prisoners and suffragists, repunctuating 'therapist' as 'the rapist' (144). The control she exerts in pursuing her refusal runs nightmarishly out of control, however, until she can do nothing but abstain. The circularity is encapsulated in a brief Godotesque dialogue she has with herself in the hospital:

I must eat. I have to get out of here.

I can't eat. I'll die. (28)

One of the peculiarities of anorexia (documented by Bruch and Brumberg) is the obsessive, self-tormenting interest anorectics demonstrate in food. Indeed, since anorexia is often coupled with bulimia, sufferers may devote considerable money and time to eating. Shute captures the compulsion; to Josie food is both enticing and disturbing:

Translucent slivers of scallop have the texture
of firm custard,
with a frothy oceanic flavor.

The veal chop is tempting, too,
thick and tender.
Try the juicy breasts of squab,
the succulent grilled quails
brushed
with hazelnut vinaigrette –
or a sole's
snowy, crisp-skinned flesh.

It's poetry; the only kind I read, tasting each word on my tongue.

The saltiness from the ham plays
seductively
off the sweet cognac.
Don't miss the silken artichoke mousse,
boosted by a lusty black truffle sauce;
or the brittle lid of sautéed potatoes
atop
melting tender *fruits de mer* –
a rousing combination.

No, it's pornography. (34–5)

In fact, what she is reading is the food section of the newspaper, but its overwritten sexual suggestiveness and luscious sensuousness give a strong indication of suppressed desire. When she does eat, in bulimic lapses, Josie's appetite is full of savagery and desperation:

I knew if I ate anything I'd eat everything . . . Desire gradually took over – not simple need, like hunger, but a taut, elastic compulsion. It took all my energy to withstand it, this urge to ravage, to tear with the teeth, to devour and destroy, to stuff the hollow skull. I knew I was lost . . . (182–3)

The use of 'lost' is revealing. When she begins to eat, something in her opens 'like a funnel', not, she says, from hunger, but to prevent a 'howl' from escaping. In case we should miss the importance of this, Shute has her associate eating three times with a cry or wail.[25] It is only when she begins to recover that Josie is able to recognise that she had a choice, unseen in her despair. In a touching little scene in the hospital she is overwhelmed by the prospect of eating porridge and finds herself asking the nurse to feed her. This is both different from compulsively filling her mouth, and progress from steadfastly keeping it empty; she is at last letting the barriers down and asking for (maternal) care. Anorexia, defined originally as loss of appetite, is widely accepted to be something of a misnomer. Here Josie is not only hungry; she is starving.

Shute makes her point about maternal care (or its lack) and about the importance of proper separation and individuation (many writers on eating disorders draw attention to failures of separation and parental interference as causal factors).[26] But her concern is with society as much as with the family. The novel attacks abuse and oppression, direct and indirect, as seen, for example, in the subordination of female desire: 'women prepare the food but mustn't eat it' (89). Notwithstanding the introspective nature of the first person narration and the individual psychological factors, the novel also lays blame on the pressures created by a goal-driven, competitive, conformist, consumer society. And, notwithstanding the introverted tendencies of the sufferer, anorexia is presented as a condition that, at some level at least, demands to be witnessed, an explanation of the phenomenon of 'hunger artists' and for the tendency of appallingly thin women to wear the most revealing clothes. Josie describes herself as a hunger artist performing for her schoolfriends (125).[27]

The purport of Josie's story (which though a novel could almost be a case history) is that her not eating, framed to herself as empowerment, is in fact an enslavement. It is as life-denying in its way as the monstrous control of *Dr Hoffman*'s Count or Buffo the clown in *Nights at the Circus*. Anorexia is fuelled by Thanatos, its occasional bulimic lapses a perverted and swiftly extinguished insurgence of Eros. The effect of not eating is indeed a literal cannibalism as the body draws on its own substance to survive, progressively diminishing the surface of contact with the living world.

There are, however, ways in which not eating may be seen as an empowerment, not for evasion but as part of growth and the development of a 'communicative' body. This is not necessarily, and certainly not wholly, a conscious, wilful act, success is not guaranteed and the cost – even risking sanity – may be very high indeed. A powerful attentiveness is required, though this is unlike the neurotic self-absorption of the anorexic disciplinarian. What is in question is not simply the ecstasy of fasting, but an almost structured pattern of breakdown, fragmentation and enlightenment that is directly related to the body, eating and not eating in a number of Doris Lessing's novels. Here the ambiguity of boundaries is not so much threatening as liberating, and what amounts to a positive embracing of the abject offers scope for personal enlargement.

The pattern is in evidence from her first novel, *The Grass is Singing*. Initially, the main female character Mary Turner bears some similarities to Josie. She employs various strategies to avoid becoming a woman, such as dressing girlishly, living dependently in a girls' club and only marrying a hopeless farmer in reaction to overheard gossip about her lack of sexuality (one of the gossipers suggests she should marry a man old enough to be her father, pointing, perhaps, to repressed desires). She fails to make good the development that marriage initiates, withholding during sex, taking refuge in a pseudo-maternal attitude towards her husband Dick and dreading the idea of pregnancy. The marriage is doomed; Mary despises Dick as a loser, hates the farm and falls prey to obsession, fixing on the weather, water, but above all on a fascinated hatred for the natives, focused chiefly on their physicality.

She is repelled by the bodies and manifest femaleness of the native women:

the exposed fleshiness of them, their soft brown bodies and soft bashful faces . . . and their chattering voices that held a brazen fleshy undertone. . . . Above all, she hated the way they suckled their babies, with their breasts hanging down for everyone to see; there was something in their calm satisfied maternity that made her blood boil.[28]

The language and suggested interior discourse here suggest she is at least doubly affronted, by their fertility and by their easy communicative comfort in their own bodies – not to mention their black otherness. Though she hates the idea of a baby, she begs Dick for a child in a desperate move to give herself purpose and companionship, remembering and empathising with how her mother had clung to her and how she had responded by comforting her mother, full of love, pity – and hatred for her father. No healthy separation here!

Dick's farming failures and persistence, combined with isolation and Mary's own intractability, repression and obsession, slowly drive her to breakdown. The crisis begins when she witnesses the 'houseboy' Moses washing. Not only is she unwillingly mesmerised by the power of his body, his size, his muscles, but she is forced into acknowledging his embarrassment: a human contact. Much against her will, her horror is slowly transformed, as an intimate personal relationship develops. Moses is gentle, fatherly, indulgent, a metaphoric replacement for her own loved and hated father. He begins to look after her; he urges her to eat as her breakdown renders her anorexic; he brings flowers on her lunch tray, his desire to please lending him power over her. She feels helpless, irrationally fearful, uneasy, subject to a 'dark attraction', and she has dreams which confuse him with her father.

Mary's fear, desire and inability to understand are of a piece with the release of the repressed. Her strange, coquettish behaviour is like a parody of femininity or a child's play-acting. She discovers herself, without wanting to, to be sensuous and physically aware. And all the time, her body is becoming thinner, more stringy, more yellow, more bony as her personality breaks down, she forgets about food, forgets to eat, cannot eat.

It may seem far-fetched to suggest a connection between breakdown, not eating and some kind of enlightening development here. The idea gains weight, however, when we look at other Lessing novels in which mental and physical fragmentation and breakdown – frequently accompanied by failure to eat, weight loss, yellowing skin and protruding bones – herald the disintegration of set mind and body models and even the attainment of a communicative body, an ideal body 'in the process of creating itself'.[29] This process might be said to reach its apotheosis in the ultimate complete transcendence of the physical at the end of *The Making of the Representative for Planet 8* (discussed further in chapter 5).

It should be stressed that Lessing's writing is by no means schematic, and she handles the question of breakdown and enlightenment with great subtlety, within complex and varied novels. In the 'Children of Violence' series, for example, she creates a dense fictional world filled with realist narrative detail. Here, body image and slimming are embedded in the fiction, almost incidentally, as part of a young woman's life, illustrating Kim Chernin's view that food obsession has become a kind of puberty rite.[30] Sure enough, before she even leaves her parents' farm, the eponymous young and isolated Martha Quest sets out to starve herself 'into a fashionable thinness', to the extent that her hip bones stick out, although she is described as plump by nature.[31]

Here again we have a dysfunctional mother–daughter relationship in which the mother is incapable of keeping out of her (resented) daughter's life. Chernin claims that a mother's anger at sacrificing herself for her child and the daughter's ambivalence about this can give rise to a symbolic substitution in which the daughter's self-starvation figures an attack on the mother's body, hiding the mother's crisis so that the daughter expresses her mother's breakdown. This analysis makes sense in relation to May Quest who projects all her resentment onto Martha, signally failing to 'mirror' her as an independent being.

By the time the young Martha is installed in town and has joined the hedonistic round of sleeplessness, club drinking and sundowner parties, described as 'delicious activity', she cannot eat, without feeling guilty and promising restitution to herself by giving up the next meal. On the other hand, she would suddenly turn aside into a shop, without even knowing she had intended to, and buy half a dozen slabs of chocolate, which she would eat, secretly, until she was sickened and very alarmed, saying she must be careful, for she would certainly lose her figure if she went on like this. (150)

Junk food guiltily eaten like this provides a classic anorexic/bulimic relapse from excessively controlled eating; the good food Martha's mother sends her she simply gives to the landlady. The image she strives towards is curiously like that of the competitive 1980s:

Just before the war, women were supposed to be tall, broad-shouldered, slim-hipped, long-legged. Martha's room may have been littered with books, but it was also plentifully supplied with magazines, where all the women conformed to that shape, and when she saw her reflection, when she imagined herself in this dress or that, she continually strained her mental image of herself upwards, thinning it, posing it; when she saw herself ideally, crossing a room, under fire from admiring eyes, it was in the guise of this other, imposed woman. (193)

Despite the implied masculinity (and suggested empowerment) of the image, Martha's boyfriend sees her as just so much raw material for him to mould, a telling instance of the disciplining practices to which a young woman's body is subject. It is only when she moves into an alternative, left-wing social group that her conventional perspective is challenged; she encounters people who are unimpressed by her fashion sense and slim self-consciousness and disapprove of endless frivolous sundowner parties.

Notwithstanding Martha's reading, rebellious tendencies and view of herself as different, she accepts the socially approved female model at this early stage in her life without question, just as she adopts the assumption that she must be 'good in bed', (simulating pleasure with both her husbands).[32] The disciplines she uses in training herself not to eat become firmly conditioned reflexes, so that her response to the body changes and the tenderness of (unacknowledged) early pregnancy in *A Proper Marriage* prompts her merely to eat less, with a perverse, self-denying satisfaction (374). Denying her body by refusing her hunger becomes an accomplishment in itself; she is acquiring a disciplined body. By the time she grows to be politically active, self-deprivation is a habit and she slips easily into a pattern of hungry irritability because she is simply too busy to eat.

Martha is never characterised as being gripped by obsession about eating. If anything, the opposite is the case. Just as Susan Bordo argues that eating disorders should be seen as a logical consequence of cultural pressures on women, so Lessing characterises Martha's slimming behaviour as run of the mill: 'she was by no means finished with that phase of her life when she was continuously thinking about food, not because she intended to eat any, but because she meant to refuse it'.[33] Her satisfaction in self-deprivation and the conditioning of her body to accept a state of semi-starvation are nevertheless indicative of eating disorders. The fine line between normal and compulsive behaviour is at its finest where eating and body image are concerned, and it is easy for the determined dieter to be quite unaware of how preoccupied and driven she becomes; Lessing touches on this most delicately.

Martha's slimming, in its conformity to a fashionable ideal, is of a piece with the commodification of women's bodies outlined earlier in this chapter. Along with hedonistic participation in the club, her banal marriage and other conventional activities and attitudes, Martha's conformity is part of a 'nightmare of repetition' which she both participates in and deplores. She is, it seems, inescapably the daughter of her mother, part of the white, ruling society of the colony, subject to the force of historical circumstance. What Lessing sets against this is the other, more unsettling aspect to Martha's personality and Lessing's project: the potential path to freedom and growth.[34]

Possibilities of growth are sketched embryonically in *Martha Quest* through Martha's 'familiar daydream' of the noble city and the painfully ecstatic interval during her emancipating walk home from the station. While the first is idealistic, even ideological, the second is distinctly mystical. Triggered by the extraordinary beauty of the landscape and occurring with the irresistibility of an orgasm, the experience is presented as a 'confused and painful delirium' (73). This is not a wholly unfamiliar occurrence, but freshly painful (because always forgotten or later mentally rewritten as extreme happiness), and difficult, as though some new conception were demanded of her. She resists her tendency to conceptualise and analyse, instead fully experiencing the process and opening herself to a different kind of understanding. Significantly, though this is as yet a tenuous link, the experience occurs after she has hesitated over and mentally rejected the possibility of calling in at McDougall's farm for an enticingly described 'wonderful Scotch tea of bannocks and griddle cakes and newly churned butter' (72). Difficult knowledge, it seems, is opposed to pleasurable eating.

Much of the following three novels is given over to the development of Martha's ideological self. In *A Proper Marriage* she has bouts of not eating, but because she progressively shuts herself off there is little in the way of physically and psychically communicative experience. She feels trapped by her husband Douglas's claims on her body, which she has only just freed from her mother, and her consequent dissociation prevents her even recognising her pregnancy. Though she envies the shadow of the integrated black woman, her 'loyalty to progress' (ideology) prevents emulation. Only her spontaneous jumping into deep puddles with Alice, in which she is surprisingly shocked at herself, suggests a release. Even during childbirth, when the native cleaner talks her soothingly through some of her pains, she must resist her body, caught up as she is within the mechanistic approach of the nursing home. This disciplined approach carries over into nurturing her daughter Caroline 'by the book', and there are great battles centred around feeding; as though anticipating Kim Chernin, Martha wonders why, when toilet training was so easy, they should battle so much over food.[35] Either, it seems, she can fight to do things by the book or give in and be numbed and smothered, a fate figured in the stodgy and flavourless meal Douglas insists upon eating on his return from the army, in preference to her omelette and stewed fruit.

Martha's physical disconnection is intensified in *A Ripple from the Storm*. In moving from a man whose degustatory self-abuse has given him a stomach ulcer to one whose eating is doggedly methodical and who admonishes her to eat because if she gets ill she will be a burden to comrades, she merely exchanges one self-deception for another. As Lorna Sage observes, Martha twice idealistically marries men who have already fallen short.[36] Martha's involvement with meetings, her general busyness and rebellious inclination make for an irregularity about eating that leaves her perpetually irritable. She is so preoccupied that she only remembers she has not eaten when she smells food, a level of absorption signalling displacement.

In *Landlocked*, Martha is once again shown dashing about, from official to unofficial meetings, to friends, to her parents. She rarely stops to eat with her mother, despite Mrs Quest's anxiously ordering supper for them both. On one occasion her mother even cooks a jam tart, imagining herself giving it to Martha, though she knows that Martha never eats sweets. This says much about May Quest's infantilisation of Martha, but also suggests that Martha denies herself the sweet things of life.[37] She airily reassures her mother she is merely in 'one of my thin phases . . . I'll just get fat again by myself' (94).

At this time, she begins to listen to her body. Noticing how her flesh begins to relax with Joss, she realises she wants to have an affair, while with her husband she wants to cover her nakedness. When Thomas Stern finds her thinness and tension attractive she understands that being with him will somehow be serious, intense, and thus for the first time she has a real love affair, her body in absolute communication (notably, she has to be thin for this to happen). She feels on the verge of being ill, as with the visionary experiences of her youth, because her body seems to take over. When it remembers Anton she vomits; her stomach, intestines and bladder rebel. On one occasion when they all go dancing she gets very drunk, and has a strange, disorienting, fragmented experience, a brief precursor of the sustained process of breakdown, defamiliarisation and growth that is worked through in *The Four-Gated City*.

Before that novel comes *The Golden Notebook*, in which Lessing explicitly explores fragmentation and breakdown, and here body boundaries are considered less discretely. The characters of Anna, Ella, Saul Green, Marion and others are not concerned with being fat or thin, drunk or sober, and attention is firmly turned away from their appearance. The body is instead intimately and inextricably coupled with questions of understanding and sanity. As language breaks down and knowledge cannot be articulated, so Anna's personality fragments; she can rely on nothing as language and the 'female creature' inside her are thrown into conflict. She must open herself to other ways of knowing, try out new perspectives, allow herself to listen.

It is not possible to do justice to the scope and complexity of the novel here, nor even to give full weight to Lessing's use of food, which has both strong mimetic and figurative functions. The twin aspects of the book most germane to the argument of this chapter are firstly the connection provided by an instinctively communicative sharing of food, and secondly eating, or not eating, in relation to connection and fragmentation: the breakdown of mind and body and how this may enable break*through*.

Connection through sharing food may be almost too obvious to mention, but is of vital importance. Mutuality in shared sensuousness makes for an unspoken communication; when Anna and Molly greedily eat bowls of strawberries, 'loaded with cream', the light, colour and texture provide a combination of shared sensations almost tangible to the reader:

'With strawberries, wine, obviously,' said Anna greedily; and moved the spoon about among the fruit, feeling its soft sliding resistance, and the slipperiness of the cream under a gritty crust of sugar. Molly swiftly filled glasses with wine and set them on the white sill. The sunlight crystallized beside each glass on the white paint in quivering lozenges of crimson and yellow light, and the two women sat in the sunlight, sighing with pleasure and stretching their legs in the thin warmth, looking at the colours of the fruit in the bright bowls and at the red wine.[38]

Here is a mixture of pure physical pleasure and friendship, comparable to (if unlike) Ella's relationship with her uncomplicated American, to whom she responds as a 'healthy savage', 'all flesh, a body of warm, abundant, exuberant flesh' (290). It is worth noting too that different ways of eating are revealing: while Anna and Molly eat their strawberries with greedy good humour, making easy their communication, Molly's son Tommy eats with a self-absorbed bullying determination that suggests a frightening – or frightened – control and isolation.

For lovers an easy relation through taste and smell has an additional dimension. The pleasures, anticipatory and actual, of shopping and cooking for her lover are deliciously evoked by Anna.[39] Her satisfaction is sensuous, even sensual, loving and communicative, indicating the kind of woman she is and the nature of her relationships (as Saul Green observes when he tells Anna she is born to cook for a man). Her rich, sensuous happiness is easily punctured however when her body registers with chill that Michael is leaving. The potency of Anna's description and her acute shifts of mood suggest the shared meal is like a statement of intent, of commitment – which is precisely why Michael does not turn up and apologises so casually.

Why should such men feel threatened by an intensity of mutuality, a shared body experience that dissolves some of the rigid boundaries of the individual? Food for Lessing's 'free women' is part of the idyll, a means of conversation; for these men it is simply a potential trap. On the straightforward level of the realist text such incidents could be taken to illustrate a male fear of commitment or entrapment (emotional or marital). On a less literal or less conscious level a man may withdraw from a sensation of infantilisation, of being mothered, as though feeling constrained to make the separation all over again. We return inevitably to the question of boundaries. One explanation suggests psychic gendering. Echoing Nancy Chodorow, Maggie Kilgour maintains that as a result of longer identification with the mother, women do not develop such strong or rigid ego boundaries as men, retaining a more fluid relationship between self and other.[40] It is precisely such fluidity that interests Lessing.

Where individual connection occurs through shared eating or sexual congress, Lessing suggests that wider communication, a significant breaking down of individualism, is desirable and even possible. This is embryonic in a simple scene such as in the 'Blue Notebook' when Anna's fellow Communist worker shares his sandwich lunch with her. But for it to happen in a major way, all kinds of fear and resistance have to be overcome. The fear of chaos that leads Anna to fragment her writing neatly into four books, bracketing off 'blood and brains' from buying tea, must be confronted, accepted and taken in. Writing stories must not be a substitute for feeling: 'if what we feel is pain, then we must feel it, acknowledging that the alternative is death' (478–9). This is no small consideration; Anna is representative, a woman in solitariness, living in the shadow of the bomb, subject to the effects of capitalism, struggling with idealism, at a time and in a situation unlike anything before.[41] Her breakdown positively offers her as one of the people with a productive 'crack' through which 'the future might pour in a different shape' (416).

It is significant that as intelligence, Anna's 'only bulwark', begins to falter, it is nurturing that provides some sort of bedrock. The one external constraint that holds her together is the presence of her daughter Janet, for whom she must cook, maintain routines and keep her own moods under control; only when Janet goes to boarding school is Anna able to give the attention to herself and Saul Green that allows her to break down, to feel, to let herself sink, experience and acknowledge the negative 'in a positive way', as her analyst Mother Sugar would have it. Although she cooks for Saul the emphasis shifts from food and eating to physical clenching (not letting anything in), coffee (an artificial stimulant) and whisky (a suppressant), though in drinking to excess – a wry touch – Anna is shocked by herself. Physical dysfunction echoes psychic breakdown as Anna becomes sick, does not cook, is not in command, is helpless because of the need to play something through.

The physicality of the breakdown is striking. Anna watches herself in the bath, her body taken over by the symptoms of anxiety and by the presence of Saul. His deathly cold in sleep is frequently referred to. Anna, too, is overwhelmed by fear, cannot breathe, cannot walk, becomes exhausted. They go through repeating cycles of fear, cruelty, spite, anger, exhaustion, sanity and a kind of knowledge. Anna tries to hold on to the 'female creature' in her body that she believes is true, but has in the end to acknowledge the protean joy-in-destruction figure of her dreams as part of herself. She discovers and accepts 'what is most discomforting about the body'.[42] Her own body becomes strange to her:

I looked at my thin white legs and my thin white arms, and at my breasts. My wet sticky centre seemed disgusting, and when I saw my breasts all I could think of was how they were when they were full of milk, and instead of this being pleasurable, it was revolting. This feeling of being alien to my own body caused my head to swim (532)

The description communicates distaste and yet Anna demonstrates that sanity depends on presence, that 'the conviction of life' requires an awareness of good physical function and pleasurable sensations. This simple, bodily understanding short-circuits the neuroses of intellectualising.

Anna's breakdown – like Mary Turner's a transforming experience – gives birth to some kind of integrity. She becomes able to write the 'Golden Notebook'. She can rerun or rewrite experience (or fiction) with enhanced perspective. The battle played out through the kitchen at Mashopi, for example, concerns not just the toppling of a colonial boss, but the hurting of a woman's feelings. Instead of caricaturing or ironising a foolish bigot she writes:

Mrs Boothby stood in the kitchen of the hotel at Mashopi, her stout buttocks projecting like a shelf under the pressure of her corsets, patches of sweat dark under her armpits, her face flushed with distress, while she cut cold meat off various joints of animal and fowl, and listened to the young cruel voices and crueller laughter through a thin wall. (550)

She gains wisdom, evident in her insights that 'a small painful sort of courage . . . is at the root of every life, because injustice and cruelty is at the root of life', and that 'the small endurance . . . is bigger than anything' (551). This is not personal but general, and stresses that her breaking down is concerned with communication and responsibility. In 'Free Women 5' Anna dreams that Janet and Tommy are both her children and Janet has all her milk while Tommy is starving. It is a recurring dream, though often with different players, and has a multitude of resonances concerning the body, nurturing, equity, self-division. Predominant among them is Anna's waking certainty that she feels responsible.

In *The Four-Gated City*, not-eating, breakdown and the communicative body are all manifest, and are still more explicitly linked. This novel traces Martha Quest's progress from her arrival in England to her death in the years after a chemical/nuclear catastrophe. The sections of the book progress through four qualities of the body, alluding to the four elements and humours: earth (most cloddish), water (beginning to flow), air and fire (leavening) and intelligence, a progress that mirrors Martha's growth into (and out of) her mind. As in *The Golden Notebook*, there is a move between fragmentation and wholeness, separation and communication; as with the supreme paradox of Anna Wulf's (re)integration through breakdown, so here understanding and growth are achieved through a reincorporation of the madwoman in the basement.

When first in London, Martha is acutely aware of the rigid stratification of English society and of the gulfs between people (to which Anna Wulf's separate notebooks offer a formal parallel). She is determined not to split herself up or keep part of herself in cold storage, a wish her sometime friend and lover Jack interprets as her old desire for the mythical city, an ideal. Mark's household, where she lives, appears fragmented, with its basement of alien people, a 'shadow world', but Martha feels it is a whole, with palpable, if strange, connections. Martha, a 'faceted mirror' reflecting qualities embodied in other people, is highly sensitized to their moods and needs in her handling of it all. The wholeness of the house (as of Martha) is literally and metaphorically fragile, however: 'everything declined and frayed and came to pieces in one's hands . . . a mass of fragments, like a smashed mirror' (371).

One way of resisting fragmentation is to focus on physical integrity and the development of a communicative body. This is what Jack devotes himself to in his post-traumatic awareness of mortality. There are danger signs with Jack, however. If, in the metaphorical scheme I am proposing, not eating is related to heightening the senses and opening the self, then Jack's crazy hunger is suspect. His appetites are an expression of Eros, yet Martha somehow feels he is not a serious man. Could it be that, like Martha's first husband, he eats to avoid knowledge? His body is, initially, immensely sensitive and responsive, so that although he cannot hear the meaning of Martha's words he can catch, sense and feel what she says. Living in the body without attempting to open himself is ultimately corrupting, however; he loses his 'subtle physical intelligence' as his unexamined and cunning mind takes control.

If the body on its own is insufficient, an existence that takes no account of it is equally distorted. Jimmy Woods is described as differently constructed from most people. He does not 'resonate', and Martha feels unable to connect with him, no matter how she tries to engage. She concludes that he is someone with one part of his mind extremely highly developed, but at the cost of everything else. His business in instruments, designed with the help of 'alternative' thought to engineer the brain for dubious purposes, is comparable to the unbridled scientism of those pure scientists who wilfully ignore the uses to which their research is put, and suggests that if alternative potential is not harnessed by reasonable people it will simply be annexed and exploited by war-mongering governments (which presumably means all governments).

Just as Jack suffers attacks of violent hunger, so Jimmy's eating reflects his career. Characterised by a 'round pinkish face, on his round (probably) pinkish body . . . his unvarying pink-rubber smile, and the surface of round staring spectacles' (536), Jimmy consumes quantities of tea and cake, 'energetically dott[ing] up loose currants on the end of a wetted forefinger' (183). His roundness and piggery suggest a physical sluggishness that is repeatedly shown to be the enemy of insight. The passengers on Martha's boat trip to England most fully exemplify this kind of enervation, not wanting to get up but nevertheless eating huge breakfasts from greed and inertia, soon going on to soup, alcohol, two hours of lunch followed by a little sleep, possibly a few games, then tea and 'masses of cakes' and finally an evening of sex and drinking. Lessing draws the conclusion explicitly: they are 'permanently heavy and dead and gone with food, alcohol and sex' (110). The 'bad time' for Martha is similarly characterised by torpor. When she is slowly working to recover the past, the hard work of it makes her fight for survival; though she never actually tells herself she is physically flabby, that she must sleep, eat and drink less, she recognises a lethargy that drags her down – and draws her own conclusions.

The converse of overfed lethargy is the sharpened senses and heightened emotions stimulated by lack of food. Martha's discovery is a revelation: 'if she walked long enough, slept slightly enough to be conscious of her dreams, ate at random, was struck by new experience throughout the day, then her whole self cleared, lightened, she became alive and light and aware' (45). Quite early on she finds herself in a real dilemma over whether to eat the soup she is faced with and begin a routine, ordered life, and risk losing her new understanding of the nature of separation and division. The lightness and clarity she experiences walking through London she regards as a reward of not eating and not sleeping, of using her body as a means of transcending her limited, claustrophobic daily life.

The step from this kind of heightened awareness to insanity is both a small and a large one. Martha attends Mark's wife, Lynda, who seems to have prepared herself for the 'task or challenge' of being ill and does not eat, drink or rest for days. Martha is drawn into the experience through Lynda's convincing rejection of Mark's rational approach. It is through their joint wordless, foodless, sleepless experience that Martha's non-rational and communicating self is confirmed. After weeks of near starvation, the two women emerge as skeletal; when they dress up and go out with Paul it is as caricature women.

Martha's own courted 'breakdown', her solitary psychic exploration, is similarly prepared for since she knows she must not eat or sleep, but keep alert, sharpen and refine her senses. Despite the danger, particularly the violence of the 'self-hater' within her, she is able to use commonsense, memory, judgement, comparison and understanding to in some way sort her unknown states of mind. An interrupting visit to a restaurant sets her back; when she returns to her room and checks her body, 'the instrument, the receiving device', she knows it will take twenty-four hours to regain her 'sensitive' state, after all that she has eaten and drunk.

At this meal Lynda orders salmon but does not eat it. Whereas Martha is able to eat or not eat at will (hence her 'thin phases'), Lynda is locked into anorexia. Even when she cooks, Lynda does not often eat, but returns to the basement. Her anorexia is part of her recurring illness, her inability to pull back into a 'normal' state. She is constantly 'tuned in' to the collective chaos of the human mind, perpetually visited by her demons, unable like Martha to move in and out of (thinness and) the landscape of pain. Whether the anorexia is cause or effect is impossible to detect: such is the circle.

The effects – generally beneficial if individually problematic – of what the women decide to call 'madness' have to do with listening, telepathic communication, intuition and a connectedness to something much larger than the individual. A confusion of human sound, mental pictures, premonitions and apprehensions of moods as colours, extraordinary beauty in the natural world and the terror and hidden unfamiliarity of ordinary, sleep-walking people, locked into themselves and eaten up with wants and needs, are the rewards and the price of being thus awakened. The novel's futuristic appendices suggest that such a chaotic connectedness offers the only hope for human survival and development.

In some ways Martha Quest/Knowles/Hesse may be said to come full circle. From her instinctive sense of connectedness to the natural world in the veld, when she perceives her smallness and the insignificance of humanity, she arrives at this ultimate perception of connection and super-personal forces. At one level it could be said that she simply grows up; as Lessing herself puts it in the Preface to *The Golden Notebook*, 'growing up is after all only the understanding that one's unique and incredible experience is what everyone shares' (13). But this is more than

a commonplace about losing egocentricity; as Martha's sexual experience with Jack indicates, Lessing is suggesting that there is a level of connectedness that reaches beyond the personal. The difference, it seems,
lies in the degree of contact and quality of the understanding. It is a
mark of her development that in the end Martha rejects the individual
and exclusive relatedness of married love and the insatiable personal
needs she sees it as breeding. The circular movement of Martha's
undoubted development is endorsed by the authoritative Rosa
Mellendip, who claims that people can never be told what they do not
already know, however hidden that knowledge might be.

In the full flood of her breakdown Martha thinks, 'If all these subhuman creatures are aspects of me, then I'm a gallery of freaks and
nature's rejects' (574). Although this is part of a realisation about sadism,
masochism, *schadenfreude* and the possibility of choice ('These things are
there. Always. I can choose to be them or not'), it touches too on the fears
about embodiment and human freakishness discussed earlier. The defa-
miliarised perception Martha has of the grotesque physicality and
strangeness of people when she goes out into the street from her session
with Lynda (like Kate's visions of animality in Lessing's *The Summer Before
the Dark*) implies that *all* humans are freakish, not just the so-called
deformed or the very fat or the very thin or the very large.

Martha's and Anna Wulf's enlightenment and ability to communicate
are achieved through their bodies, but paradoxically at the expense of
their physical needs. There is something disturbing, even dehumanising
about this, and it runs directly counter to the sensuous communication
through food discussed earlier. But elsewhere Lessing offers an enlightened growth and communication that is deeply rooted in the physical,
embracing perceptions of freakishness as relative. This enlightenment is
achieved precisely through ministering to the body's needs and hungers.
The major example is in *The Diaries of Jane Somers*, which confronts
morbid undercurrents of fear about embodiment.[43] The two novels that
make up *The Diaries* focus on the body both as revealed in popular
culture (Jane Somers, or 'Janna', is editor of a women's magazine) and
as a disturbing, deteriorating reality. Few novelists, it must be said, dwell
so directly or so movingly on the physical details of old age and debility.

The instinctive repulsion of the healthy from the alarming 'freakishness' of the very old or very sick is encapsulated in Janna's withdrawal
from her husband when he dies of cancer, looking 'like a boiling fowl'.
Her claim that she can't stand 'physical awfulness' suggests fastidiousness, but the sick and panicky feelings that accompany it reveal a refusal

to acknowledge mortality, and deep unease with embodiment (the 'what is most discomforting about the body' of Jacqueline Rose and of abjection). Her inability to tend to her dying mother demonstrates a similar reluctance to acknowledge the realities of decay; as she admits, she refused to see old ladies, for fear of being like them.

The substance of *The Diary of a Good Neighbour*, is the breakdown of Janna's distaste, fear and aloofness from the contingent realities of ageing. Janna is representative as well as specific; through her, discomforts, preconceptions and embarrassments about the ageing body are examined. Lessing clearly states the problem through Richard Curtis in *If the Old Could* . . . when he observes that that we do not, in contemporary western society, much care to be reminded of mortality: 'the very old are too frightening, too much of a threat, we can't stand it, *mementoes mori*, one and all' (354), and so we keep them out of sight or infantalise them. The detailed narrative of growing friendship between Janna and old Maudie Fowler both brings into focus the painful physicality of old age and endorses the crucial communicative importance of food.

Janna's initial overtures to Maudie Fowler are fraught with difficulties born of her own ignorance (she brings fruit that Maudie cannot eat because of her teeth) and Maudie's prickly dignity and pride. These difficulties are compounded by the women's relative positions of privilege and poverty – and class: 'I thought how one did not have *friends* with the working classes. I could be many things to Mrs Fowler, including a Good Neighbour, but not a friend' (46). (By the end of the novel Janna's achievement is to proclaim herself truthfully as Maudie's friend.) Janna is embarrassed to appear Lady Bountiful, and ashamed of the luxury of her own lifestyle, especially the bathroom, which Maudie, with her kitchen tap and outside lavatory, eagerly dwells upon. There is a gradual increase in physical intimacy between the two women as Janna overcomes her distaste for drinking tea out of grimy cups and repugnance at Maudie's sour smells and begins to help – making tea, shopping, feeding the cat, cooking Maudie a piece of fish, sweeping the floor, emptying urine from the full commode.

The women regularly take tea and cake together, and Janna encourages Maudie to reminisce about her early life, much of Maudie's nostalgia centring on food. The climax of the women's intimacy comes not with eating, however, but in connection with malfunctions of the digestive tract. Maudie dies from stomach cancer, a disease figuratively in keeping with the details of her life: the pains and indignities she has had to swallow, her periods of near starvation, the connection established with Janna through food and lavatory care. When Maudie hints that she would like to be washed, Janna is confronted by the inescapable facts of defenceless old age. Maudie's body is pathetic: fragile, skeletal, with yellow skin and thin, pendulous breasts. Worse still, she has 'shat her pants, shat everything', so Janna must cope with the smell, the mess, the washing and Maudie's suffering at the invasion. She is struck, above all, by the contrast between her own self-love and Maudie's pitiful helplessness and deep embarrassment.

Maudie's body is a disturbing reminder of what is to come and how the ageing body is a burden. Lessing evokes the difficulties of weight, stiffness, effort, panic, weariness, numbness, emptiness and the labour and difficulty of moving, reaching or bending, to feed the cat or make the fire. With everything such an effort, solitude is itself an affliction, giving rise to fantasy and depression. The arrival of 'Meals on Wheels' is an event for all the old women in the *Diaries*, partly for the fleeting social contact, but also because eating is almost their only physical pleasure. Lessing makes the most of its poignancy, here in the case of Annie Reeves:

The two little oblong containers are sitting one above another, on the sill. Annie carefully opens the first, and she is sick with disappointment. It is Wednesday, she had forgotten; Wednesday they bring this great sog of a pie, all damp crust with some dubious mince in it, a spoonful if that. She loathes cabbage. She hates carrot. She picks at the mince, her face squeezed up with distaste. No, she cannot. She investigates the pudding. It is a sponge, in custard. 'On a hot day like this, you'd think they'd give us a bit of salad,' she moans. And eats slices of white bread and jam and biscuits, one after another, till she's full. (427)

But there is also real pleasure, often in defiance of the 'experts', tellingly demonstrated by Vera Rogers' story of the ninety-four year old who responds to her advice on nutrition with the question, 'And how old did you say *you* were, dear?' (112).

For Annie and Maudie food offers both present pleasure and happy recollection. They recall details of meals eaten sixty or seventy years previously: dumplings in sheep's head stock, boiled puddings with fruit and sugar, eels and potatoes, batter pudding with meat and then again with jam, to fill hungry stomachs cheaply. Maudie reveals periods of deprivation, when she was so poor she took bread from the birds, or when she thought she was being poisoned by her father's 'fancy woman' and refused to eat, an inability to stomach the facts of her mother's death and father's inconstancy. Janna empathetically labels this to herself: anorexia.

But food is not just pleasure; it is both literally and metaphorically a sustainer of life, and these old women's preoccupation with food keeps death at arm's length. When, on an impulse, Janna takes Maudie to the Rose Garden Restaurant for tea and cakes, her unspoken gift to Maudie is more than rewarded by Maudie's relentless eating and fierce delight in everything she sees, the world as a 'gorgeous present' (120). Maudie eats to feed her cancer; she eats to make up for all the times she could not eat; she eats because she can. The hunger, the pleasure, the fierceness are expressions of an appetite for life itself. The two repeat the visit when Maudie is very ill and can barely walk, and she again eats her way methodically through a pile of cakes, to Janna's incredulity, given 'that little yellow belly' (212). When Maudie is dying, shortly before she finally goes into hospital, they go to visit her odious sister and here too she eats, more than anyone, 'demolish[ing] every last crumb' (218). Which is very much the way she dies, fighting, complaining, refusing to let go:

'Wait a minute,' she had muttered, or cursed, or cried, as life went surging on, leaving her behind, but life had taken no notice and had gone on past her. (255)

Janna, supportive to the end, does not understand Maudie's rage and her sense of injustice at losing life, but believes her own incomprehension may have something to do with being fifty and not ninety. Understanding, really understanding, one's own mortality is something the body is remarkably reluctant to allow, for too much acceptance might sicken the appetite and extinguish the fire.

The second Jane Somers novel, *If the Old Could . . .*, reaffirms the difficult aspect of eating, showing that young bodies may be as problematic as the very old and confirming the view that freakishness depends on perspective. Janna's niece Kate has developed a 'mirroring body', constantly seeking to deflect pain. Janna never really understands or gets through to the unhappy Kate who, for quite different reasons from Maudie Fowler, is equally unable to cook, bath or pull herself out of passivity and dependency. Though she seems to appreciate firmness and order – she is covertly pleased by Janna's ultimatums – she responds with passive resistance, shielding herself by attempted suicide, drunkenness, comfort eating and plugging in her earphones.

Her eating is a far cry from Maudie Fowler's simple appetite, and – like Josie's binges in Shute's *Life-Size* – is largely out of control: she puts all the stew on her own plate, leaving none for Janna; she buys samosas, a dozen Mars Bars and six large packs of crisps, all of which she eats in one evening; alone with Janna she either wolfs down her food and retreats behind her earphones, or cannot eat the enticing supper Janna has prepared because she is full of biscuits. In the small hours one morning, Janna finds her in the kitchen chain-eating shortbread with both hands. Such compulsive eating, according to Bunny Epstein, is a sign of anger about denial in childhood:

The compulsive eater symbolically 'stuffs her anger down her throat' with food she neither needs nor wants. She does not feel herself to be a whole and separate person. The boundary of self and other is blurred ... Metaphorically speaking, many women are starving but they cannot eat and enjoy the feast that lies before them in present time because they are so hungry for the food they didn't get as children.[44]

Epstein's description of compulsive eating in terms of symbolism and metaphor suggest the suitability of compulsive eating as a literary device. Here psychologist and novelist concur: Kate attaches herself, limpet-like, to her sister or Janna; she fills her mouth with food and ears with music to seal herself up and deny her pain; she has 'a great gaping pit or hole somewhere in the region of her solar plexus, all need and craving' (333).

Yet Kate also represents something more than one child's dysfunctional upbringing. She is portrayed entirely through an external mode so unlike Josie in *Life-Size* reveals no perception of herself, and neither are Janna's efforts at understanding illuminating, ending as they do in defeat. Does Kate represent the 'generation gap', a breakdown in communication between old and young in modern society? Or is she a child who cannot be explained by parents (or a society) programmed only for successful offspring; is she a prototypical foreshadowing of Ben in *The Fifth Child*, a creature who simply cannot be accounted for by liberal/psychological/cultural explanations? Certainly, she is an isolated creature; her earphones prevent both self-communication and contact with the outside.

Kate's lethargic inhabitation of her body is the antithesis of the vital engagement and receptiveness attempted by Anna Wulf and Martha Quest. As so often in Lessing, excessive eating is a danger sign, though she connects this here with being dulled rather than becoming fat. Fat appearance, indeed, may be presented positively; old Annie Reeves is 'comely, does not sag, is all comfortable rolls and curves' (426). Jolly appearances are deceptive though; Annie is starving for want of activity and attention, and all her eating can do nothing to assuage that hunger.

The most shocking image Lessing gives of the body is Janna's disabused view of Annie's absolute physicality:

I look at Annie's gaping mouth, making words, words, and I see it as the opening into a conduit that runs, convoluted and disgusting, to the opening that is her anus and which looks, probably, the same. (497)

She concludes that we are essentially 'containers of dirt-filled intestines', a nihilistic attitude that she resists, but which reflects the trials of caring for the old and sick, and asserts the ultimate grotesqueness of the human body as flesh. Love, friendship, connection make all the difference; whereas the engagement with Maudie's physical processes leads Janna beyond repulsion into a bodily conversation, a mutual connection, Annie's comfort eating, mirroring Kate's, is self-centred, non-communicative. As for Annie, it is as though her real personality becomes progressively submerged by her misery and disavowal; metaphorically, she becomes buried within the accumulations of her own body fat.

The perception of Annie's body as grotesque, her anus resembling her mouth, and Janna's insistence that we are simply producers of faeces recalls the processes of abjection delineated by Kristeva. In a complex exploration of the female grotesque, Mary Russo makes a similar connection. The grotesque body Russo outlines functions in two ways. One is as a projection of an inner state and relates to the uncanny. In the other (more in keeping with the carnivalesque of Bakhtin discussed in chapter 5) the grotesque body functions socially, in connection with all that is 'low' – the body parts, processes and substances of abjection. The figure of the fat woman would seem to embody both personal and social abjection, on one hand as a repository of individual 'shame and repressed desire' and on the other as a literal abjection of society's overconsumption, what Russo calls the 'disavowed aspects of production and "dangers of overproduction"'.[45] In simple terms, the fat woman is a scapegoat.

The cult of the slim, firm body discussed earlier is certainly defined in opposition to all that is fat and uncontained (and lacks firm boundaries – just think of all those corsets and workouts). Unlike the equation of physical substance with wealth and status in other places and periods, fatness in contemporary western culture is regarded as generally disgusting; studies have suggested that fat people are stigmatized, held to be somehow morally responsible for their condition.[46] There is class bias here, too, partly because poverty, poor diet and obesity may go together, but also because popular images (music hall, slapstick, comics, seaside postcards) frequently combine comedy, fatness, and the (usually female) working classes. Even in a novel that purports to explode the slimming business, *A Matter of Fat*, it is the working-class character, Maureen, who is fat, self-deceiving and quite without self-discipline.[47] Fat women, according to Edwin Schur, are particularly subject to critical judgement, perhaps because women's clothing puts their bodies more permanently on show than men's, so that fatness is seen as a failure (or refusal) to please through conforming to shape and size conventions.[48]

By the same token, the very transgressive nature of fatness may be seen as a source of power, a potential deliberately exploited by feminist comedians making a virtue of the eating, defecating, copulating, grotesque female body. If the fat body represents a cultural abject, then it contains a disruptive potential parallel to that of the psychically abject: it constantly threatens to break back in to the prevailing order. How this highly intangible source of menace may manifest itself in powerful practice is more problematic. In the face of social opprobrium, what can a fat body do?

In terms of literary strategies, there is scope. Margaret Atwood's protagonist in *Lady Oracle* finds some empowerment in using her bulk to torment her mother, but it is a negative power, born of unhappiness, and it insulates her from life. Angela Carter's rumbustious Fevvers is an unequivocal example, combining the grotesque – her freakish wings, her gross physicality, size and appetite – with the spectacular, to confute the 'clean and proper body' of socially acceptable femininity. She eats, drinks, laughs – and yawns – with gusto; she has 'Elizabethan' table manners and is generally larger than life, offering a female embodiment that contrasts sharply with both the traumatised abbreviation of the anorectic and the forlorn bulk of a comfort eater. Size, here, equals power, and is no barrier to elevation. Nevertheless, even Fevvers does not entirely address the dilemma of the fat woman. She is a big girl, certainly, but more brazen than bloated, and her power in any case relies on her feminist-Communist magicking mentor, the wizened Lizzie.

Molly Keane takes a more realist approach in the novel *Good Behaviour*. Here the protagonist Aroon St Charles is caught between her large, ungainly body with its swinging 'bosoms', her hopeless appetites and a constricting upbringing that prioritises adult comforts over children's needs. Aroon's desperate, hot desires are firmly repressed, so that all she certainly knows is how to behave, 'believe me, because I know'.[49] Keane contrasts this enforced good behaviour with all that is abject; Aroon's response to repression is to turn herself into a freak: 'the fat woman in the fairground; the man who chews up iron; the pigheaded woman; anything to escape from hopeless me' (85). She becomes a gargantuan eater, indulging her appetite and making herself a joke acceptable to her brother Hubert and his adored friend Richard, while at the same time burying the pain of emotional exclusion. Eating, for Aroon, takes the place of all the passions that 'good behaviour' forbids her to express, and these unexpressed feelings make her swell to ever larger proportions.

Aroon is the very figure of powerlessness, victim of parental neglect and her mother's distaste, of her own naivety and of Hubert's and Richard's heartless manipulation as they use her to conceal their affair. She is constitutionally unable to engage in the dynamic of the household, sensing herself always to be outside the charmed circle. Her two (very physical) pleasures, dancing and eating, are spoiled by her size and her wretched bosoms, and by her mother's carping insults and restrictions.

Yet from all her defeats and humiliations Aroon plucks a victory. Her ultimate empowerment comes economically, when her father – periodically solicitous and confidential, always delighted by her appetite, finally touched by her fate ('I'm on your side, sweetheart' (195)) and maybe by contrition – unexpectedly bequeaths her almost everything. The revenge of 'kindness' she wreaks on her mother, though couched in the codes of good behaviour, is nothing less than a return of the repressed, a recursion from her marginal, abjected status. She moves the household to a small Gothic folly clinging to the cliff-side, situated appropriately on the margins of land, sea and air; she installs her invalid mother in a room of her own design, insisting on her being 'scrupulously clean and washed and scented' (5) and (torment for a semi-anorexic woman) well fed. In short, she takes absolute control. The death of a mother who always begrudged her appetite is induced through the medium of exquisitely cooked food, but it is a dish made from rabbit that her mother cannot stomach and that is abjectly indeterminate, having been 'forced through a fine sieve and whizzed for ten minutes in a Moulinex blender' (4). Appropriately enough, her mother dies on a surge of vomit.

This reading of *Good Behaviour* asserts the power of a fat woman *as* freak and misfit. The novel begins with the deathly ending in which Aroon frankly seems a monster; the rest of the novel, framed as Aroon's attempt to 'understand', traces the family history from nursery days. Whereas Aroon is initially seen as powerful and monstrous, by the end of the novel her abject sufferings and humiliations through early life (even allowing for her gross self-deceptions) render her transformation grimly satisfying. Her elevation does not mean she is laudable or even likeable; it is the extent of her bulky impotence and dejection that endows her with pathos and makes her ultimate retaliative empowerment gratifying. It is worth noting, however, that only one and a half of thirty-four chapters show this big/fat woman as empowered. The major part of the novel focuses on Aroon's sense of inappropriateness and her social exclusion, an emphasis that foregrounds the prevailing views and practices of twentieth-century western society as a whole.

Hillel Schwartz ends his excellent analysis of these very views and practices by spinning a utopian fantasy, a 'fat society' in which dinners would be delicious and sociable and children well fed when hungry, where fat people would dress expressively and be forthright about the body, and women especially would 'wear their weight with new conviction'. Such a society would be comforting, more caring, less 'harshly competitive, less devouring', a consumer's society without unsatisfied desire: 'In a fat society people would consume for the sake of the company they would keep. Consuming would become satisfying to the degree that it became social, generous and unburdening.'[50] Well, it's nice to think so.

Casting a retrospective look at this chapter in the light of Schwartz's utopia, anorexia shows up as a dystopian phenomenon, partly on account of anorectics' total absence of body fat, but chiefly and more seriously because what little eating does occur is unbearably and obsessively private. Anorexia is a refusal, not only of food but of social connection. Margaret Atwood presses the point in a short story, 'Spring Song of the Frogs', in which the aptly named but diminished Will, seeking 'generosity', is assailed on every side by a lack of flesh.[51] The story is partly about Will's own passivity, but registers an edginess in these pale, secretive, non-eating women who keep checking their image in the glass. The story associates unwillingness to eat with narcissistic withdrawal, implying a trend. More disturbingly it intimates the death of Eros, a warning echoed in the diminished wooing song of the frogs.

The feeding and fasting of Doris Lessing's characters is more equivocal. They eat in company, take pleasure in the communicative potential of food and may or may not break down and fast in company. The resulting efforts and processes, moreover, are focused at a level beyond the narrowly individual, and are directed towards what is most profoundly, if obscurely, social. It is such eating, social in its widest sense, that flavours the second half of this book.

CHAPTER 4

Sharp appetites: Margaret Atwood's consuming politics

The perspective of the first part of this book has been largely personal, focused on the individual psyche or body, or on how cultural influences and power relations affect the individual. This chapter begins to open out that view by considering the cumulative effect of a single writer's use of food, eating and appetite, how they embody her particular vision and sense of engagement. Highly distinctive and widely varied in form and content, Margaret Atwood's writing spans and reflects themes and preoccupations discussed throughout this book, from predatory cannibalism to self-starvation and the body, the force of conventions and the significance of foods.

In a 1982 interview, Atwood said: 'Politics, for me, is everything that involves who gets to do what to whom . . . Politics really has to do with how people order their societies, to whom power is ascribed, who is considered to have power.'[1] 'Everything that involves who gets to do what to whom' is pretty comprehensive. Clearly Atwood, like Carter, considers herself to be an essentially political writer, one for whom politics suffuses all activities. She has said more or less as much in several interviews.[2] By looking right across her work it is possible to put together a picture of how food, eating and appetite in her fiction relate to 'how people order their societies', on micro (individual, interpersonal) and macro (cultural) levels, not just in specific instances, but woven into an overall political analysis or vision. It is in this sense that we may speak of a politics of appetite or a politics of eating. Atwood's political analysis is mediated through a sophisticated, mutating and complex feminism that – eschewing narrow and sexist censure – indicts the predatory but also castigates passivity, asserting women's ability, even duty, to rise above the perception of self as innocent victim.

Atwood's publication in 1987 of *The CanLit Foodbook* testifies to her interest in food, both literal and literary, and her lively awareness of its history and presence in Canadian writing. She has a shrewd view of its function: 'authors put [various foods] in because they reveal character, slimy as well as delectable, or provide metaphors or jumping-off points into the ineffable or the inferno'.[3] Food in her own writing has an important part in character revelation, and the ineffable and inferno are occasionally evoked, but it also bears a varied and ultimately more exact burden of signification. Atwood focuses a remarkable variety of cultural and political issues through eating and female bodies and these combine to expose differences and dislocations between culturally constructed roles and experienced realities.

Atwood's first novel *The Edible Woman* is permeated with food. Characters stumble through breakfasts, women cook for each other, female employees share the catering for an office tea party, people hold more or less unsuccessful – even farcical – dinner parties; all these occasions manifest complicated relationships among and between the sexes in the precisely delimited society of place and period. More specifically, Atwood brings food and eating (or not-eating) into direct relationship with gender and cultural politics, using food and its activities to problematise assumed gender roles of the late 1950s and 1960s in urban Canada. She emphasises the predatory nature of appetite and, perhaps more importantly, the protest signalled by its lack. In doing so her narrative invests the body with interpretive capacities in excess of its cultural definition, allowing physical recognition and a refusal of oppressive definitions. In other words, the body is given its own, subversive, voice.

Atwood renders the experience of her young protagonist, Marian MacAlpin, explicitly in terms of consumption; the overt symbolism of eating interweaves not only carnivorousness and cannibalism but involuntary self-starvation and the metaphoric significance of particular foods. At the beginning of the novel, Marian is represented as an unquestioning omnivore; in the first dozen pages she consumes or samples milk, cereal, bread, peanuts, vanilla, caramel and orange flavoured canned rice puddings, coffee and toasted Danish – all before lunch. She is connected with food indirectly too, through her work in consumer research for a company whose hierarchical and static structure she describes as 'layered like an ice-cream sandwich', signalling both the (nutritionally) surplus quality of the firm and the impossibility of women's upward movement from the middle 'gooey layer' to the (male) executive level.[4] The goods tested by the company are related to the body (razor blades, sanitary napkins) or are edible (canned rice pudding, laxatives, instant pudding-sauce, beer). Marian's close relation to food – and to consumerism on a cultural scale – suggests both women's traditional association with nutrition (in the middle layer, feeding others, catering to their tastes) and their role as a consumable.

Marian's pathway is more or less that of any young educated woman of the time: university, work, marriage. The novel effects a critique of the convention of the period, that women give up paid employment on marriage (indeed, Betty Friedan's *The Feminine Mystique*, which Atwood admits along with de Beauvoir's *The Second Sex* to have been an important influence, identifies this as a salient factor in the 'problem with no name' of women's alienation and domestic depression).[5] The social and sexual attitudes that underpin this convention are laid bare in a semi-drunken vision of the future in which Marian sees a middle-aged, balding Peter at the barbecue (a nicely gendered and faintly atavistic cooking image) and herself notably absent from the garden. The Marian–Peter relationship is from the outset signalled as problematic. Peter's contradictory reactions indicate the conflicting roles their gender requires them to inhabit; he is fearful of being trapped into marriage yet resentful when Marian doesn't cook 'proper' meals. When Marian tries to flee, however, he pursues her and tries to pin her down (hence the imagery of weaponry, hunting, traps and photography). Marian's ambivalence is focused at an unconscious level; while she believes she means it when she tells Peter that she would prefer to leave the big decisions to him, her body is in full rebellion.

Marian's doubts and discomforts take various forms, but the most dramatic is the refusal of food. In a classic hysterical pun, she becomes unable to swallow, or stomach, the facts and implications of her situation. Her first food refusal is framed as a response to the unnatural position she is forced into as a bride-to-be: submissive, domestically focused, approving, deferential, maternal. She sits in the restaurant with Peter considering her aptly distorted reflection in the bowl of a spoon, almost entirely passive, having abdicated to Peter even the choice of what she will eat from the menu (he prefers red meat). Distancing herself and contemplating him coolly as he pontificates, she becomes acutely aware of his precision in cutting the steak, concluding that this is a highly violent action, albeit disguised and decontaminated. Encapsulated here and at issue in the novel is the containment and encoding of the essentially brutal realities of gendered power politics of the late 1950s and 1960s. Marian's associative chain of sanitised and horrific images – the too-neat Moose beer advertisements, a random mass-shooting, the cow marked in sections in a cookbook – leads her to perceive her steak as muscle, flesh, cow, and no matter how she tries she is unable to continue eating it. Politely exercised private power in an apparently peaceful setting – a romantic dinner for two – is suddenly tilted into a different frame, indicating savagery and ruthlessness.

Gradually, further foods add themselves to the list of what her body refuses: meat, eggs with their reproductive resonances, sentient-seeming carrots, finally even processed foods. Some of the givings-up are highly symbolic, such as the Valentine's cake shaped like a heart that she buys in guilty response to Peter's roses and which her body rejects with an empathetic shudder, perceiving its texture to be that of tiny lungs. Marian's rejection of eggs is precipitated by the hysterical reaction of Len Slank to the predatory Ainsley's revelation that she has deliberately used him in her plan to have a child (a comic, gender-reversing parallel to Marian's own flight from the predator). His reaction to the physical realities of pregnancy is a distraught infantile outburst about his mother having once forced him to eat an egg which had a little chicken in it. Marian is initially contemptuous, but the next morning her body overrules her intention, her mouth closes 'like a frightened sea-anemone' and her throat decides that her egg is alive (161). She is represented, like Len, as hysterical; she cannot contemplate the physical realities, and responsibilities, of gestation and birth.

Eggs are an obvious symbol of reproduction, but here they are also associated with Marian's embryonic identity; after she is engaged, her breakfast egg breaks, 'sending out a white semi-congealed feeler like an exploring oyster' (84), rather as she begins to do. She similarly characterises Duncan's confessional monologue as like an uncooked and formless egg. Although her food-revulsion is framed as reverence for life, her reaction to flesh and the curiously repellent language she uses to describe Clara's pregnancy ('like a boa-constrictor that has swallowed a watermelon' (31), 'a strange vegetable growth, a bulbous tuber' (32)) suggest a disgust with mature femaleness and the generation of life that places her alongside the teenaged anorectics discussed in chapter 3.

Duncan's role is crucial. He offers an alternative masculinity to Peter's machismo (as does Joe), and is a sort of mentor, giving Marian permission to transgress and ultimately reject the unwritten rules of the Peter pathway. But he also mirrors Marian's anorexic self; he is thin and fleshless and equally unwilling to embrace adulthood. He is drawn to the child-like, foetally curled skeleton in the museum's mummy room, though he warns Marian in the hotel bed that adopting the foetal position solves nothing. Both reflect a desire for the clean and proper body indicative of abjection. At the office tea party, Marian is fascinated, repelled and finally appalled by the women's bodies, their lumps and bulges, their coarse skins, their lack of containment, the 'continual flux between the outside and the inside'. In the end she feels 'suffocated by this thick sargasso-sea of femininity' (167), a conclusion directly paralleled by Duncan's passing complaint in bed that 'There's just altogether too much flesh around here. It's suffocating' (253). In this respect, adult human contingency overwhelms them both.

It is clear that Marian's anorexia is not appearance-driven, for she is not interested in looking thin; her not eating is simply a refusal. What she is refusing is not clear to her since her condition is not willed: 'Whatever it was that had been making these decisions [it was] not her mind certainly' (152). Her refusal of food is repeatedly attributed to her mouth, her throat, her body's decision.[6] Atwood seems to be rewriting the female body in such a way as to draw together biology and culture, reinvesting the body with the power to determine eating – and thus living – practices. Marian's actions, if not her understanding (she seems to be on automatic pilot) are prompted by her body. In this sense, she is really not anorexic like Josie in Jenefer Shute's *Life-Size* or Jane Somers's niece Kate or even Martha Quest; she has a peculiarly symbolic form of anorexia which, though it is inconvenient and manifests one or two of the usual symptoms, causes her no actual harm. She does not even lose much weight.

The effect of starvation on Marian's body is never an issue. What is more important is the metaphorical stripping of her ability (or desire) to consume. When Duncan leads her to a wilderness place in the ravine they come 'as near as possible to nothing' (263), in effect an existential void. She understands that what she had really wanted had been an impossible and inappropriate safety. This can be seen as the crux of the novel; significantly, it immediately succeeds the final extinction of Marian's ability to eat and drink. Though she responds to Duncan's withdrawal with 'desperation', Marian accepts responsibility for herself and ceases to be passive. It is here as much as in the relations between characters that Atwood makes her most incisive and damning criticism of the sexual politics of the 1950s and early 1960s. Rejecting simplistic feminist views of this period as characterised by male oppression of innocent women (the predatory Ainsley and caring Joe equally refute these stereotypes) Atwood suggests that women collude in their oppression (in being edible), through passivity and the assumption of innocence. It is a claim that comes to bear increasing weight in Atwood's later novels.

The mould-breaking action Marian takes is archetypally feminine and simultaneously subversive, as she invites Peter to tea and bakes and decorates a cake in the shape of a luscious woman. While the cake cools she grins at herself in the mirror, showing her teeth – perhaps for the first time. Apostrophising the cake as though it were herself in her party clothes, she condemns it: 'You look delicious . . . Very appetizing. And that's what will happen to you; that's what you get for being food' (270). Marian has learned assertiveness, that sexual politics means 'eat or be eaten', but although her cake has the desired effects of frightening Peter away and returning Marian's appetite, it does not address the conundrum of how she can live without either being consumed or becoming a predator. As with much of Atwood's writing, there are no simple answers; the ending is open, the emphasis on possibility rather than solution.

There are plenty of questions left unresolved. The dangers on the one hand of self-consumption (whether through narcissism or abnegation) and on the other of both subjective and objective commodification are ever present. It is, after all, Marian who eats most of the woman-cake, and with gusto. Being a consumer entails empowerment (her not eating is represented in terms of passivity: she *cannot* eat), but the use of this trope throughout the novel also portrays eating as both an act of aggression and a participation in the *status quo*. Individual responsibility (here the claiming of subjectivity) raises questions: to what extent do victim and persecutor collude and what are the possibilities for action for a woman deeply implicated in a consumer culture that casts her as the (passive) filling in a sandwich? Even in this first novel, Atwood's critique is not limited to individual and sexual politics but relates to the cultural and political meanings of apparently individual actions. The significance of who is trying to eat whom, of submission (and protest) is general. Marian's relationship with Peter is entirely conformist (she is the foodstuff) until she withdraws from collusion (through anorexia) and resists reincorporation (becoming a consumer). Marian and Ainsley, caught up in the value system of western capitalism, spend much of this novel packaging themselves for male delectation; there is a parallel with Marian's employers packaging their presentations, the brewery advertising their beer and manufacturers marketing their toilet-paper.

A different kind of packaging (but one equally central to contemporary western society) goes on in *Lady Oracle*, which is concerned, in part at least, with the false solace offered by both escapist fantasy and comfort eating. The predatory eating of *Edible Woman* is followed through more equivocally in this novel to include cultural preoccupations with physicality and pressures to conform, manifested through the internalisation of 'norms' as well as through external coercion. The novel channels these pressures explicitly through the protagonist Joan Foster's mother, but also indicates their presence in the prevailing culture, among whose instruments are the Gothic romances Joan herself writes. The appetite catered for by 'Costume Gothics' is, Joan claims, a 'quintessential need' to escape from hard and disappointing ordinary lives. Joan says she deals in hope – obliterating the defects of the real bodies of her readers and transforming them into beautiful romantic heroines – but this is at the cost of reinscribing idealised models of femininity. Writing the novels is an escape for Joan herself, compensating for the lack she experiences and allowing her to compartmentalise her life, though ultimately she concludes that they are bad for her, indulging a compulsive, escapist appetite. Atwood stresses the commercial status of the Gothics; they are marketed as a product, like the decorated toilet paper Marian deplores in *The Edible Woman*.

Popular romances are part of a general commodification that works towards reinforcing a particular female image, a construct resting upon a notion of something essentially feminine. This notion is partly what *Lady Oracle* (like *The Edible Woman*) attacks; de Beauvoir's 'One is not born, but rather becomes, a woman' informs Atwood's unpicking of the feminine construct, as she questions how women come to be placed as objects in relation to men.[7] The slim body ideal and a specific created 'feminine' appearance (predating but not unlike those identified in *Life-Size*) are objectifying pressures espoused by Joan's mother. She conditions her child: Joan is regularly invited to sit and watch her mother 'put on her face', which includes lipsticking over the borders of her thin mouth, giving her a (literal and figurative) double mouth.[8] Joan's fantasy Fat Lady is encased in a fluffy femininity which Joan acknowledges as a 'destructive' mould, preventing acceptance by self and others of who she really is. But as she also says, things are not so simple and women themselves desire what a culture constructs as desirable, however pernicious: 'I wanted those things, that fluffy skirt, that glittering tiara. I liked them' (103).

The relationship between Joan, her mother, the body, hunger and eating is intricate, and relates both to the wider culture with its commercial and political pressures and to mother–daughter power relations, which are foregrounded. A psychological and physical aetiology is also indicated, rooted in the mother's expressed wish that she had aborted

Joan. Joan portrays herself as deprived of maternal love, taking refuge in eating which she learns is a weapon she can use in the chronic power struggle with her mother, a struggle focused on her body. The mother attempts strategic moves to persuade Joan to slim: diet books on the pillow, bribes, remarks, appointments with specialists, laxatives. Joan portrays increasing efforts by her mother to control her and increasing efforts on her own part to provoke her mother. The futility of the conflict is clear at Joan's moment of triumph for, although she makes her mother cry, she is undermined by her mother's arrogation of blame: 'What have I done to make you behave like this?' (88).

Joan's size and appetite are ostensibly endorsed by Aunt Lou, whose relation to Joan is both nurturing and problematic. Apparently unconcerned by size, Aunt Lou provides treats: gumdrops, shared popcorn at the movies, cotton candy at the National Exhibition and lavish, mouth-pleasing snacks after the movies or church: shrimp sandwiches, grilled crab-meat with mayonnaise, cold chicken salad, hot chocolate, petit fours. Joan is indulged, allowed her escape in eating, and she feels nurtured by Aunt Lou in ways she never does by her own mother. All this is called into question, however, when Aunt Lou dies and leaves Joan $2,000, on condition that she lose a hundred pounds in weight. Does this mean Aunt Lou didn't like her as she was, wonders Joan, or was she simply being pragmatic? Is life in fact easier for the slim? Or, to nod to de Beauvoir, is capitulation a part of the inevitable process of becoming a woman? The money opens for Joan the way to escape her mother, but at the expense of surrender to her mother's (and the culture's) valuing of slim and youthful appearances. Atwood neatly encapsulates the dilemma for women in a culture of appearances and consumerism: you cannot escape from your culture's values, its exigencies won't go away, so you have to find some way to deal with them. The price of freedom is engagement.

The battle between Joan and her mother is only superficially about Joan's size; it centres on identity and control. Far from being pleased about Aunt Lou's legacy, Joan's mother is infuriated, trying to sabotage Joan's slimming by means of strategically placed pies and cookies and manifesting increasing signs of distress, from heavy drinking to verbal abuse. The climax, in which Joan announces she is moving out and her mother desperately stabs her arm with a kitchen knife, is a dramatic culmination of this struggle for control, a struggle enacted almost entirely through food. Despite Joan's departure, though, her mother remains victorious, for her control is internalised by Joan. Joan's narrative's relentless focus on her mother is testimony to the power of her presence and influence. After her mother's death, when Joan returns home, she even binges on the contents of her mother's fridge, half-hoping, half-expecting her mother to reappear with her inescapable 'disgusted, secretly pleased look' (178). Joan's dilemma is self-imprisonment; only when she realises that she herself maintains her mother's power is she able to let go.

There is, notwithstanding, a transformation in Joan, the first stage of which is physical. In adolescence she is the 'fat duenna', protecting her girlfriends from unwanted boys and popular by dint of 'personality', her schoolfriends duped by her appearance into thinking she herself has no feelings, no desire. Despite the denial of self, there is a kind of numb safety in this wonderfully phrased 'magic cloak of blubber and invisibility' (141) which allows her to remain a spectator, evading men (and therefore maturity) as well as enraging her mother. By fits and starts, however, she exposes herself to the world. Bodily transformation (her slimming) and a long slow shift from consuming to perceiving provide the vehicle. Joan describes herself as an 'escape artist', and from her faked suicide at the beginning of the novel, back through her history of miserable childhood and adolescence, affairs and marriage, her story is one of dissembling, evasion and flight, all of which re-enact in some sense her original concealment through flesh. For if her eating is partly in mitigation of her accidental status (her conception being unwanted), which renders her very existence precarious, her doubling and dissembling allow her to try out identities and continue avoiding commitment.

Joan's reluctance to take charge is evident not only in the submersion of her own body in fat but in other areas concerned with food. Her failure to cook properly is a form of deceit, for she privately considers her disasters to be successes, 'secret triumphs over the notion of food itself' (209). There is a fantasy element too. The archetypally American (and therefore suspect) Kentucky Fried Chicken is strongly associated with dissembling. Joan and the Royal Porcupine eat it when they have been dressing up and dancing, so that, along with Coke, it becomes part of their fantasy world. As their relationship begins to falter and he becomes morose, she tries to reinject some fantasy by suggesting they go out to buy KFC. When she has a bad conscience and decides to confess to Arthur, she brings home a family bucket which, though he calls it 'American crap', he nevertheless eats with gusto, and Joan's resolve disintegrates at the sight of his defenceless, greasy pleasure. Her appetite for fantasy and romance is at this stage evidently stronger than her appetite for truth.

Throughout the novel Joan is portrayed as having a strong sense of herself as victim. As a child she is a target for bullies and she is rescued several times by strange men, including her subsequent lover Paul. She feels more or less victimised by Fraser Buchanan, by Arthur, by the Royal Porcupine perhaps, certainly by Signor Vitroni, by her publishers and even by herself: 'Why did every one of my fantasies turn into a trap?' (334). Such a self-perception precludes the taking of responsibility, as Atwood stresses in this 1972 interview:

If you define yourself as innocent then nothing is ever your fault – it is always somebody else doing it to you, and until you stop defining yourself as a victim that will always be true. It will always be somebody else's fault, and you will always be the object of that rather than somebody who has any choice or takes responsibility for their life. And that is not only the Canadian stance towards the world, but the usual female one.[9]

Here Atwood draws a logical conclusion from de Beauvoir's analysis of the objectification of women, fused with an Existentialist politics of responsibility. Women may be denied their own subjectivity, may indeed have internalised a perception of themselves as objects, but acceptance and passivity are a kind of bad faith. Rejection of the 'innocent victim' is crucial to Atwood's work and part of what the current chapter seeks to demonstrate is that it lies at the core of her politics of appetite. Atwood's protagonists must learn that 'who gets to do what to whom' *is* their concern, that they cannot evade responsibility. Marian and Joan do not get very far with this, but at least they achieve some sort of perceptual shift.

By the end of the novel, Joan's perceptions begin to catch up with her body's transformation. She realises that faking suicide has solved nothing (and has created pressing problems of its own). Her crisis prompts a series of semi-comic resolutions as her past and her fantasies begin to cohere: the Fat Lady reappears as a threat, Joan has a vision of herself fattened up with pasta as a huge Fellini whore and she rewrites the end of her Costume Gothic, conflating her desired men in a way that suggests they are all to some extent her own romantic creation. Her mistaken Cinzano-bottle assault on the journalist provides a caesura, enabling a fresh start, a planned restitution, truth-telling (the novel itself) and Joan's acknowledgement of mess. Like Marian, Joan reaches a point of perception, but not much further; although she has conscientious plans, the book ends on a highly equivocal note, without her putting any of them into action.

These two novels emphasise both the female body as a medium for transformation and the externally conditioning forces of society, seen in consumer commodification and internalised models of femininity. Joan's and Marian's understanding is experientially and physically achieved; it comes through their peculiarly female bodies, but in relation to culturally defined female eating, cooking and starving practices. Atwood is steering a course between resolute anti-essentialism and an empowering of the body that acknowledges sex as well as gender. Appetite, and its connections with action and responsibility, is complicated and mutable.

Life Before Man's concern with appetite, in terms of 'who does what to whom', is located in the ostensibly private sphere of sexual relations in and around the dying marriage of Nate and Elizabeth. In this novel appetite manifests power (and powerlessness) and reveals characters' attitudes towards themselves, others and the world in general. The dinosaur-obsessed Lesje, for example, sees herself as a timorous herbivore, though the passivity of the daydream in which she imagines a Gorgosaurus about to devour herself and William is couched in terms that could suggest a projection of her own deepest desires: 'The Gorgosaurus wants, wants. It's a stomach on legs, it would swallow the world if it could.'[10] The fact that she regards it with 'friendly objectivity' only confirms that she is accustomed to dissociating herself from desire, a passive detachment reminiscent of Joan Foster's fat status as an 'onlooker' in life. In the light of this, her ultimate 'act' of getting pregnant – although in one sense a passive one, an act of omission – is an engaged and subversive way of forcing an issue.

The gorgosaurus of Lesje's imagination is later more clearly embodied in Elizabeth, though Lesje herself does not make the connection. Elizabeth's appetite is given a fluctuating history. In the aftermath of the suicide of her lover Chris, Elizabeth is so stunned and insulated that she is unable to recognise or experience her own appetite, eating only by way of routine care, like servicing a car. Though she lacks appetite this does not inhibit her eating; on the contrary, she eats too much, as though incapable of physical regulation. Her body is dulled, mechanical, fails to communicate with her consciousness. This is very like the perilous overeating in Doris Lessing's novels. Elizabeth's appetite for nurturing is also affected; she fails, for example, to make the usual Hallowe'en cookies for her children. The kitchen is 'no longer familiar' and the fridge silts up with unused and rotting food – a trope invariably suggesting dysfunction in Atwood's writing. Nate's mother's distrust of Elizabeth for 'vitamin deficiencies' (for which read maternal deficiencies) reinforces the point: the apathetic Elizabeth cannot cater properly for her children's appetites.

This negative eater is the inverse of the hungry Elizabeth seen elsewhere, wrestling with powerlessness. As a child and teenager, she responds to her father's flight and mother's sodden helplessness by going out and buying bread and cheese to eat, furiously, in place of the dinner her mother fails to cook. She copes with dutiful adoption by her monstrous Auntie Muriel and Uncle Teddy and protects her sister like a street fighter, so stimulating her hunger to win. Her appetite is voracious; she meets boys in the drugstore for necking purposes, but food is always involved. This is the most extreme hunger that Atwood portrays, a hunger for everything missing from Elizabeth's life. When she picks up a boy after her mother's death, he watches her eat a waffle 'as if she's never seen one before' (178), and she subsequently urges him to full penetrative intercourse. Atwood complicates matters further by entangling this avid appetite with guilt: when Elizabeth returns home it is to find her sister comatose, possibly suicidal, possibly insane, and in a pitiful act of contrition, Elizabeth voids the contents of her stomach.

This is the tough background to Elizabeth's undoubtedly predatory appetite for power and her complicated and often manipulative attitudes to food. During her ostensibly open marriage she regularly lunches Nate's mistress Martha, strategically at first, in case Martha should prove to be a threat, and subsequently as an act of malice and control: 'You wanted to *supervise* us', accuses Martha later (147). When she discovers that Nate is seeing Lesje she lunches William, unsure at first whether to tell him or bed him. She chooses the latter as a sort of mutual consolation prize, though in comparison with the unpredictable appetites of Chris she finds him bland and unsurprising, like processed cheese. With Chris she exposes her 'refugee's desperate habits' (150), letting him see her power and his deficiency, leaving him naked and defenceless – treating him, she later reflects, as men so often treat women.

The dying of Elizabeth's marriage to Nate intimates how long and varied power conflicts may be. Though she loses the battle to keep him as husband and resident father, Elizabeth struggles keenly to wield power over Nate. She plays upon his difficulty with separating, giving him 'news' of the children as though he were a distant uncle and she drives a wedge between him and Lesje by repeatedly springing the children on them unexpectedly for meals or weekends. The cost of these skirmishes is high even for Elizabeth; she has to fight to keep her grip on material reality, clinging for dear life to her cup of chicken Oxo and slice of toast and peanut butter. Even apparently monstrous appetites have both their causes and their reverses. As time goes on Elizabeth's appetite softens and she gives up trying to manipulate events. She also ceases to accept invitations to dinner: 'she's no longer willing to be that bored simply to eat. If she wants to devour the ground-up livers of deceased geese, the plucked carcasses of birds, wild or domestic, the pancreases of young cows, she can buy them herself' (260). The language here suggests a move away from predatory carnivorousness, and indeed Elizabeth recognises that she does not want to torture Nate, merely to win, though the winning looks more like a defeat for Nate than a victory for Elizabeth.

Nate is set up to lose in such a confrontation, since he is the 'carer' of this novel, associated from the beginning with activities such as cooking the children's favourite, macaroni cheese, and clearing the abandoned and rotting contents from the fridge. His own appetite is as much for comfort as possession and he is well aware of the processes of substitution: popcorn and cigarettes for a double Scotch, the double Scotch for Lesje. Throughout the novel, he consistently cares, cooks and provides – mostly, it seems, peanut butter sandwiches – for his children, and also at times for both Elizabeth and Lesje. He even cares for Chris, offering him beer when he comes to beg for reinstatement with Elizabeth. Nate seems the most ineffectual of the characters, especially in the long period when he is strung out between Lesje and Elizabeth. But it would be a mistake to confuse decisive action – carnivorousness, perhaps – with goodness, and to forget that responsibility can pull in (at least) two directions. Nate does after all suffer, his 'sentimental, unbearable' pain discounted by both Lesje and Elizabeth. Further, he stands in for his mother, gets involved with her political campaigns, takes Martha for supper when she has helped him to a job, and turns up, unbidden, at Auntie Muriel's funeral. He is something like a good man.

Nate's actions qualify him as a conscientious striver, but it is Elizabeth, victim turned persecutor, who makes the longest journey. Atwood's emphasis is on the significance, rather than the magnitude, of actions and perceptions. When Auntie Muriel turns up to bribe Elizabeth and Nate back together, Elizabeth is incandescent with rage, not only because of Auntie Muriel's interference but because this recalls her real mother having 'sold' her to Auntie Muriel. Her ejection of Auntie Muriel is deeply, carnivorously, cathartic: 'She feels savage, she could eat a heart' (218). When Auntie Muriel is dying and Elizabeth visits her in hospital, she re-examines her own motives, considering her longstanding appetite for revenge, but is still unable to forgive, is repelled. Yet as Auntie Muriel crumples up and weeps, Elizabeth takes her hands and, despite feeling sick, soothes them, offers comfort. After the funeral service, when Elizabeth falls unconscious and Nate helps her up, she allows herself to feel relief, to realise she is alive, just about solid, able. She takes the children home for tea and peanut butter sandwiches, a Nate-flavoured connection with their real appetites and her own capacity for nourishment.

Giving children tea is a small, but necessary, act. In Elizabeth's case it represents a turning outwards, from preoccupation with her own miserable hungers to the needs, however humdrum, of those (children, friends, fellow humans) to whom some obligation is owed. Atwood's next novel, *Bodily Harm*, altogether widens the scope, geographically, politically in the community it features, and in terms of the existential choices it offers the protagonist on her path from morbid self-absorption to a very different contemplation of death. The epigraph to this novel, from John Berger's *Ways of Seeing*, claims that while male presence is active, a woman's presence is defined as passive (so: men claim subject-positions to which women are objects and if men are violent then women are victims). The burden of this novel suggests that while social structures may be responsible for this state of affairs, men *and* women are complicit in its perpetuation. Atwood uses appetite and food to lay bare both suspect activity and passivity and to offer a possibility for crucial individual action that engages both body and appetite.

The protagonist is Rennie Wilford, victim of a partial mastectomy, the departure of her boyfriend and a threatening visit by an intruder. Rennie perceives her body as not so much a medium for change as a fifth column, unexpectedly unreliable, whose malfunction has plunged her into an unwelcome confrontation with her own mortality. Her reaction is to withdraw both from friendship and from her boyfriend, into a childlike state in which she longs for the doctor who operated on her, who had 'known' her from inside, to become her lover/mother/lifesaver. Her desired status as a non-participant is illustrated when, in response to the doctor's reassurance that radical mastectomy is only performed in cases of 'massive involvement', Rennie quips that massive involvement has 'never been my thing'.[11] Going to the Caribbean to write a frivolous travel piece is merely an extension of her withdrawal.

Rennie becomes involved through food, eating and the reinhabitation of her body. She is introduced to the other players through food. The intruder whose visit begins the whole process drinks Ovaltine in her flat, a curiously domesticated, suburban choice which aligns him rather with ordinary life than fantasy (abusive fantasy had been the alarming keynote of her relationship with boyfriend Jake, a devotee of sinisterly exotic foods and possessor of vampirically long canines). Dr Minnow on the aeroplane engages Rennie in conversation about the corrupt sequestering of tins of ham donated by the Canadians for hurricane relief, while himself taking only a single fastidious bite of the airline sandwich. The aspiring politician Prince's grandmother offers her cheese puffs in the airline queue, Paul engages her in conversation over the repugnant hotel food and even Lora first smiles invitingly at her while she is waiting for dinner. One effect of such food-linked introductions is to locate issues of abuse and corruption at the heart of ordinary exchanges and communications.

The food Rennie eats on St Antoine is uniformly bad: leathery beef, indeterminate greenstuff, chalk-flavoured lime dessert, undercooked eggs, burnt cheese sandwiches. This is food for tourists, for the non-involved. When Rennie is persuaded by Lora to collect the package of 'medicines' from the airport, thereby missing her breakfast, her errant taxi driver returns with a huge roti, the juicy filling dripping down his wrists. Though extremely hungry she doesn't ask him to get her one, and cannot bring herself to ask for a bite, for this would be 'borderline familiar' – though he only eats part, throwing the rest on the ground. By eating separately, or alone, Rennie remains apart; familiarity invites involvement.

Within this metaphorical scheme, Rennie's alimentary seclusion is attacked on three fronts. Dr Minnow takes her to a Chinese restaurant to ask her to write about what she sees on St Antoine. Since she is carnivorously hungry, she accepts the lunch, but when he manoeuvres the conversation round to his request, she backs off, loses her appetite, finds excuses. She only does 'lifestyles', she tells him, sketching a definition. With a lovely shift in meaning, his reply is exact: ' "You might say that I also am concerned with lifestyles," he says. "It is our duty, to be concerned with lifestyles. What the people eat, what they wear, this is what I want you to write about" ' (136). When Rennie goes to Ste Agathe, Dr Minnow reappears, like a conscience, in the Lime Tree bar, telling her of more abuses. Just before he is assassinated, she admits that he is a good man, but acknowledges to herself that she finds him austere, like a diet that provokes her lust for chocolate mousse and cream.

Like Dr Minnow, the more elusive Paul also takes her for a meal with a purpose, when he warns her away from the politically provocative Dr Minnow. Since Paul's status is dubious (he may be a CIA agent, a drug-runner, a friend to the rebels), his intention is unclear; it could be political (to find out if *she* is CIA), strategic (getting her to unwittingly help import arms) or personal (lust or protectiveness), or some combination of the three. Once Rennie travels to Ste Agathe (where the food – cream cheese and banana bread sandwiches, rum and lime, papaya, tropical fish – is better and notably less colonial) she is en route to involvement, initially in the form of a liaison with Paul, whose sexual skill and unconcerned acceptance of her truncated breast enable Rennie to reinhabit her body. She stills both her physical qualms and fears of getting involved, however, by reassuring herself that she is committed to nothing; as a tourist, she is untouchable, 'exempt'.

The third assault on Rennie's self-containment comes from Lora, the person she likes least. It is Lora who drinks with her and engages her to collect the (arms) package from the airport, Lora who offers her bread to settle her stomach on the boat ride to Ste Agathe, Lora who turns up crisp and fresh with ingredients for breakfast the first morning Rennie wakes at Paul's. Lora, with her abjectly chewed fingers, scrounged drinks and unwelcome confessional monologues, provides valuable lessons for Rennie. Lora's life is one of survival; childhood beatings, escape, rape are not indulgences or fantasies but realities for her, and she discovers early the truth underlying all oppression: her mother's boyfriend hit her not because he was intrinsically evil, but because there was no one to stop him.

When the political powderkeg blows up, it is incarceration with Lora that finally leads Rennie to discover that she is not exempt: 'Nobody is exempt from anything' (290), a phrase that could sum up Atwood's entire oeuvre. In their grim cell, Lora talks and talks and smokes until Rennie is desperate for escape, overfilled with reality. It gets worse as the bodily discomforts pile up: there are bugs and rats; they are hungry and thirsty; the tea is made with salt water (deliberately, '[b]ecause they can', says Lora), the water tastes of rancid butter and the lunchtime boiled chicken backs are undercooked; the cell stinks. Atwood shows the two women slowly accommodate themselves to the life they have, making the best of physical proximity. Rennie maintains some boundaries; she condemns Lora for trading sex with the guards for news, cigarettes and chewing gum and is mortified by Lora's angry reaction. But from initially fastidiously passing her rejected underdone chicken to Lora, Rennie comes to

depend on the lunchtime tin plate. And after witnessing the brutal treatment of prisoners outside, she solicitously picks up the chicken Lora has
spilled and wipes the dirt from it, urging Lora to eat in a spirit of shared
survival.

The freedom of action of the two women is severely limited, their
choices reduced to almost nil. Their presence, to recall the Berger epigraph, is defined as passive, their subjectivity effectively denied.
However, after Lora is beaten up and flung more dead than alive onto
the floor of the cell, Rennie acts. The motif of curative touch, predominant in Elizabeth's stroking of Auntie Maude's hands in *Life Before Man*,
is used again as Rennie recalls her grandmother's dementia and her own
childish inability to respond to the old woman's distress by taking her
hands and pulling them to her attention. Now Rennie pushes through
her invisible physical boundaries, overcoming her revulsion at blood,
pulp and faeces and taking Lora's body in her arms, holding her, pulling
against death and willing her to live. Her action is a consummation, with
a flavour of oxymoron: 'this is a gift, this is the hardest thing she's ever
done' (299).

The ending is ambiguous. Whether Rennie is actually freed and goes
home hardly matters; the important thing is that she becomes a 'subversive'. She has looked, she has witnessed, she is a reporter. Her inter-
connection with the human race is achieved in minimal space, with
almost no scope for action, in desperate circumstances but in essential
connection with food and through the body. No matter how narrow the
limitations of choice nor how extreme the circumstances, we may conclude, political responsibility is intimately acquired through our most
basic eating, sharing selves.

It is only at the eleventh hour that Rennie's possibilities for choice
become so restricted, however. There are numerous earlier points at
which she is shown to avoid engagement. The overtly political context
accentuates both her attempt to maintain her self-image as unique
victim and the absolute necessity of taking responsibility for actions and
perceptions, to bear witness. Extreme circumstances, in particular those
involving severe restriction and incarceration, are manifestly of interest
to Atwood, returning as she does to such situations in both *The
Handmaid's Tale* and *Alias Grace* – indeed, imprisonment may be taken as
a metaphor for women's condition, especially when 'woman' is constructed as a threatening Other who must be contained. Restriction and
incarceration pose tricky questions about appetite, choice and responsibility. Do people behave better or worse in captivity? What happens to

appetite? How do external restrictions impact upon the body? Is the capacity and desire for connection with others diminished or enhanced? Does the denial of liberty alter the relationship between reality and fantasy? *Bodily Harm* offers some answers, but Atwood has more to say.

In her dystopian novel *The Handmaid's Tale*, Atwood creates a longer-term framework of restriction by effectively incarcerating her protagonist not only physically but within a highly determined and codified life style. Gilead society, a nightmarish actualisation of right-wing puritanism and biological essentialism, is segmented into discrete classes or groups, women being further restricted according to their prescribed function. Handmaids are valued only in their ancillary, utilitarian capacity as procreative hosts. The restrictions on Handmaids – special clothing to announce function and conceal their bodies, prescribed behaviours and a high degree of isolation – apply also to food. Unlike the food in *Bodily Harm*, the Handmaids' food is good. Offred is given boiled eggs, chicken, vegetables, salad and canned fruit, sandwiches and fruit juice, bland food but healthy, as she admits. It is, in keeping with the puritan ethos, a restricted diet, though restrictions have as much to do with the power of the restricters as absolute health considerations for potential mothers. At Janine's birth party, for example, the Handmaids are given milk, sandwiches and grape juice, while the Commanders' wives have a buffet with ham, cheese, oranges, fresh breads, cakes, coffee and bottles of wine. Handmaids are not allowed either coffee or alcohol, but at the birth party a blind eye is shrewdly turned when someone pinches a bottle to enliven the grape juice: 'We too need our orgies.'[12] A sanctioned orgy (one bottle of wine between twenty-five or thirty women!) is almost by definition drained of revolutionary potential.

The restriction of food in Gilead contrasts most vividly with the freedom of choice 'before', and Offred wistfully remembers the profligacy of ordering food and drink in the hotel with Luke before they were married: 'I could lift the telephone and food would appear on a tray, food I had chosen. Food that was bad for me, no doubt, and drink too' (61). The freedom taken for granted in the old world is exemplified in this ability to choose what is bad or unhealthy as well as what is good. 'Going for a beer' with Moira in the old days equally becomes synonymous with the freedom to dissent. The sheer variety of the fish Offred remembers (sole, haddock, swordfish, scallops, tuna, lobsters, salmon) stands for the diversity of ideas, beliefs and discussion, now suppressed. Erstwhile freedoms include the frivolity of aesthetic choice; Offred's little girl chose her ice creams by colour. Offred perceives such visceral memories of 'before' as treacherous, as are the maternal and sensuous associations aroused by the smell of bread and memories of the fleshlike texture of dough, for these are recollections that tempt her to despair. But their potency may also be seen as that of appetite, of fundamental connection, something that propels resistance.

As though in anticipation of such resistance, the Handmaids' appetite is subject to official control. Not only must they eat exclusively the blandly nourishing food, they must eat all of it, even when it is unpleasant (such as the 'inevitable' breakfast egg tasting of sulphur). No allowance is made for the vagaries of appetite or for stress, and even on the evening of the Ceremony when she feels nauseous with dread, Offred (unlike the Commander's Wife) must leave nothing on her plate or Cora will report her. As she says in her parodied Lord's Prayer, she has enough bread, the problem is to get it down. Such infantilising force-feeding is an admonitory reminder of disempowered status, echoed in the restriction of Handmaids' cutlery to spoon and fork.

Restrictions surrounding food inevitably invest the foods themselves and associated transactions with importance. The one small freedom the Handmaids are allowed is symbolic shopping walks with food tokens, and although this is a parody of the erstwhile housewife's powerful role, the minimal contact between Handmaids is enabling in several ways. Offred is able to bring home news of what is freshly available in the shops and gossip about what other Handmaids buy. More importantly, a conduit is established, albeit shakily, for the underground. For the 'Marthas' in the kitchen, too, food provides a means of expression; Offred's chicken can be over- or undercooked to express disapproval and small acts of generosity – the giving of an ice cube to suck on a hot day, the disguising of wasted food and broken glass on a dropped tray – become humane gifts.

Food is a weapon and a means of communication in this world. But more than this, forbidden foods themselves become a measure of delight, of transgression. When Offred is induced to play Scrabble with the Commander, the forbidden pleasures of language are described as voluptuous, 'candy', 'peppermint', 'lime', 'The letter C. Crisp, slightly acid on the tongue, delicious' (149). Lorna Sage calls this an 'erotic charge' and it is, a highly oral one.[13] But it is more, too, the very unattainableness of these mouthwatering tastes invoking the luxury of liberty and sharply delimiting a world of sensory deprivation. The associations conjured by the rich vocabulary are spelled out more fully further on: '*café au lait* at an outdoor table, with a brioche, absinthe in a tall glass, or shrimp in a cornucopia of newspaper' (164); what Gilead lacks is the richness, variety and corruption of the old world.

The glimpse of other life afforded by the Commander's transgressions and Offred's brief sharing in these form part of a pattern of small openings in Offred's sequestered life that are all that make it bearable. The trip to the brothel (including the illicit gin and tonic the Commander gives her) is part of this, and it reunites her with her friend Moira, though it also shows that Moira's bid for liberty ended in a very relative kind of freedom. Offred's hoarding of butter to use as moisturiser is another small but nourishing infraction. The evidence Offred sees of black market activity, notably the Commander's wife's (and Nick's) cigarettes and the Commander's magazines, offer a hope rooted in the knowledge of human greed. Even her own urge to steal something from the sitting room, with its suggestion of appetite, offers a crumb of power.

The importance of these slivers of transgression, these holes in the tight fabric of the Handmaids' life, is that they offer possibility. The degree to which life is otherwise controlled – and the appalling sanctions in force – makes possibility problematic: when a doctor offers to impregnate Offred she is terrified by the implications of choice. Her body, reduced to a single function as it is in her role as Handmaid, becomes something she does not wish to be reminded of, yet it also empowers her. She is driven to survival by its hungry craving after she witnesses the public killings, appetite strongly reasserting itself in the face of death. Her awakened need for sexual exchange, love even, drives her again and again to Nick, whose connectedness – glimpsed in his whistling, surreptitious touching of Offred's foot with his boot, drinking, smoking, black market activities and involvement with the Mayday underground – in the end offers her rescue. Like Marian in *The Edible Woman* she is led by her body; its sensuous and maternal memories and appetite resist regulation and maintain her subjectivity.

It is this sensory subjectivity, rather than specific actions, that makes her subversive. Gilead's oppressive but contradictory essentialism cannot tolerate women who do not conform to defined 'women's roles', even when their resistance is tacit. And women themselves are instrumental in this oppression; Atwood has much of the persecution and all of the training effected by women (the Aunts) so there is no possibility of drawing simplistic conclusions along gender lines. As suggested earlier, Atwood's political analysis allows no easy answers; Offred ruefully reflects that her mother's desire for a woman's culture has, in a perverse way, been realised.

Atwood pursues the question of women's responsibility as persecutors (and victims) in *Cat's Eye*. Here the restrictions under which the protagonist labours are those of little girls' cruel friendship, for Cordelia, and to a lesser extent Grace and Carol, persecute Elaine almost to the extinction of her sense of self. The portion of the novel – and of her childhood – during which Elaine so suffers is comparatively small, but the strength of her misery and powerlessness, her consequent self-consumption and the reversal following from breaking the spell resonate throughout the novel.

The misery and contortedness of Elaine's period of subjugation is thrown into relief by the idyllic background of nomadic family life in the north. Lunch on a groundsheet – bread and sardines or cheese or jam – exemplifies its simplicity. Cans of Habitant pea soup heated in a dented pot and nights under canvas or in rundown motels, games of war and sharing the chores with her brother all convey an unquestioning and unselfconscious innocence. Even after they move to town, something of this is maintained by visits to the university laboratories where the children surreptitiously examine their body products under the microscope, and by the family's summer visits to the north, where outdoor meals of fried Spam and potatoes and lumpy milk mixed from powder offer respite and comfort. It is worth noting that Elaine's relish for the lumpy milk, her pleasure in scrutinising scabs, earwax, snot and blood and her happy collusion in burping and farting competitions with her brother give no indication of the conflicts of abjection. Her demolition by Cordelia, Grace and Carol is a persecution coming from the outside.

Elaine is induced to feel that she is nothing. This begins when she is tricked into being buried in a hole of Cordelia's digging; she experiences utter powerlessness and a passive despair. Her appetite for life is abruptly stunted and her childish pleasures disfigured; she subsequently has no memory of her ninth birthday party, only an enduring vague horror of pastel icing. The immensity of Cordelia's power over Elaine is partly explained by this early passage as Cordelia transfers her own feelings of negation and helplessness onto her friend; the friendship disarms Elaine, for the feelings of friendship are confusing, mutable, and irresistible. The girls' malignity is dressed up as amelioration; they purport to help Elaine become 'normal', to 'improve', to pass some unspoken and ongoing test. There is no implausibility in Elaine's victimisation; it is simply, the adult Elaine insists, what little girls do to each other.

A sense of powerlessness may manifest itself in overeating (Joan) or not eating (Marian). Here, the persecution of Elaine kills her normal appetite. Though she concentrates on the pleasurable minutiae of breakfast in a vain attempt to delay the onset of the school day, her body rebels against the simmering porridge: 'my stomach will contract, my hands will get cold, it will be difficult to swallow. Something tight sits under my breastbone.'[14] She knows however that she will somehow eat it because she is expected to; it is this well-behaved compliance that allows her persecution, ensures her silence and restricts her protest to the involuntary. Her dread provokes nausea, the inability to eat, physical dissociation, sickness, bouts of escapist fainting, self-hurt and self-consumption. She unsuccessfully attempts avoidance by covertly clinging to her mother, and propitiation ('atonement') through giving licorice and sherbet and jelly beans to her friends, which buys her a transient moment of love. The sheer relief of legitimate illness, when she vomits in the snow and is confined to bed, gives rise to further bouts of sickness, time out in a place of safety, a 'pleasant' interlude of rest and coolness: absence from school and friends.

Elaine's behaviour shows a strong streak of self-punishment and mutilation, her appetite turned inward against her own body. She relates how, during the 'endless' time of Cordelia's power, she peeled skin from her feet as a deliberate infliction of pain, to give her a focus, something immediate and physical to concentrate on. Her thought of putting her finger into the burning toaster is a similar counter to psychological distress and dissociation. She chews and tears at her fingers, especially in situations of embarrassment or divided loyalties, such as the Sunday lunches at the Smeaths. The parallel with Mr Banerji is instructive: at Christmas dinner in Elaine's house, he too bites his fingers and picks at his food, an alien in an incomprehensible landscape, uncomfortable in case his behaviour is inappropriate and fearful of what he might be required to eat.

Elaine feels alien, has a distorted sense of herself in the other girls' world. If by eating we absorb the world, then it is fitting that this bullied child should find it difficult to swallow. Her attempts at withdrawal, her sickness, her self-laceration and even her eating of herself (both literally in the familiar taste of blood from chewed fingers and metaphorically in her solipsistic distress) are attempts to minimise the interface with that world as well as to reduce her self. Eating normally involves incorporation of what is other, so eating oneself becomes an attempt to reduce intake of the other, paradoxically signalling resistance and the protection of boundaries at the same time as engaging in self-mutilation and self-destruction. Elaine's feeling that she is nothing is a denial every bit as powerful as that of Carter's cannibalistic negators or Jenefer Shute's Josie; she is both subject and object, her self-consumption an unwilling surrender to Thanatos.

Atwood has focused specifically on pre-pubescent girls in this examination of persecution. There are several things to be said about this. Children are proverbially more easily and routinely cruel than their elders, and they certainly dissemble less. The exertion of power is more nakedly seen, more raw. The same is true of the effects of such power, especially their relation to primary oral relationships to the world. If teenage eating disorders are the expression of identity problems in relation to culturally derived conceptions of self, then Atwood is pulling the individual back into a more fundamental arena in which culture is filtered through the powerful dynamics of the (far from benign) peer group and the individual's sense of boundaries is far from clear. Atwood locates deprivation, intimidation, *starvation* in the midst of ordinary life and at its most impressionable stages. Children are cruel, women are cruel, people are cruel, and this, she stresses, can be perfectly routine.

The intensity of focus, the self-consumption, the remembered pain of childhood and its long-reaching effects on Elaine's adult life ensure that this relatively short passage dominates the novel as a whole. Because it is located before the brink of adolescence, it is also – immediately, at least – easily relinquished, and Elaine is simply able to walk away from Cordelia and the girls once she sees that she can. Like the oppressors in *Bodily Harm* the girls have power because there is nobody to stop them; they torment Elaine 'because they can'. Nobody can help Elaine, in fact, except herself, for it is she who lends Cordelia power. There is a clear implication of women's collusion in their own oppression as well as of the need for refusal and protest, something that Elaine achieves and Cordelia signally does not.

Elaine only realises that Cordelia is herself a victim later in their adolescence. Two dinners are revelatory: one in each household. At Elaine's house, her father dishes out beef stew, his monomaniac conversation barely faltering, such is his didactic passion for the environment. He is seen as quirky – by Cordelia, and consequently by Elaine – but is involved and nurturing, as his actions and educative conversation demonstrate. At Cordelia's house there are different kinds of dinner: slapdash, careless eating when only women are there, but formal, ritualised eating with candles and flowers when Cordelia's father is present. This father is imposing, frightening and charming, requiring conversation from his daughters and guests. It is here that Cordelia reveals herself desperate and frightened, 'somehow the wrong person' (249) who can never please him enough. Elaine's anger that Cordelia is so 'abject' indicates the inversion of their childhood relationship.

Cordelia is progressively represented as troubled and dependent. She moves through schools and tutors, comfort eating, drinking, smoking, experiencing anorexia, breakdowns and attempted suicide. The real Cordelia is a mess, last seen when Elaine, in her twenties, visits her at the clinic and takes her out for coffee and Danish and is surprised by her own fury at Cordelia's plea for rescue. But the mythical Cordelia does not yield power. Elaine continues to feel and to fear her power, recognising that it may have transferred to herself. At the very end of the book, when, hungover, she revisits the scene of her childhood torments, she achieves a visceral understanding in keeping with her original reactions: 'There is the same shame, the sick feeling in my body, the same knowledge of my own wrongness, awkwardness, weakness; the same wish to be loved; the same loneliness; the same fear' (419). The difference is that she finally recognises these feelings as Cordelia's own desperate, unassuaged appetite.

The interactions between these girls are personal and psychologised, but they also represent a wider social reality. The girls' behaviour, specific but typical, is influenced by the expectations of western society. It is significant that neither Elaine nor her brother experiences any such intense manipulation in relationships with boys; boys deal with things differently, Elaine insists. Boys, of course, are subject to quite different cultural pressures. Grace sticking pictures of household commodities from the Eatons catalogues into scrapbooks and precocious Carol, whose mother has 'cold wave' and wears twin sets, are emblematic of idealised female roles (domestic and sexual) in the 1950s, roles bound up with commodification and the perception of women as consumed and consumers. Cordelia leads Grace and Carol in a parodical induction, designed to turn Elaine into the docile, feminine, anxious-to-please creature patriarchy arguably requires. It is worth noting, incidentally, that the tenor of such feminist argument – or at least its extension into a polarisation of the sexes – is later rejected by Elaine herself, when she recoils at her women's group's segregation of pain and blame (female pain is sanctified; men must take the blame). Indeed, Atwood makes much the same objection elsewhere in her own voice (with a typically culinary metaphor) when she writes of the oversimplifications of the early years of the Women's Movement in North America, with a 'tendency to cookie-cut . . . to write to a pattern and to oversugar on one side'.[15]

Elaine's story concerns women's pain and the restrictive roles foisted on them by patriarchy, but it also affirms their culpability as persecutors and even as victims.

We have seen how Atwood uses appetite to figure escapism, power/lessness, commitment, connection and transgression, and lack of appetite to signal dysfunction and protest. But what happens when appetite is let loose, unchecked? The acme of unrestrained appetite, of women's bad behaviour, has to be that of the *Robber Bride*. In Zenia, Atwood posits a voracious sexual adventuress who likes challenges: 'breaking and entering . . . taking things that aren't hers', Tony, one of her plundered victims, ruefully recognises.[16] Zenia's motives are variously ascribed, but Tony firmly says that, like Attila the Hun, she just has 'appetites'. She is an embodiment of rampant appetite, not friendly, not nice. Like Atwood's abusers, in other words, she does it because she can. This is a distinctly Gothic tale of the invasion of the good safe place each of the three protagonists seeks to create, by the horror of a predatory Other Woman. The foods associated with each of them say it all: Tony painstakingly cooks outdated tuna casseroles, Charis eats only virtuous health foods, while Roz stokes up on snacky comforts (thick toasted-cheese sandwiches, toast with honey and jam, pickles and popcorn, creamy coffee, alcohol). Zenia, by contrast, is associated with blood. The blood is part of a cluster of vampiric and carnivorous imagery attaching to Zenia, a Gothic note introduced from the beginning when Tony reflects that, for Zenia's funeral, a bowl of blood would be more appropriate than flowers. Tony's perception of Zenia at the Toxique restaurant is of something between model and vampire, with bleached out skin, huge deep eyes and a full 'red-purple mouth', an imperceptible wind accompanying her everywhere; later she imagines Zenia having lured West to bed again to suck out his blood. Roz, too, perceives her in this light: 'Zenia . . . is looking terrific. Doesn't she ever age? thinks Roz bitterly. What kind of blood does she drink?' (438). And Charis believes Zenia has powers connected with eating live animals, an image that spans the vampiric and the bestial. These carnivorous, cannibalistic images hint at animal gratification; both Tony and Charis see Zenia as a bird seizing a worm, and the weasel in the henhouse suggests a perversion of appetites: mayhem for pleasure.

Zenia not only indulges her own appetites – for fine food, for beer, martini, rum and steak, for destruction, for men, for adulation, in short for power – but appeals also directly to the appetites of others, whether for sex (Mitch's appetite, for example, is a pale shadow of her own), or for approval, comradeship, glamour, to rescue or nurture. Tony believes Zenia's appeal is in her rawness, contrasted with her own 'parboiled' and tamed quality, and she likens Zenia to gin at midnight. More potent is the notion that Zenia represents whatever her victim is hungry for. In this sense she is irresistible.

One effect of Zenia's path of destruction is that Tony and Roz and Charis all rescue and cherish and look after each other. Roz feeds Tony soup, pudding and baby foods; in turn Tony looks after Roz with tuna casseroles and chocolate, while Charis brings physical succour and health foods. Roz and Tony together help Charis to sort out her life and they become godmothers to her child. Ultimately, the three women meet regularly to eat together and monitor their Zenia-battered lives. It is as though she has kindled their appetite for her, and for each other. Roz reflects to herself, 'Food should be shared. Solitary eating can be like solitary drinking – a way of dulling the edge, of filling in the blanks' (390); unlike Roz's comfort eating, the three women together do share, but around the blank of Zenia.

One possible reading of this mutual deliverance and support is of a timely female solidarity. Certainly the friendship and sympathetic action between these three women stands out in Atwood's fiction where, by and large, women are not mutually supportive and indeed can frequently be competitively fractious, if not downright abusive. But it is also true that Atwood is at pains to avoid prescribing modes of behaviour, particularly when these might be claimed by ideology, and there is no question of ideological proselytising.[17] The point about this particular trio is that, although they have contributed to their own victimisation, their consequent fellow feeling gives them the strength to learn and to resist, if only because they realise that no one else is going to rescue them (least of all the men implicated in their various sufferings).

An alternative reading suggests something more complicated, linking with the Gothic, vampiric and psychological aspect of the story. The vampire itself is a highly ambiguous figure of both fear and desire (Dracula, for example, has been read as figuring both hysteria and suppressed homosexual craving[18]). Zenia can in a similar way be read as a projection of the desires of the three women, an interpretation underlined by the fact that her hotel room changes with each of their final visits. Both Lorna Sage and Coral Ann Howells draw attention to the process of *splitting* in much of Atwood's work; here each of the three characters has a join or split of some sort in her life.[19] Tony's backward language is her 'seam . . . where she's sewn together . . . where she could split apart' (19); Charis splits from Karen who 'returns' at times of extreme stress and Roz's life is 'cut in two' when her absent father comes into her life. These splits are described by Howells as 'the space of repression occupied by their "dark twins"', an 'edge of desire and lack' which is where Zenia operates.[20] The expression 'dark twin' suggests complementarity and it is certainly the case that an element in each woman identifies, half reluctantly, with Zenia. The ambivalence is encapsulated in the child Tony's horror-stricken reaction to her mother's disappearing downhill on the toboggan:

> "No! No!" she screamed. (Unusual for her to have screamed: she must have been terrified.) But inside herself she could hear another voice, also hers, which was shouting, fearlessly and with ferocious delight:
>   *On! On!* (137)

Zenia doesn't just pillage and torment and use the women as fodder; she *is* their own darkest appetites, what they fear and most secretly relish. Tony reveals a trace of this when she admits to feeling an affinity with ancient kings drinking wine from the skulls of their enemies. Seen in this light, the women's friendship may seem more problematic than simple supportive sisterhood.

Alongside the generally destructive manifestations of appetite, the novel contains a good deal of nurturing. But just as Zenia is an equivocal figure so nurturing in this novel also raises questions. How 'good', for example, is the nurturing? To what extent does it disempower the recipient? Is it important to be on the receiving end as well as dispensing care? Roz, for example, finds difficulty in being looked after by her friends, because her own caring role (doing the 'hen things') is usurped. If nurturing can put the recipient at risk, it can also expose the nurturer. Zenia is able to manipulate Charis precisely by appealing to her caring nature and her myopically held belief in health food, meditation and generally New Age cures. All Zenia has to do is feign illness and Charis feels privileged to feed and heal her.

Rescuing is a strong element of nurturing for the women in this novel, and one way or another all except Zenia feed and rescue men. Charis rescues Billy. Tony rescues West twice from Zenia, though at the cost of infantilising him, his childishness demonstrated in guileless reactions to breakfast eggs and Tony's protective response. Roz rescues Mitch financially, though aware of the dangers of disempowering him by too readily filling his needs, and speculates that the appeal of Zenia could be the opposite, that she presented herself as a vacancy or 'starvation'. The

women's friendship and support is more mutually adult than their relations with men; the women's initial rescue in each case develops into an
attempt to help the victim restart her life and regain autonomy: spoon-
feeding gives way to meeting and eating.

The notion of rescue is intimately tied up with the question of taking
responsibility. For the most part rescue is not forthcoming in Atwood's
writing, unless it involves some taking of risk and sense of personal and
social obligation. Staying safe and waiting for someone to come along
and solve your problems is not an option. What Atwood's writing cumu-
latively suggests is that no degree of external confinement or coercion
extenuates failure to take responsibility. Hence Atwood's progressive
reduction of her protagonists' scope for action and detailed evocation of
their reduced circumstances. In these situations it is the body and its
appetites or women's special relationships with food that provide the
medium for taking responsibility. We have already seen, in *Bodily Harm*
and *The Handmaid's Tale*, two different forms of incarceration where
freedom of movement is curtailed, where eating is controlled and even
bodily functions are regulated. In *Alias Grace* imprisonment, regulation,
restriction and impoverished diet are virtually permanent, for the eponymous protagonist is serving a life sentence for murder. Imprisonment
formally deprives Grace of liberty and future and the penitentiary practices further restrict her behaviour. The only scope for freedom of action
lies in her wits, through finding favour within the system or, through
external agency, by rescue.

Dr Simon Jordan offers a possibility of rescue. But he also represents
risk, or even temptation, since to cooperate fully with him Grace would
have to relinquish the only area of control she maintains: over the contents of her mind. With heavy – and multiple – significance, at their first
meeting Dr Jordan offers her an apple, which she indeed takes to be a
kind of trade, though fending off any questions that evoke symbolic or
religious associations. Her reluctance to engage on his terms – though
she becomes willing and even eager to talk – initiates a struggle that Dr
Jordan comes to perceive as a battle of wills. Looked at slightly differently, it is a conflict between the discourses of authority and those of
domesticity (a conflict that might similarly be cast in terms of class, race
or gender).

Grace's life is dominated by the discourses of authority. Her life is
shown as externally regulated, especially where food is concerned (about
which there is considerable detail in the novel), from her poor childhood through emigration and her life in service and into her life in the

penitentiary. Imprisonment intensifies the brutality of the regulating discourse: starvation is 'calming to the nerves'; 'overfeeding' stimulates the
'criminal organs of the brain'; whippings are best before breakfast to
avoid mess and waste and give the guards an appetite.[21] Simon Jordan,
by contrast, brings Grace into direct relationship with the more subtle
discourses of authority, through his questions and, more particularly, in
the answers he attempts to elicit from her.

The discourses underpinning Dr Jordan's enquiries include those of
the medical establishment, lunatic asylums and the Church, together
with those of less respectable practices which he does not rule out, such
as Mesmerism. He is committed to a belief that he can unlock the secrets
of the mind through associative patterns and so discover from Grace the
truth about the murder. His principal intended stimulus is root vegetables, which he believes will trigger a downwards connection (cellar/
underground/graves/corpses) leading her to reveal, or to remember
and reveal, the events of the murder. What ensues is a comic series of
attempts whereby he puts a carrot or turnip or potato on the table and
asks Grace what it makes her think about. This invariably turns out, to
his disappointment, to concern cooking and eating.

Even when Dr Jordan tries steer her responses through leading questions, her replies are resolutely practical, those of commonsense. A question about potatoes growing underground produces only private scoffing
(where else would they grow?), and further suggestive probing about
what else is underground is met with the disappointing answer beets and
carrots, because that is where they grow. Similarly, an ill-informed
attempt to lead her by observing that parsnips are kept in cellars provokes the negative response that they are better kept outside as they are
improved by frost.

There is a clear clash of discourses here; Grace's responses are contained entirely within the world of domestic service and do not begin to
engage on Dr Jordan's terms. He is obscurely aware of this but cannot
successfully adapt his own discourse to hers. When he attempts to give
her the initiative, asking what vegetable she thinks he should bring next,
she suggests a radish. His immediate associative speculation about its
redness is punctured by her revelation that this is what she would most
like to eat. The experiment dwindles to a small and wittily 'dispirited'
turnip that they both ignore, but by this point Dr Jordan has discovered
that the more Grace remembers, the more difficulty he has in keeping
track of the details. Instead of her narrative being contained within his
explanatory discourse, her discourse has subsumed his own.

By holding fast to the safe details of cooking and cleaning and sewing, Grace resists wholesale surrender to the temptation of believing in rescue by Simon Jordan. In a curious echo of Grace's own story, it is Simon himself who falls. He becomes obsessed not only by Grace's story but by Grace herself and the fact of her mystery. Added to this, just as Grace fails to satisfy his hunger for knowledge, so his landlady and her cook fail to satisfy his hunger for a decently cooked breakfast, blighting his morning with under- or overcooked eggs and consequent stress. Considerable space is devoted to Simon's eating habits: his breakfasts are a daily disappointment; his mother expresses concern in her letters that he should eat well; he writes to his friend about the awful meals he has at a local inn; he is acutely aware of the quality of sherry he is given. When, like the men in *The Robber Bride*, he responds to a show of weakness – in the landlady Rachel Humphrey – he finds himself cooking for and eating with her. He subsequently yields to a confused temptation and becomes sexually embroiled with Mrs Humphrey, projecting his Grace-awakened lusts onto her.

Food for Simon is clearly demarcated: there is what as a doctor he knows people must eat; there is his own comfort and pleasure; there is that which has symbolic or metonymic value which he uses in his work. Through his relationship with Rachel Humphrey he is also exposed, a little, to the world of working people, as he falters his way about the market to buy food and learns to prepare it. For Grace, by contrast, food has been a major and time-consuming part of life, in her childhood because of its scarcity and the need for contrivance and later because its procurement and preparation is a fundamental part of her work. The restricted diet of imprisonment has strong effects: her memories of good food or plentiful food are sharp and nostalgic.

It is against this background of conflicting discourses and experiences that the other major food symbol in the novel operates. The apple that Dr Jordan offers Grace at their first meeting, with his question 'is there any kind of apple you should not eat?' (45), is heavy with symbolism. Her refusal to give the 'right answer' is prompted by suspicion of the doctor and the small power she gains in withholding. But the apple's biblical symbolism and Dr Jordan's 'riddle' are only part of the story. For the incarcerated Grace its associations are also those of freedom and the outdoors, its succulent taste and the culinary possibilities to which she has no access in prison. On top of these, she has a very specific memory of Hallowe'en and the superstitious throwing of apple peel with Mary Whitney, to see who they would marry. Thus, as well as temptation (and the Fall) the apple is associated with doom. The discourse of the Judaeo-Christian tradition is overlaid by those of superstition, folklore and personal narrative.

Grace returns to Dr Jordan's apple at the very end of the novel. But apples reappear earlier in her narrative, when she describes the culmination of her birthday walk in the orchard at Richmond Hill. In this tranquil place she comforts herself in her loneliness by looking at the plants and flowers and the apple tree with its miniature green apples. It is an Edenic scene as Jamie Walsh joins her and befriends her, asks to be her sweetheart and they make daisy chains. Knowledge and temptation are present but only embryonically, in the ungrown apples. The innocence of the afternoon is tainted only by subsequent probing and sneering interest by the household in what she has been up to. Grace represents herself as innocent: she has taken no apple and is ignorant of Kinnear's and Nancy's goings-on.

In the end, Grace thinks she has understood the significance of Dr Jordan's 'riddle'. She recasts the Bible's Tree of Knowledge and Tree of Life as a single tree, suggesting that death will be the result whether or not you eat the fruit, and drawing the conclusion that it is preferable to die less ignorant. Her own quilt of the Tree of Paradise will aberrantly include snakes. This is a very different interpretation of the Fall story from that of established religious discourse. It concurs with the apparently extraordinary conclusion Grace draws that it is victims who are responsible and who therefore need to be forgiven. There is a logic in what she says:

they are the ones who cause all the trouble. If they were only less weak and careless, and more foresightful, and if they would keep from blundering into difficulties, think of all the sorrow in the world that would be spared. (531)

Victims are culpable. No one is going to rescue women (or men) but themselves. This is very like Atwood's own recipe of responsibility, though its validity is tested by being placed in the mouth of a possible murderer. Grace herself is a victim of her past and her time and her social status, yet she strives to claim her piece of space, to exercise her own appetite and cook (or cook-up) both nourishment and narrative. If she never admits guilt for any part in the murders, she nevertheless takes some responsibility for her life, and her life story.

CHAPTER 5

Food and manners: Roberts and Ellis

Food is an essentially social signifier, a bearer of interpersonal and cultural meanings. It is, and has been, constructed as symbolic in all sorts of ways, either intentionally (Passover, the Eucharist), through custom (harvest suppers and hot cross buns) or by commerce (the 'ploughman's lunch'); the resonances are, initially at least, culture-specific. (These resonances may change, of course: hot cross buns began their life in ancient Egypt as bread marked with horns for fertility.)[1] Both the acceptability of particular foods and what they signify are part of cultural identity. Not only might raw fish, witchetty grubs or blancmange be repellant to people from cultures that do not eat such things, the cachet or dreariness of a particular dish or titbit is likely to be overlooked by outsiders. What, for example, might a passing Martian make of a cake topped with burning candles?

The socially constructed significance of food is many-layered, and increasingly multicultural. Peter Farb and George Armelagos claim that since eating is something we normally do every day, it is a major means of self-definition, as well as an important channel for the transmission of culture, eating habits being the most conservative of behaviour patterns. Eating is influenced, they claim, by the whole cultural system: by the means through which a society adapts to and exploits its environment; by social structures created for order and to train the next generation; and by ideology, the world-view of the particular society.[2]

The effects of ideology in relation to food are more easily seen at a micro than a macro level, although particular food conventions are sometimes used ideologically, as in the British 'digging for victory' campaign in World War II, for example, or the prohibition of alcohol in Islamic Arab countries. More generally, ideology permeates food and eating practices almost invisibly, through family and social structures which perpetuate particular patterns. Gender is clearly a factor; not only have women traditionally done the domestic cooking in western culture (while male chefs annexed the more celebrated aspects of culinary exhibition), food is also subtly categorised. Men barbecue steaks and carve joints, hearty slabs of meat being deemed masculine; caring mothers produce comforting soups and stews and sweet puddings. So, more or less, run the stereotypes.

In British culture some foods are inextricably bound up with class: the exclusivity of grouse, lobster or venison, the middle-class nicety of cucumber sandwiches and the sustaining comfort of Lancashire hotpot bear only partially on the cost of the ingredients. A 'mixed grill' and a 'fry-up' may both centre on bacon, sausages and chops, but inescapably connote middle-class order and working-class informality (complete with recycled leftovers) respectively. The contrived, transnational egalitarian connotations of MacDonald's burgers with relish and French fries entirely lack the specificity of the English, historically generated associations of fish and chips and pickled onions.

In Foucauldian terms, food is given meaning within specific discourses and discursive practices, including recipes, reports on diet and health, advertisements, government rhetoric, newspaper articles, 'foodie' literature, religious rules and cultural rituals (not forgetting those of class). Less obviously ideological but of no less influence are parental guidance, peer group advice and self-made regulations. Food itself is not bound within any single discourse, but becomes impregnated with meanings from the many and various frameworks within which it figures – and this is a major reason why it is so rich a resource for writers.

The intricacy of meanings and influences both enriches and complicates eating, making it difficult to always understand the conventions of any particular eating situation. All participants at a gathering need to subscribe to the same discourse and 'read' the situation in the same way, so that the implicit rules, codes and interpretations are equally understood. In the same way, readers must learn to decode the significance of the foods and eating occasions in fiction. There is a potential problem here: how can a writer assume a shared cultural understanding with his or her readership? Toni Morrison, in whose writing cultural differences are of the essence, confronts this problem head-on, referring to 'strawberry shrug' and 'raised bread', 'goobers', 'cobbler' and 'meal-fried porgies' without explanation.[3] She makes no apology for writing specifically and overtly for an African-American readership, for whom these (and many other things) do not need to be explained. They may be only partially decoded by other readers, but this, she suggests, is part of the deal; if others choose to read her work then understanding it is their problem: 'I would not footnote the black experience for white readers. I wouldn't try to explain what a reader like me already knew.'[4] Though less obviously, this is the dilemma of all writing and reading, for strangeness is most vividly felt in relation to food. Part of what Morrison is doing, it seems, is to evoke (eating) experiences in which her characters and a proportion of her readers feel very much at home; those who do not can experience what it feels like to be an outsider.

What it means to feel at home in a culinary tradition – where the practices are understood and some of the meanings attaching to foods are familiar – is important to many women writers. Angela Carter often deliberately locates her fictional characters in relation to archetypal English food, Melanie with tea and cake in *The Magic Toyshop*, for example, and *Wise Children*'s Chance sisters with 'cockney' food: eel pies with mash, bacon sandwiches, sausages rolls. Margaret Atwood's comfort eaters have recourse to simple foods: the peanut butter and jelly sandwiches of their childhoods, oatmeal porridge, toast and jam, boiled or poached eggs, apple sauce. These, like the comforting stews, corned beef, mashed potatoes, canned peaches and even Tony's tuna casseroles, are the unsophisticated meals of post-war North America.

For Michèle Roberts, writing between French and English traditions, the question of location within a cuisine is a major theme. But I will come back to this, after considering more broadly why food seems to be of such importance and how Roberts handles it in her novels, for she evokes food almost as a constituent of female sensuousness and contingency, suggesting a knowledge and understanding more visceral than cerebral. The multiplicity of foods' associations is central to her fiction. Certain foods recur: bread, soup, wine, eggs, grapes, lamb, dried fruit, water and fish all have particular weight, incorporating not only existing associations (such as Christian resonances of bread and wine) but significances that are discovered, teased out and elaborated by Roberts, and some that she effectively creates through her poetics.

The egg is a good example, inherently laden with potential for symbolic use. As suggested earlier, the egg represents rebirth, new life, the containment of future possibilities. In its very essence embryonic, its unbroken state none the less suggests completion and wholeness. It is as discrete an item of food as you could hope to find, yet, at the same time, one of the most versatile (an Alice Thomas Ellis character, citing mayonnaise in proof of the existence of God, lists meringues, omelettes, cakes, custards, soufflés, poaching, frying and boiling).[5] Out of their shells, raw eggs are slippery, slimy, semi-liquid but lumpy, suggestive of all that is antithetical to the cool shape of the unbroken whole. It is, of course, broken eggs that Michèle Roberts is drawn to focus on in her explorations of femaleness.

In Roberts's *The Wild Girl*, a rewriting of the story of Mary Magdalene, the ten-year-old Mary, intoxicated by the rhythm and strength of her mother's beating eggs on a summer evening, is impelled to join in somehow, and tosses her basket of eggs in the air so that they 'crack and splatter in a splendid gold mess on the yard's stone flags'.[6] The rhythm lives on in the slaps of her punishment, leading her to discover her gift for songs, but the occasion also suggests a transition, a birth, a dramatic rupture, even a mixing together of elements previously separate – all of which could be taken as prefiguring the disruptive events to come, and especially Mary's embracing of mess and contingency.

Such mess is for Roberts quintessentially female, and the later travails of Mary explore, through the 'mess' of myth and dream, the problem of understanding and embracing a womanhood that includes both female spirituality and sexuality. In Roberts's hotpot of women's histories, *The Book of Mrs Noah*, the Re-Vision Sibyl's cooking meditation, while she listens to evensong on the radio, puts a more physical gloss on the problem, emphasising the Church's traditional discomfort with women's bodies. Imagining the choirboys 'in frilly white drag' she senses the chilly misogyny of the male choir:

She breaks egg yolks into a bowl, whips them with sugar and flour, boils them with milk. Beats and beats with her wooden spoon to remove lumps. Lumpy female bodies. Lumpy bellies and breasts. Eggs breaking and splattering, warm mess of sweetness on the sheets, warm flow of sweat and blood. We can't have *that* in our nice Anglican chapel. Only male chefs please.[7]

The 'breaking and splattering' eggs and 'mess' recall the infant Mary, but they also suggest sexual activity and childbirth, rupture and conjunction, breaking up and mingling. In this metaphorical scheme, it is *scrambled* eggs that Hattie and her lover enjoy after close and trusting coitus in *In the Red Kitchen*,[8] having on first meeting eaten *fried* eggs on toast, the unshelled and spread out but whole egg forming a sensuous bridge between the potential of an unbreached egg and the intermingled quality of scrambled egg or omelette. (Hattie's lover falls in love with her in response to her appetite.) The Re-Vision Sibyl's earthy categorisation of the inviolate Church as antithetical to female 'mess' is echoed here, with the image of the enclosed space of the abbey at Fécamp 'empty yet full as an egg' (10) – unbroken, presumably.

It is not simply a question of female contingency (an arguably essentialist characteristic in any case, though one suggested both by post-Freudian stress on the pre-Oedipal and sociological analysis of body types outlined in earlier chapters); in focus are a particular female physicality, sensuousness and sensibility, all profoundly related to food. In *Daughters of the House* the young teenagers Léonie and Thérèse take a secret midnight feast of mouthwatering leftovers up on to the roof:

Fingers greasy with lovely chicken fat, mouth attacking the crisp salty skin, the flesh scented with maize and herbs . . . They made sandwiches of Roquefort and sliced peach. The cold veal, meat jelly and rice, scooped up with their fingers, was one of the best things, they agreed, they'd ever eaten. Léonie licked Thérèse's fingers to see if they tasted the same as her own . . . (79)

They toast themselves in unwatered red wine, which they are determined to like although it makes them choke. Not only is this tactile episode an antidote to the terminal illness of Thérèse's mother, Antoinette, and an exquisite bonding (for the girls have recently quarrelled), but a rite of passage, pointedly completed with the onset of Thérèse's menarche. Food, feelings, femaleness, the body's rhythms are all connected.

Elsewhere in the novel, specific foods become a sort of pathetic fallacy. Thérèse struggles with stuffed tomatoes at supper, not only because she hates her puppy fat but because she is bursting with grief and anger at her mother's terminal illness. Tomato and child here uncannily mirror each other. Later, Léonie abandons stripping the tomato plants so as to accompany Thérèse to the cemetery. Tomatoes thus become metonymically associated with death, a connection repeated in the image of the dead rotting 'quietly, like the dropped fruit you found hidden under the leaves of the tomato plants' (107).

This is not to suggest that there is any absolute relationship between food, or any particular foods, and women (though there is certainly a semiotics of food in which women may figure). It is rather a question of the way Roberts writes about food conveying profound physical, emotional and imaginative, as well as socially constructed connections. Any food may develop potent associations according to the nature of a particular occasion, or become temporarily imbued with certain characteristics related to a cook's mood or emotions. At the beginning of *The Book of Mrs Noah*, the Babble-On Sibyl, still mourning a stillborn baby, perceives the salmon she is preparing as 'dead', on a silver 'bier', anointed with a 'home-made chrism' of mayonnaise (28). There are several things going on here. There is the projection of grief onto the fish (not unlike what happens with the stuffed tomatoes). Then there is the connection of dead food with dead bodies, a vegetarian observation (the ethos of this novel being dominantly vegetarian) which also recalls the waste matters of abjection. Finally, there is reference to women's roles in cooking and laying out the dead, roles which are linked to the female body when, towards the end of the novel, it is Noah's wife who must kill, gut and prepare the 'Gaffer's' fish for cooking, both because this supper involves the taking of life, and because it is a messy, bloody task that the Gaffer sees in terms of 'some hideous pagan menstrual rite' (189). The preparations for cooking thus become something arcane, mysterious and feminine, as well as being associated with death and female sexuality, the smell, mess and menstrual associations of the fish adding to its mythological and Freudian sexual symbolism.

The Gaffer's perception represents the unease of western religion with both femaleness and the messier aspects of incarnation, a species of holy abjection, perhaps. For Roberts is concerned not only with food in relation to women's bodies and lives and sense of self, but with the effects of its various 'external' meanings and their cultural resonances. In *The Wild Girl* she affords lamb very much the religious and teaching significance to be expected in the Judaeo-Christian tradition: following the roast lamb provided by Nicodemus, Jesus recalls the lamb as it had been alive, using this concrete image as the beginning of a lesson about the food of eternal life that will culminate in the first communion with bread and wine. By the end of the book the Passover lamb has become transformed into an anniversary remembrance of the Lord's death, and Jesus is referred to unselfconsciously by his band of followers as the 'Lamb of God'. Roberts embroiders only a little on the grafting of Christian symbolism onto the pre-existing Jewish associations of lamb, so as to underscore Mary's holistic polemic. As suggested earlier, culturally established meanings adhere to food, whether or not they are overtly evoked. For the lapsing adult Léonie in *Daughters of the House*, the Christian connection with lamb is vestigial, but the link is still tenuously there: she goes conventionally to Mass every Sunday with her husband and children and afterwards sips her *apéritif* bathed in the smell of roasting lamb.

In recent years, meat has come to have increasingly less innocent resonances, and Roberts's fiction reflects this too, characterising deadanimal flesh very much in relation to its bodily origin and the revulsion that this may cause. In *The Book of Mrs Noah* Jack's wife refuses to allow more death after the flood and will not agree to sacrifice a lamb (curiously recalling – or, biblically speaking, anticipating – the terms of Jesus's lesson on the lamb in *The Wild Girl*). Her stomach confirms her belief: the meat stew nauseates her 'as though it were boiled up from dead babies' (85), her 'body knowledge' paralleling that of Lessing's Anna Wulf or Atwood's Marian MacAlpin. Thus strengthened and confirmed, and with a dream of the harmony of all living things, she separates from the others and takes to a vegetarian life. Later in the novel, Roberts includes a further dig at the inconsistencies of a body-disciplining, abjection-inducing, animal-slaughtering religiosity as the Correct Sibyl remembers being told to eat up her meat by the nuns: 'think of the starving millions who'd be glad of your leftover scraps of gristle and fat. Mortify your body. Spoon up the food that revolts you . . .' (102).

If the given meanings of meat are contradictory (embracing both redemption and culpability), women's involvement is also shown as ambiguous. Mrs Noah confesses that reading meat recipes used to be her form of pornography, a revelation that calls to mind Jenefer Shute's *Life-Size*, Angela Carter's *The Sadeian Woman* and Atwood's comments on the 'sybaritic voyeurism' of cookbooks.[9] The Re-Vision Sibyl focuses on torture. She begins to avoid butchers' shops, 'those white-tiled laboratories of death' with their smell of blood, cruel hooks, 'sloppy piles of purple liver, dripping red hands fumbling for change in the till' and 'dishes of tripe like white knitting' (130). This last is a poetic image, defamiliarising, even enchanting, but it is also more; along with the hooks, the dripping hands, the reference to meat as 'corpses', peered over by 'terrible women', it evokes the spectacle of public torture and execution, the knitting a product of some *Madame Defarge des animaux*. Meat, in this book, is inseparable from death and corruption, while vegetarianism is grounded in an empathetic connection with human flesh. Women are associated with both.

So far, the emphasis has been very much on the material reality of food. Equally important is the symbolic freight of certain foods, how their figurative meanings impact on women and how Roberts uses and manipulates these meanings. The most symbolically saturated food in western culture is probably bread, heralded as the essential food and widely used in metaphor: 'give us this day our daily bread'; 'don't take the bread out of someone's mouth'; 'you must earn some bread'. Christianity is a major source of the symbolic use of bread, most obviously in the association of bread with Christ's body at the last supper and the ensuing Mass or Eucharist, associations that, though usually unexpressed, give bread a special status in western culture. Bread has

connotations of intimate communion too; as Michèle Roberts and Alice
Thomas Ellis both point out, 'companion' means someone with whom
bread is consumed (Latin: *com* = with; *panis* = bread).

Roberts invokes bread's symbolic and metaphorical associations and
she also adds a few of her own. She offers bread as a basic necessity; the
story of Meg Hansey in *The Book of Mrs Noah* has Meg sending her wages
home to provide bread for her brothers and sisters, and the narrator of
the book recalls surviving on brown bread and carrots as an impoverished student. Roberts also makes a connection with the powerful and
sometimes nostalgia-inducing associations of childhood – indeed egg
sandwiches act as a sort of Proustian *madeleine* in both Roberts's and
Alice Thomas Ellis's writing. In *The Visitation* Roberts sketches idyllic
after-school teas in the garden, with marmite and cream-cheese sandwiches and chocolate cake, but she also details inedible 'thin slices of
white bread soaked and glued into sandwiches with lemon curd' in the
unappetising paper bag of tea thrown from an upstairs window to Helen
in the garden by her mother when they visit her godmother.[10]

Bread is associated with the boredom of long meals by the children
Roberts places in France; in *A Piece of the Night* and again in *Daughters of
the House* the children make grey bread-sculptures while longing to leave
the table. In both novels, however, jam-soaked *tartines* offer the children
comfort as well as sustenance. The childhood associations of certain
forms of bread are so strong that when the narrator of *In The Red Kitchen*
sees some 'modernised' nuns eat and gossip over tea, their bread and
marmite somehow emphasises a childlike quality in their homeliness.
Bread has both a literal, stomach-filling and a metaphorically sustaining
role, instinctively felt by the unnerved adult Léonie in her longing for
fresh bread, butter and apricot jam to 'wall off the uncertain future. To
shore her up.'[11] The obverse of this walling *up* is a walling *in*; teenage
Léonie stuffs her mouth with bread on the day of the Mass for dead
Antoinette to separate herself from Thérèse and Louis, but also to
prevent her feelings bursting out, a taking of bread that ironically echoes
the actions of the Mass she is not allowed to attend.[12]

If many of these bread associations tend to emphasise the personal
and the familial, the combination of bread with wine unfailingly calls up
the religious and Roberts explicitly uses the elements of the Catholic
Mass, both in relation to its participants (Julie in *A Piece of the Night* taking
the 'thin white disc', knowing she 'must never chew it, for it would be the
Christ she gnashes and mutilates'),[13] and, more radically, to its creators.
In *The Wild Girl* the 'new rite' of bread and wine, flesh and blood, that

Jesus invites the mystified disciples to join in at the Last Supper is perceived by Mary Magdalene as a union of the spirit and the word, of
understanding and wisdom, of female and male.[14] Thus, as well as sat-
urating the ritual, and therefore the bread and the wine, with broadly
spiritual meanings, Roberts backdates a politicising of the practice,
investing the combined food and drink with contentious significance
when she has Mary perceive the prohibition on women offering 'the
supper of bread and wine' as running directly counter to Christ's teaching.

Mary's experience of wine suggests the two contradictory associations
of release and communion. Roberts represents wine in Mary's early life
as deeply disturbing to her, 'smeared on women's mouths like blood' at
a Dionysiac feast (55); it is a token of ecstasy and an unstable communi-
cant, as she discovers to her cost through her own wine-fuelled indiscre-
tion. However, her passage through the underworld, a personal
marriage of heaven and hell which contrasts a vision of unity to the separation, hierarchy and murmurs of witchcraft promulgated by the male
disciples, is consummated with the drinking of a special wine. And wine,
with bread, continues to symbolise communion for the women and their
followers in exile, as they combine the elements of their simple lives into
a ritualised, almost pantheistic remembrance.

Elsewhere, Roberts inverts existing associations, this time by suffusing
wine in its unconsumed state with danger. In *Daughters of the House* the
wine and cider the villagers have hidden in the basement are laden with
the associations of German occupation, collaboration, resistance,
secrecy and guilt. The wine becomes substituted for the hidden Jews;
indeed, the imprisonment of the Jews in the upstairs back bedroom of
the house sets them as polar opposites to the concealed bottles: discovered, taken and, as it were, consumed by the Germans. Through the
cooperation of the villagers the wine is saved; because – within the
village and fracturing its community – the priest is an informer, the Jews
and Henri Taillé are slain and, metaphorically and metonymically, wine
becomes associated once more with blood, with dissension and with
religion. Wine's public significance is imbued by Roberts with connotations of peril and betrayal as much as with the religious associations of
communion and fulfilment.

Betrayal is a concept that seems to have a ready affinity with food,
though not necessarily with any one particular food. There are various
possible explanations. To begin with, both cooking and eating experiences always run the risk of disappointment, of the mild betrayal of

hopes and expectations. Eaters are always vulnerable, since eating is an act of trust, and history and literature are full of poisonings that show such trust betrayed. Then, too, there are the betrayals that take place during the course of a meal, a common arena for dissent, especially within families. To go back to the Bible, the Last Supper is so drenched in imminent betrayal it is not surprising that Christ is referred to in terms of the slaughtered Passover lamb. It is only curious that lamb as a food has emerged unmarked by such association.

With some sagacity, Michèle Roberts picks fish for imprinting with betrayal in *Daughters of the House*. As already seen, fish has psycho-sexual connotations as well as an interesting history of mythological connection with women.[15] Fish also has strong Christian resonances, including the use of the Greek word for fish as a mnemonic by early Christians[16] and the widespread featuring of fish both literally and in parables in the New Testament. The gospel according to St Mark, in which Jesus recruits the fishermen Simon and Andrew to be 'fishers of men', contains the famous miracle of the loaves and fishes (reframed by Roberts in *The Wild Girl* as a parable of good housekeeping) and in St John's gospel the story of the risen Christ advising Peter and the other luckless fishermen to cast their nets on the other side of the boat, where they are filled, is followed by a meal of fish cooked on a fire of coals on the beach, a sort of spiritual barbecue. There is also, of course, the practice of eating fish on Fridays, a fixture in the post-war Catholic France of *Daughters of the House*.

On the day that Thérèse's father Louis returns from the clinic after his stroke, the lunchtime mackerel becomes embroiled in the most complex cross-currents of power and desire. Thérèse half-prepares it; robbed by her aunt Madeleine of the chance to get her father's room ready for him, she imagines herself coaxing him to eat, and decides upon a herb sauce as more original and more tempting to his appetite than mayonnaise. But as she cooks, her thoughts are filled with her aunt, rival for her father's attention and, Thérèse feels, usurper of her dead mother's place. The mustard she splashes reminds her of Madeleine's bright yellow dress and reflects her own fiery and unhappy feelings. In the event, Madeleine appropriates the looking-after and coaxing of Louis, feeding and petting him, while Thérèse is driven to enact a revenge on them all, and on her mother for dying, by asking the Bishop for permission to enter a convent as soon as she is sixteen. For, while Léonie and the others have completed the cooking, Thérèse has been glorying in the shrine in the woods and it has become the Bishop's lunch.

The sexual associations of the fish (played out in the Electra triangle of Louis, Madeleine and Thérèse) becomes overlaid with the Christian and worldly manifestations of the clergy.

The fish is inscribed with multiple betrayals: of Thérèse's desire for her father; of Louis's hopes for his daughter and Madeleine's for her niece; of the Bishop's pretended humility by his greed – and, more distantly, there is the betrayal of Christ himself. Underlining the food/betrayal connection, it is when the Bishop raises his glass to Thérèse and congratulates her on the fish soup with *rouille* and the poached mackerel in its delicious sauce that she makes her punishing request. But there is a further and more poignant betrayal over the fish: the betrayal of Léonie by the whole company. She is wrongfully denounced by the curé as mistaken, muddled and, worst of all, 'half-English' for having spoken of her own (sincere) vision; here, even her mother speaks not a word in her defence for she is absorbed with stroking and reassuring Louis. After waiting in vain for deliverance, Léonie goes out to fetch the salad.

It could be argued that the food is really incidental to the events here, and indeed nowhere do Roberts's characters explicitly associate fish with betrayal. Nevertheless, the pre-existing associations of fish, along with Roberts's metonymic manipulation, do help to create a figurative density in the five chapters spanned by the cooking and the lunch, so that fish, sexuality, religion and betrayal become, in effect, enmeshed. The interplay is subtle and suggestive like the food itself, and it is only afterwards, when the girls quarrel over the washing up and Thérèse burns her mother's old letters, that accusation becomes overt, as Thérèse cries 'They've betrayed me. I don't want you as my sister. I want Papa' (148).

Writers take advantage of the pre-existing associations and significances that food is impressed with and may, like Roberts, elaborate their own, but even common associations are mutable, and foods can take on certain characteristics according to the occasion. The meat pies, sausages, bacon and ham that the nuns eat for breakfast on Sister Veronica's 'wedding day' in *A Piece of the Night* are special by virtue of the fact that the normal diet of the nuns is frugal. Similarly, with Christmas food: in the Victorian Milk household of *In the Red Kitchen*, the smells of boiling pudding cloth and hot sweet punch are inseparable in Flora's memory from the extravagantly cheerful holly, ivy, candles, red berries and wafting smell of pine from the tree. Christmas teatime is special; there is a whole list of food: 'slices of boiled ham, bread and butter and watercress, custard tarts sprinkled with nutmeg, fruit cake covered with marzipan stuck with sugar roses, mince pies' (32–3). At Flora's wedding, along with (then inexpensive) fresh oysters and crab patties, watercress and boiled gammon make their appearance again, cheesecakes closely replace the custard tarts, and the plates, a synecdochal reminder of the Christmas decorations, have ivy leaves around the rims. Luxury in this relatively poor household results not only from the comparative richness of the ingredients and from the inclusion together of dishes that would normally be served as alternatives, but from the association of particular foods with festivity.

Roberts's writing of food is not only a matter of female consciousness and symbolic richness, however. Food provides, as Farb and Armelagos so importantly note, a primary means for the transmission of culture, establishing habits and confirming patterns of behaviour and expectation within the discourses of class, gender, nationality. In his introduction to *All Manners of Food*, Stephen Mennell stresses that taste is not innate but acquired, sometimes in the face of initial revulsion (as is frequently the case with coffee, caviar or cigarettes, for example).[17] This is an anthropological observation, not a psychological one; approved responses are determined by particular groups, rather than the individual, and include amongst others hunger, pleasure, disgust and even (see Farb and Armelagos) intoxication. According to Lévi-Strauss's classic analysis in *The Raw and the Cooked*, methods of cooking are equally tribally determined (a general principle borne out in this country in the class and cultural differences between, for example, the 'roast beef of old England' and boiled beef and carrots).[18]

The reasons for a group's approval or otherwise of particular foods or cooking methods are in British society inextricably bound up with class, and Roberts reflects this. When, at the Hannibal Dining Rooms in *In the Red Kitchen*, Flora and her sister choose kidneys and peas and tripe and onions, followed by apple dumpling with custard and suet roll with butter and sugar, they are opting for simple, sustaining meals for working people, redolent of cheerful bluntness and commonsense. Flora scathingly contrasts such food with the middle-class dinner party fare her patrons will eat: 'while Minny's picking her way through some dainty mess in a French sauce we'll be feasting on a nice bit of boiled beef and carrots' (74). Boiled beef is an archetypal English working-class dish, as are the suet puddings, steak and kidney pies, mutton chops and treacle tarts favoured by Flora's husband, George (though it must be said not in fact eaten with any regularity in this period by the poorer working class, whose diet was meagre and monotonous). Poor people must eat cheap, readily available foods and those who work physically must be well supplied with fuel, hence the popularity of suet and batter puddings, pies, stews, potatoes and bread. Minnie, by contrast, prefers more 'delicate' food. Exclusivity depends on rarity and expense, but also on lack of necessity; the most 'upper-class' foods are the most unobtainable or expensive and are valued precisely for this reason, especially if they are quite inessential to a healthy diet and thus truly luxuries.

In much of Roberts's writing, enculturation has particular significance for women, because it so often occurs through the preparation as well as eating of food and because it involves special rules. Food preparation provides not only a means of training young women but an inculcation into some of the mysteries of adult female roles and perceptions. In *Daughters of the House* Roberts constructs a web of social interaction around the 'hill of beans' which the two girls help Rose and Victorine to prepare at the kitchen table. The descriptions of topping and tailing or shelling the different varieties of beans are painterly and sensuous, detailing the 'fresh green smell' of one sort, the 'silky inner case' of another and the pink speckled beans 'like tiny onyx eggs', evoking the pleasures of trickling shelled beans between the fingers and speculating about the delicious ways in which they might be cooked (69–70). For Léonie the activity is not only pleasurable on account of the beans themselves, but because she can absorb the conversations of Rose and Victorine. Their talk is largely gossip, but it is hugely important, for it is by means of this food-handling dialogue that they rehearse, process, absorb and come to some kind of understanding of their lives:

While their fingers flew in and out of the earthy heap of beans Rose and Victorine talked. They described village life to each other in intricate detail. They passed it back and forth. They crawled across their chosen ground like detectives armed with magnifying glasses. They took any subject and made it manageable. They sucked it and licked it down to size. They chewed at it until, softened, it yielded, like blubber or leather, to their understanding. They went over it repeatedly until it weakened and gave in and became part of them. Tragedy, disaster; they moulded them into small, digestible portions. (70)

Léonie, silently listening, feels invisible and powerful because the women converse intimately as adults and she is witness to a discourse from which she would normally be excluded. She also feels empowered because she is able to increase her knowledge, her piecemeal understanding of the world, in particular those aspects of it that have previously been concealed from her. The food preparation and the eating metaphor together give the impression of a nourishing and sustaining ambience, the repeated activities providing both the security of familiarity and the thrill of overheard gossip and digestible portions of adult knowledge.

A similarly enlightening process, but this time concerned with a major historical and political issue, occurs over the *gâteau à la peau de lait* that Léonie helps Victorine to make, for she punctuates the cake-making with questions about the bones found in the woods and about Germans and Jews. This cake, 'everyone's favourite' also crops up in 'Une Glossaire' (Roberts's French inventory in *During Mother's Absence*) under the entry for 'crème', but in the novel the juxtaposition with the story of the Jews spikes the appetising description with sinister suggestion.[19] When Léonie weighs the flour there is a full paragraph describing the scales; scales connote justice, and the little weights, like children '*herded* into line' (119, my italics), reinforce the implication of *in*justice. To reinforce the point, when Léonie asks why the Germans hated the Jews, Victorine balances the cake tin on the palm of her hand, frowning at it. In this context, Victorine's *beating* of the cream, *slapping down* of the cake tin, greasing it with *rapid strokes* and *clattering* it into the oven all somehow suggest, like background noise, the brutality of what had taken place. Even the name of the cake, with its evocation of goods made from human skin, has an echo of Nazi atrocity.

What is most thoroughly and indelibly learned through food is a feeling of belonging and this is something that Roberts, with her own childhood shared between England and France, is acutely aware of. The contrast between the two traditions and the potent familiarity of certain foods, which gives that sense of belonging, reappear several times in her novels. When in *A Piece of the Night* Julie Fanchot compares the sauces, stocks, wines, eggs and cream of her childhood with the pork pies, fish and chips, bread pudding, haddock and greasy sausages she experiences at Oxford it is the high-minded contempt of the Oxford scholars for food that she remarks. The richness and complexity of French rural middle class gastronomy contrast sharply with a cultivated English intellectual asceticism. Later in the same novel, though, when Julie returns to England, her thoughts are of eggs and bacon and hot tea: home.

The sense of being at home in a culinary tradition is particularly vivid for children, an explanation, in part, for the nostalgic persistence of the remembered food of childhood. The insecurity and divided loyalties of a bilingual (or bi-nutritional) upbringing in two countries are acutely illustrated in *Daughters of the House* by the conversation between Léonie,

Victorine and Thérèse over the making of potato soup, *gougère* and a cake for supper:

> French cakes, Léonie mused: aren't as good when they come out of the oven as English cakes. No currants and raisins. No icing. No hundreds and thousands or anything.
> French cooking, Victorine asserted: is the best in the world!
> Her blue eyes narrowed to marble chips. She pushed back a long fair curl with one hand. She whacked butter and eggs with her wooden spoon.
> Suet pudding with slabs of butter and white sugar, Léonie recited: fried eggs and bacon, fish and chips, kippers, marmalade, proper tea, Eccles cakes.
> Thérèse flicked a piece of muddy potato peel across the table.
> Everyone knows that English food is terrible, she stated: soggy boiled vegetables in white sauce, overcooked meat, I don't know how your mother could stand it, having to go and eat stuff like that. She stopped being really French, everyone says so. The English are just heathens, aren't they Victorine?
> Heathens was a word Victorine applied to foreigners. Who were not Catholics. The people in the famous circus, for example, that she was always telling them about.
> Léonie frowned very hard so that she would not cry. She concentrated on her potato, gouging out its deep black eye with the serrated tip of her knife. The potato was called Thérèse. (46–7)

The skill of young girls in applying verbal torture is keenly caught. Léonie's dreamy speculation, her thoughtful balancing of the one tradition against the other and her dispassionate but judgemental rebuttal of Victorine's sweeping statement (*'proper* tea') are all nullified by Thérèse's dismissal of English cuisine, the attack on Madeleine and the imputation that as part English – and thus guilty by association with 'terrible' English food, 'stuff' – Léonie is simply beyond the pale.

Food, clearly, is a signifier of belonging. Though Léonie might feel herself to be part of two traditions, she is made to feel she belongs to neither, for she is not French (her mother having 'stopped being really French') and English cooking is too awful to associate with. When the conversation turns to outsiders – gypsies and then Jews – Thérèse announces that Jews were responsible for the crucifixion, that they were 'as bad as the communists' and must be prayed for. As Léonie licks cake mixture from the bowl she remembers going to tea with Jewish school-friends: 'delicious food. Bagels with cream cheese and smoked salmon, pumpernickel bread, gherkins, rollmops, chollah bread, pastries rich with poppyseed and cinnamon' (48). As with the Milk family Christmas, the presence of a list signifies pleasure. Silenced by Thérèse's assertions, however, Léonie denies this memory for its connection with her English self and with a despised ethnicity – thus adding her personal betrayal to the history of the Jews. (It is after this conversation that Léonie's mother tells her about the hidden wine, initiating the metonymy that trades Jews for wine.)

Léonie's denial and self-denial deprive her of richness. The need to belong, to be unequivocally included in the family, to be part of the village, to be French, impels her to deny membership of a larger community, and, indeed, to deny the knowledge offered by the voices of the dead Jews in the back bedroom, until Thérèse's return forces her to re-examine the past. The irony is that she cannot become wholly French either, for she is who she is. As a child even her palpable enjoyment of eating is impaired by her knowledge that it is *English* eating, that she eats too fast and doesn't adequately savour the food. For, Roberts suggests, alimentary belonging really *matters* and these childish claims do not go away; when Thérèse returns and Léonie claims to cook just like Victorine, Thérèse muses to herself, 'You think you've laid a real French supper . . . but you haven't got it quite right. I know that. But you don't. You grew up in England, don't forget' (15).

If food's associations are generally culturally specific and to a large extent understood, the (sometimes convoluted) surrounding conventions, taboos and manners carry even more weight. When the adult Thérèse, returning to the house, doesn't eat much of the leek and potato soup, roast veal and *petits pois* that Léonie has cooked for her, claiming she is used to eating simply, Léonie, feeling rejected and disempowered, points at Thérèse with her fork, commenting on how thin Thérèse has become, and asking if she is ill. While pointing a fork is not quite as nakedly aggressive as pointing a knife, it is certainly threatening, and is invariably considered to be bad manners. In her cultural history of eating, Margaret Visser makes a great point of the fact that meal times are so hedged around with etiquette precisely because of their potential violence.[20] Forks share the prohibition on pointing; they may be less threatening, but are rude by virtue of having been in our mouths. The fork here recalls Léonie's toying murderously with the cooking knives while waiting for Thérèse to arrive; her pointing with a fork is aggressive and accusatory, though it does make some concession to the proprieties.

Léonie and Thérèse are *jeunes filles bien élevées*. The girls may play with their leftover bread at the table, but they obey the bourgeois rules, talking to each other in low voices, never interrupting, speaking when they are spoken to and remaining seated until dismissed. Dinner time rules are of great importance in western bourgeois culture; over the centuries there has been a progressive imposition of spatial boundaries at table, (individual plates, upright chairs, keeping the elbows tucked in, not taking food from another's plate), with the result that conversation has become the major or even sole channel for expressions of community and inter-connection (or indeed polite animosity). Conversation, so heavily loaded, is therefore hedged round with protocols concerning content, vocabulary, precedence and the participation or otherwise of children.

Léonie chafes at the restrictions and the conventions, fantasising about the freedoms she will indulge in when she grows up: she will eat fast, read at the table, talk loudly and lengthily, lay the table as she pleases without being corrected for laying the cutlery the wrong way up. There are two important things about this fantasy. As with the accepted symbolism and associations of certain foods, so here the humour and poignancy of the fantasy depend upon the reader's appreciation of the conventions and on the foregrounding of rules of behaviour that might otherwise be taken for granted. The restrictions under which Léonie suffers draw attention to differing conventions in table-laying and to a locally fierce adherence to these conventions as 'correct'. From the child's point of view, these rules are restrictive, even oppressive, and this raises the second point: instilling a code of manners, especially where the quiet behaviour of children or young women is concerned, is a matter of discipline, control and the cultivation of conformity. Polite behaviour is characterised by the difficulty of what is attempted, such as sitting very upright or balancing food on forks, and the appearance of effortlessness in actions which in fact require considerable physical control.

Good manners are highly conventionalised, as anthropological research, etiquette manuals and almost every travel book testify. Ostensibly functioning to facilitate social ease and order, manners are ideally based on awareness of and consideration for others, but underlying this is the reality that, if we share the same standards – as with rituals, eating customs and food preferences – we feel secure. The conventions work two ways, however: they may facilitate, ease and comfort, but they can also exclude and put people in their place – as both *Good Behaviour* and *Daughters of the House* illustrate. The internalised rules of eating behaviour effectively function as a means of maintaining the *status quo*, which often means an inferior status for women and children, though the rules also reinforce other hierarchies to do with family, community, class and privilege.

In practice (and certainly in literature), the *status quo* is frequently

assailed, at least locally, through manipulation or even outright challenge
of the conventions. Foucault's model of power as not monolithic but
manifested through a network of 'micro-powers' suggests how this
works.[21] Every interaction with the various discursive practices surrounding food and eating (including 'good manners') allows the possibility of challenge and therefore of shifts in overall power relations. This is
both a danger for the unwary and an opening for the opportunist. When
both (or all) parties are aware of a struggle for supremacy, it may become
a linguistic game, participants manipulating the particular discourse in
attempts to gain advantage. There is an element of this in some of
Roberts's writing – baiting the Gaffer in *Mrs Noah*, the verbal skirmishes
of Léonie and Thérèse – but Alice Thomas Ellis brings such struggles to
centre stage.

The exercise of power through food is, traditionally at least, a peculiarly female activity (which is not to say there have been no powerful
male chefs). Cooking, like sex, has been considered a mode through
which women can express their feelings, rewarding the husband with a
special dish, or producing a late or unpleasant dinner as a punishment.
As suggested earlier, too, the cook is rendered powerful through the
eater's trust. As Visser points out, poison is a female weapon in all folklore, whereas men have knives – emblems of the private and the public
respectively. Ellis's fiction fully occupies this private, female domain,
which it takes for granted as the most important (to the extent of mar-
ginalising men and generally reducing them to ciphers). She thoroughly
annexes the lethal power of the cook. Indeed, her characters happily
speculate about invisible methods of despatch: tigers' whiskers in the
case of Mrs Munro in *The Skeleton in the Cupboard* (89) and various
methods of poisoning by Aunt Irene in *The 27th Kingdom* (104). The power
gained even in the imagination provides a source of self-satisfaction not
always easy to categorise. These extreme solutions may be fantastic, but
the covert sway and manipulative skills of Ellis's kitchen impresarios are
far from illusory.

The power and power games that Ellis details have several strands.
There is the food itself, its content, preparation and serving; there is the
manipulation, or sabotage, of the associations attaching to foods as discussed earlier; there are linguistic play and battles involving particular
customs and codes of manners. Within the various power displays and
struggles can be detected a plethora of personal motivations, assumptions and prejudices, as well as revelations concerning class, culture,
gender and value. Power is not merely oppressive, imposed from above,

a means of maintaining a fixed and unthreatening social order, but positive; according to Foucault, it produces reality, and is inseparable from knowledge.[22] Power and knowledge are self-evidently mutually necessary, not only for the wielder of power or dominant party, but for whoever subverts power (and thus claims it).

Ellis's use of food, though in a manner quite unlike Roberts's, is potent, its effectiveness relying on a degree of implied knowledge often hidden from the other characters, and not always spelt out for the reader. The pre-cricket match dinner in *The Sin Eater*, a planned sabotage, achieves its effect both through linguistic voodoo (the main course conjuring 'out for a duck') and because it is a disingenuously lavish meal, with excessively rich ingredients: 'Evidence of ill-will lay openly, but unrecognisably, on the table: numerous egg shells, orange peel, chocolate wrappers, heavy cream, oil and butter and sherry, three ducks thawing flaccidly on a charger in a cold pink pool of blood.'[23] There is no mistaking the intention here, nor the (sardonically narrated) concealment: 'While there were many ways of killing a cat, the easiest was to choke it to death with cream: it involved no coercion, no show of force, and even looked like kindness' (99).

The appropriation of power often involves manoeuvres that are tacit, covert, unrecognisable except to the initiate, and that rely upon the major English sanction of embarrassment. Closely allied to shame, the effects of embarrassment can be both physical (blushing, stammering, trembling, nausea) and psychological (ostracism, humiliation, wretchedness). It is thus a highly effective form of social coercion. Ellis's game-players, who frequently use impeccably good manners as a front for being diabolical, seek to create embarrassment in their victims by outdoing them in a fastidious conformity to accepted etiquette, by parody, or by flagrant transgression, reinventing the rules for themselves and carrying this off by sheer bravura. The one taboo they invariably break is the injunction not to behave oddly or draw attention to another's oddity (a solicitude eccentrically evident in the many versions of the etiquette story of a host who drinks the water in the finger bowl so as not to embarrass a guest who had ignorantly done so).

Rose, in Ellis's first novel *The Sin Eater*, is positively dedicated to drawing attention to what she perceives as other people's oddity, and embarrassing those she sees as offenders. Her chief weapons are culinary theatricality and parody. She prepares prawn cocktail, steak with decorative chips and pavlova for a Midlands client of her husband, a 'nice man' who doesn't realise he is being mocked. She gives boiled eggs to Cousin Teddy when his head is bandaged following an accident, so that he appears, metonymically, to be cracking his own skull. Most ambitiously, she organises a faintly anachronistic plebeian post-cricket match tea complete with sandwich spread, meat and fish paste, sausage rolls, packet biscuits, swiss rolls and tea from an urn. She only regrets her action when the 'gentry' arrive, for whom she would prefer to have provided a 1930s tea, as self-conscious as its description implies: 'a cake disguised as a tiny cricket pitch and little rolled sandwiches with flags describing their contents' (152), or a grand formal Edwardian tea on the lawn to frighten her sister-in-law Angela.

Rose wishes to frighten Angela because she perceives her as a self-serving, self-righteous and stupid snob. She contrives to mock, anger or discomfort her on every eating occasion, parodying her with damp cucumber sandwiches and unsettling her by switching from clichéd 'drawing room' cups to thick white china which make Angela think, uncomfortably, of a 'lorryman's caff'. Such instances are accompanied by a constant but subtle baiting about class, religion, nationality, permissiveness – general subjects, but each of which pertains directly to Angela. Angela is uneasily aware that Rose is goading her, but does not take full measure of the parody and pastiche, and neither does she have the wit to play Rose at her own game. The purchase Rose achieves, and her unfailing ability to manipulate Angela's responses, reside precisely in this gap; Rose's detachment permits her to see and play upon English upper-middle-class mores without herself feeling controlled by them, whereas Angela is fully defined by her class-bound lifestyle.

Rose's combination of wit and unscrupulousness nevertheless require, theatrical as she is, an audience that has *some* grasp of what she is up to (a condition that applies equally to Ellis's readership). The over-excited young visitors at the pavilion tea, for example, are beyond Rose's control, protected by their own innocence and inexperience; they do not understand the nuances of ritual, tradition or expected behaviour, and so cannot *read* the cricket tea as we are induced to and as Ermyn and one or two of the older middle-class visitors do. The common ground here is missing; these young people are unembarrassable.

So what are all Rose's efforts for? Why is she dedicated to catering as parody, self-display and the subversive exercise of power? Ellis twice supplies a cook's agenda that provides part of the answer. In *The 27th Kingdom* Aunt Irene is described as 'an artist . . . [who] needed an appreciative audience' (14) and for whom people form part of the 'raw materials' in her domestic and culinary art. Rose, similarly, is: 'greedy and clever and cynical, qualities essential to a good cook, and sometimes she used her ingredients like a witch, as social comment, to do mischief, or as a benefice' (17). Ellis's cooks' purpose is thus partly aesthetic but also involves social comment, wicked satirical fun and endorsement of certain specific values and relationships, such as a mother's care for her children.

Rose's more particular motives are also hinted at: an outsider by virtue of her Catholicism, her Irishness and the finer gradations of class (she is the daughter of a vet), she enacts a kind of revenge, confirming her exclusion from and sense of superiority to the secular and class-bound English. She insults Angela's husband, implying a lack of manliness and the failure of both aesthetics and nutrition in his background: 'I expect he had rickets. So many upper-middle-class kiddies did, because their nannies fed them on rice pudding and boiled cod' (51). And through her catering, she manipulates people into behaving like caricatures of themselves, thereby manifesting the most unlovely aspects of English upper-middle-class manners. The negative, repressive, self-selecting, exclusive and sometimes simply preposterous nature and effects of such manners are thus highlighted, taking Rose's 'purpose' distinctly beyond the personal.

Two points are worth adding here. The first is that Rose, who refuses to go back to work or education, is portrayed as relishing the highly domestic power she wields; through cooking and catering she increases her dominion and transforms a disempowered position into a nearly invincible one. The second point is that her battle with Phyllis, the (Welsh) family retainer, is quite different from her baiting of the upper classes, since both dislike the English, are unembarrassable and unscrupulous, have strong maternal (or grandmaternal) feelings, and are eerily kindred spirits, inexplicably laughing together in the kitchen at night. These two engage in a contest whose unspoken rules they equally understand.

Many of the conflicts centred on cooking, food and eating in Ellis's writing seem to revolve around class, but class seen not so much from a political as an ethical or moral point of view. Part of what she draws attention to is a singular *lack* of awareness displayed in some upper-middle- or upper-class manners, the mindlessly arrogant assumptions that allow a young girl visitor to demand, 'Well, I want something to eat . . . Where's the little man with the goodies?' (85), or an Angela to claim complacently, 'I think it's marvellous how class distinctions have completely gone' (107). Such attitudes betray a thoughtless, smug and self-deceiving perception of social structures. Angela's mother can play at slumming by eating jellied eels at a street party without losing any of her own social prestige because of a profound confidence that an increase in equality will not require her to relinquish anything of her own privilege and position (the inverse, incidentally, of Lessing's May Quest, who cannot afford to slum precisely because of her psychological and economic insecurity).

With a perception of social structures and power relations as static, it is easy enough to cling to customs and precepts that reinforce the *status quo*. Rose's rule-breaking eating occasions are designed so that conventions will not protect, for example when she breaks with the tradition of an exclusive pre-cricket match lunch, opting instead to serve a buffet in the kitchen. The effect of this kind of lunch is to erase the distance essential to the maintenance of class distinctions, a distance so constituted that if the upper classes condescend to socialise, the lower orders must nevertheless know their place. Not only does this lunch satisfyingly antagonise Angela, it also reveals the pettiness and stupidity of meanly class-bound behaviour, as Jack and Gomer, smartly dressed in their whites and aware of the special occasion, are nevertheless at home and quite comfortable, blithely impervious to both Angela's acid observations and Michael's patronising sociability. The class battles in Ellis's writing are by no means clear-cut, just as they are not necessarily political (at least in the sense of class war). Mutual game-playing is a common form of middle- or upper-class power struggle, acted out through the medium of 'good' behaviour or polite manners, and it is apparent in several of Ellis's novels (as it is in *Good Behaviour*). Lydia does it in *Unexplained Laughter*, as does Lili in the trilogy, in which Mrs Munro is also tempted to; Kyril, in *The 27th Kingdom*, is annoyed that Valentine will *not* play, so unaware is she of his worldly game.

In the same novel, Aunt Irene and her appallingly genteel cleaning lady Mrs Mason engage in a running warfare; Mrs Mason, as acutely aware of position as Angela, is at pains to demonstrate that she is middle class (impoverished maybe, but not *really* a charlady), and Aunt Irene that she is above class (though possibly of grand descent). Once again, the struggle is played out through food:

Mrs Mason was having a little snack when they got back home. She had put a lace tray cloth on the end of the oaken kitchen table and chosen a Spode plate and matching cup and saucer to place her biscuit on and drink her tea from. She behaved with grotesque politeness, putting down her biscuit after each nibble and her cup after each sip and folding her hands in her lap like a child pretending to eat and drink.

Aunt Irene felt like pulling out the tray cloth and jumping on it. She ate because she liked eating, not as a demonstration of manners: sometimes she put her elbows on the table and waved her fork to emphasise a point. Now she took a biscuit and bit it with her right-hand teeth, keeping her mouth open and causing crumbs. (35)

Even the language used to represent Mrs Mason's actions is deliciously and horribly genteel: the 'oaken' table and 'placing' of her 'little snack' and the fact that she 'nibbles' and 'sips', whereas Aunt Irene is described in much more robust terms. The battle represented here is between two displaced women whose relationship is hardly at all defined by the respective roles of employer and domestic help. Mrs Mason loses no opportunity to inconvenience or annoy Aunt Irene or enhance her own position (telling the tax man she is Aunt Irene's 'housekeeper', for example), just as Aunt Irene does everything she can to distance herself from Mrs Mason, deciding to cook a *daube* rather than cold food for her party, for example, simply because Mrs Mason has suggested 'a cold table' ('"Cold table" indeed! It sounded so hideously refeened' (98)).

When it comes to working-class characters there is undoubtedly an element of stereotyping in Ellis's women – the clever char with a heart of gold – but this is offset by instances of criminal behaviour, malice, stupidity, appalling taste, involvement in the game-playing, and the fact that nobody is immune from Ellis's satirical and ultimately misanthropic eye. Untrammelled by class pretensions, her cleaning women are frequently the most perceptive and sensible of her characters, and are equally the most robust cooks. The watchful Phyllis in *The Sin Eater*, diligent dispenser of pastry, corned beef, bacon, eggs, fat tomatoes, bread and cakes for her son and grandson, is the first to identify Michael's homosexual relationship with Gomer. In *The 27th Kingdom*, Mrs O'Connor, who makes ferociously strong restorative tea, efficiently doses the Major's DTs with concentrated orange juice, recommends hangover remedies and recognises Aunt Irene's horse-meat stew with a down-to-earth commonsense and generosity, is also the first person to perceive and revere Valentine's miraculous powers. Edith, in *The Other Side of the Fire*, who despises Claudia's purposeless lifestyle and fancy food, and herself provides for a husband who demands traditional working-class food (three meals a day, all prompt and all with meat, not forgetting Yorkshire pudding on Sundays), is the only person to realise that something is going on between Claudia and Philip. Her perception itself is powerful; Claudia reacts by cooking 'bangers and mash' for lunch, as though metonymically influenced for the moment by Edith's plain cooking and ungarnished self.

Edith displays the same hearty contempt for Claudia that almost all Ellis's working-class characters express for the ineffectual middle classes, and she is triumphantly delighted to see a fall in standards when Claudia buys a frozen shepherd's pie. There is a kind of complicity, however, between such characters and the more raffish and rebellious middle-class women: Rose and Phyllis in *The Sin Eater*, Aunt Irene and Mrs O'Connor in *The 27th Kingdom*, Mrs Munro and Mrs Raffald in *Skeleton in the Cupboard*. Mrs Raffald and Mrs Munro, in particular, have an equality and an intimacy that Mrs Munro recognises with satisfaction would be deemed shocking by the prevailing mores of middle-class Croydon.

It is the particularity of the tastes, rituals and rules of behaviour of any exclusive group, however small or large, that is likely to give rise to friction and awkwardness in dealings with other groups in the community. Ellis states this explicitly through the partially reformed Lydia in *Unexplained Laughter*: it is 'the constraints of formality, the manners and *mores* of different groups that caused alienation'.[24] The suspicions and hostilities between Welsh and English in *The Sin Eater* and *Unexplained Laughter* are similar to class inasmuch as discord and embarrassment may result from social or cultural expectations as well as from deliberate actions. Discomfort, tension and conflict can even be so common as to become embedded in occasions themselves, rather as symbolic meanings are imprinted on foods. This chapter will conclude with three such eating occasions: afternoon tea, Christmas dinner and the picnic.

Afternoon tea is potentially the most awkward eating occasion, especially in English culture, and one which writers have frequently exploited for maximum social unease. Oscar Wilde's teatime battle between Cecily and Gwendolin in *The Importance of Being Ernest* is the very pattern of a mealtime conversational struggle for supremacy. Though afternoon tea has fallen from its formal height at the beginning of the twentieth century, it has always been what Angela Carter acutely describes as 'that uniquely English meal, that unnecessary collation', and Ermyn, in *The Sin Eater*, muses that the Devil presides over the tea table, since it is a less necessary and thus less convivial event than supper.[25] Afternoon tea is the most public and artificial of meals since its function has more to do with social intercourse than nourishment, and its rituals of tea-pouring, cake-passing and polite conversational exchanges are not really conducive to intimacy. Thus Aunt Irene's conventional friends in *The 27th Kingdom* hold the view that eating with 'original' people is only permissible at tea time. Even where children are concerned, tea is the most public occasion, the time at which they may eat in friends' homes, which is why Ermyn's bleak childhood teas in *The Sin Eater* set her insistently apart, rendering her almost dysfunctional; when she arrives at the Plâs at the beginning of the novel, she sits just out of reach of the tea-table.

If its function is very often to do with children, afternoon tea is nevertheless associated very much with women. The combination of female space, ritualised intercourse and the (literary) association of teatime with battle almost prescribe certain kinds of exchange. Both the overtones of formality and veiled hostility are in evidence at the uncomfortable afternoon tea Ellis provides in the trilogy for the elderly Mrs Munro, her unwilling daughter-in-law-to-be and Lili. Ellis does not develop the tensions into any kind of sparring: this particular tea party is a disaster because so much is *un*spoken. Its silences and lacunae instigate action, however, as the unspoken undercurrents begin the process that draws Lili and Mrs Munro seditiously together, gives Mrs Munro licence to indulge in drinking and smoking and leads to Lili's exhibitionist rescue of Margaret from marriage to the odious Syl.

Mrs Munro's ultimate desire in *The Skeleton in the Cupboard* is to 'ride across the boundaries which separated the done from the not-done thing',[26] a phrase that presupposes a thorough understanding of which is which. What is 'done', approved, is conventional, the proprieties depending once again on class, ethnicity, nationality, family and culture. As Mrs Munro's tea party demonstrates, what is 'done' may even contain or herald its opposite. By sketching the ritualised eating occasions, Ellis demonstrates how they are ideally constructed and suggests some of their cultural freight; she measures and tests her characters against the events as they are culturally conceived and holds these constructions up to scrutiny in the light of the pressures they bring to bear on women's lives.

With the exception of weddings, the most pressurised occasion in British culture – with widespread and deeply embedded rituals and traditions, some religious, some commercially induced and some culinary – is Christmas. The core traditions – cards, tree, presents, Christmas dinner – are common to Christians and the irreligious, and are surprisingly consistent. The eating of a roast turkey or other large bird or joint with traditional trimmings, followed by a dark, fruity and spicy pudding, is so well-established that mass catering (schools, hospitals and canteens) almost always features a 'Christmas dinner'. Obviously, there are local variations, but there is an entire etiquette of festive behaviour, a compound of social and family traditions dictating who should carve, who be served first, how children should behave, when crackers should be

pulled and so on. As with the ceremony of the main meal of the season,
so with the whole Christmas package, from ritualistic shopping to tacit
expectations of over-indulgence.

The combination of Christian remembrance with pagan celebration
has become gradually altered and overlaid – to the point of cliché – with
commercial excess, greed, inertia and indulgence, and this is at the core
of Ellis's *The Birds of the Air*. Not only is the religious element of
Christmas largely overlooked, she suggests, but egalitarian carnivalesque
is reduced to the hollow gestures of parties, family politics and petty
drunkenness. Ellis has a Catholic agenda that is not part of my concern
here, but she also sees Christmas in secular terms as a time at which
resentments and disputes come to a head; there is certainly nothing of
the nostalgic charm Michèle Roberts evokes in *In the Red Kitchen*, though
a similar regard for appropriate celebration may well underlie both representations. Social intercourse in Ellis's Christmas world is simultaneously forced and restricted, by culturally sanctioned custom, internalised
expectations, commerce and, once again, the fine discriminations of
class.

Christmas involves expectations that cannot possibly all be met and
which place particular burdens on those who cook or entertain; both the
expectations and the burdens are in evidence in *The Birds of the Air*. Office
parties or their equivalent also often provide unwelcome revelations.
Barbara organises two Christmas gatherings: pre-lunch drinks for a few
of Sebastian's undergraduates, and a party for his colleagues; both occasions represent aspects of her duty to her husband. The first is part of
the 'relentless hospitality' shown to unfortunate or unpopular students
who have not gone away or home and holds no pleasure for any of its
participants. The party for Sebastian's colleagues is for Barbara striated
with anxiety and apprehension about her teenage son Sam's looks and
behaviour and filled with hospitable obligations towards people who
seem quite alien to her. To cap it all, she witnesses her uncharacteristically 'playful' and 'lascivious' husband Sebastian feeding a piece of
turkey to a colleague's wife, thus learning through food of his extramar-
ital affair.

Expectation, ritual and duty here clash with shock and transgression;
amidst the sharply satirised exchanges, through which the adolescent
Sam promenades as a mute critic with his tape recorder, Barbara strives
to dissemble, to perform her expected part, to be like all the others who
seem to be enjoying themselves. She conflates infidelity with rudeness,
gasping at her own temerity when she pretends that a guest's smoke is

responsible for her tears: 'Oh, she thought, I wasn't brought up like that. I was brought up to be faithful and polite' (34). Barbara is paralysed by the inability to divorce her feelings from the rules of behaviour she has thoroughly internalised, and it falls to her son Sam to disrupt the party by broadcasting the unflattering and hugely amplified tape-recorded conversations of the guests, thus loudly and rudely expressing his mother's feelings through his own distress.

A number of factors apparent within this party recur on Christmas Day, including a foolish adherence to preconceived expectations of what the occasion will be like. Ellis provides a typically unstable mix. Barbara's mother, Mrs Marsh, is determined to have a traditional 'family' Christmas complete with snow and everyone being cheerful and nice to each other, a foolish but culturally endorsed fantasy. The family circumstances are particularly inauspicious: Barbara's grieving sister Mary simply doesn't care about the occasion; Barbara herself is fully prepared for her mother's expectations, but, still stunned by the knowledge of Sebastian's infidelity and perpetually anxious about Sam's non-conforming adolescent behaviour, is tranquillized; Sebastian, like Mary and indeed Sam, wonders rather desperately how he will survive the few days; Sam, in adolescence preternaturally sensitive to the pain and discomfort of others, can only manifest his feelings disruptively.

The comedy is black. Mrs Marsh is propelled – by loss and a pained inability to adapt to change, by a sense of motherly duty, by awareness of social position and by a total absorption of cultural expectations – to pursue her ideal of benevolent Christmas. Mindful of the proprieties, she is almost overwhelmed by the logistical difficulties of organising such a disparate, disaffected and increasingly inebriated group of individuals through the lunch, tea and evening drinks she has planned. Despite the authority vested in her as senior member of the family, mother and hostess, she has no power at all. There is a parallel here with the limits of Rose's power in *The Sin Eater*: the very sad (Mary) or the very drunk (Barbara) may be immune to constraints policed by embarrassment.

The social dysfunction resulting from a combination of unexpressed negative feelings, alcohol and a paralysing expectation of conformity to polite good manners is so acute that Mrs Marsh is reduced to coercion, announcing for example that 'lunch *must* now be served' (110, my italics). Ellis neatly illustrates that power depends on others' compliance and that people generally expect everybody else to conform, even if they grant themselves licence. Mrs Marsh, after learning of Sebastian's infidelity, takes the pepper mill from him to show him how to use it, grinding a lot of pepper over his food in a childishly transgressive act of judgement.

These apparently decisive actions are, like Barbara's ineffectualness, a function of Mrs Marsh's disempowerment and her frustration that she cannot control events. Unable to regulate the quantity of wine being consumed, she frets about timing and serves the pudding in a spirit more chivvying than generous: 'She dumped glass bowls in front of everyone, splashing a few spots of freshly melting brandy butter on Seb's cardigan. He dabbed at it, tutting, instead of ignoring it as a proper man would have done' (120). She even neglects to offer the Stilton and biscuits, deciding resentfully that they would make too many crumbs and rationalising to herself that everyone has had enough to eat anyway. The kitchen, too, is beyond her control, cluttered as it is with part-filled dishes and glasses and the disordered evidence of her neighbour Evelyn's slovenly helping. Mrs Marsh is worn out: by the cooking, the anxiety, the desire to make everything 'nice' and the impossibility of realising such niceness. She is exhausted by the responsibility. For although she wants to be in command she does not have Rose's interest in power; she feels responsible for everybody. As their hostess, their temporary provider, she owes them a duty of care. Aunt Irene, in *The 27th Kingdom*, has a similar view: 'once you'd fed people you had admitted responsibility, like saving a life' (53).

This is a moralist's perception of the cook's role, diametrically opposed to that of Rose's power games and closely related to models of nurturing. Responsibility is undoubtedly connected with power but the two may operate independently, and indeed conflictingly. Women's sense of responsibility for others' needs (as daughters, wives, mothers and carers), for example, is arguably a construct of patriarchal power. Morality may conveniently be invoked, in other words, for political manipulation. While Ellis's novels display a lively sense of morality, her more feisty protagonists are at pains to distinguish true goodness from commonly approved and regulated behaviour, to shun a disempowering, conventionally ascribed responsibility. These women's self-conscious manipulation of the roles of guest, hostess and cook, and their disruption of accepted mores represent a refusal of the burdens Mrs Marsh unwittingly takes upon herself and a rejection of the controlling effects of conventional good manners; their interest is directed firmly towards empowering themselves.

Lydia in *Unexplained Laughter* is just such a protagonist, eschewing responsibility for her guest, Betty, who herself takes on the cooking and cleaning in a spirit of 'looking after' the lovesick and jilted Lydia. This is not because Lydia cannot cook (her culinary skill is sketched by reference to her bread sauce: 'the best bread sauce in the world with a great deal of butter, nutmeg and black pepper')[27] but because she reacts by opting out in the face of Betty's domesticated earnestness. While she recognises that Betty is really much nicer than she is, Lydia nevertheless indulges her own spite and pleasure in power in true Ellis game-playing fashion, baiting and manipulating her guest. Power and responsibility are split: Lydia wields and seizes power; Betty assumes responsibility. The one occasion on which she demurs is in the preparation of Lydia's pheasant, a refusal which, given the lack of any such request from Lydia, underscores her self-appointed role.

Lydia is aware of goodness, both common humanity and the fierce unworldly innocence of the trainee priest Beuno, whom she carnivorously labels 'not for human consumption' (82). The trouble is that behaving badly is more fun. It is also more empowering. This is why Lydia cannot resist the idea of staging a picnic near the priapic rock drawings of Dr Wyn, to his potential disgrace. She is ambivalent, however, and almost immediately decides to make it a 'nice picnic'. She vacillates between several positions: indulging her spiteful desire, wishing she had not conceived of the picnic at all, realising that she can have it as an ordinary picnic and seeing her mischief-making plan as sad and trivial by comparison with the prospect of engaging in battle with her ex-lover Finn. If Lydia's attempts to be good represent responsibility and her succumbing to mischief-making a pursuit of power, then the two can be seen as fluctuating throughout her approach to the picnic. Betty, by contrast, is all responsibility, making quiche and cake, boiling eggs, mashing sardines, slicing bread and tweaking and prodding at Lydia's conscience.

The etiquette of picnics is quite unlike that of other meals. Normal rules and hierarchies are overthrown as people sit on the ground and eat with their fingers; the possibilities of gaining power through parodic manipulation in the Rose manner are limited. The event is nevertheless orchestrated to some extent, and Lydia does decide upon and take credit for the venue which, in a concession to goodness and responsibility, is situated away from the rock drawings. She even makes an effort to keep a desultory conversation going, though Betty has to come to the rescue by producing the food.

By the time the food is eaten, however, Lydia has relinquished both responsibility and power over the picnic through quarrelling with Finn, the group has begun to disperse and Dr Wyn and April have gone off for a walk in the direction of the rock drawings. A vestigial sense of culpability makes Lydia cry 'Hell', but it is too late. Her original abandoned plan is now fulfilled so successfully that she even feels sorry for the doctor, and she regains control by 'mercifully' releasing him with the announcement that it will soon be time to go. In charge once more, she orchestrates the post-picnic leave-taking. Ever adept at engineering slight shifts of power to her advantage, she also stifles the possibility of a relationship between Finn and Betty by 'blessing' them and smiling knowingly. Even though she offends all those closest to her, she is able to reclaim both power and affection through her intimate understanding of what is expected, by her unstinting manipulation and as a result of occasional spontaneous benevolence; an easy moment's sincere warmth at parting secures Betty's loyal goodwill. Power, for this hostess, is a sustaining game.

CHAPTER 6

Social eating: identity, communion and difference

As in the previous chapter, the focus here is on social eating. But while chapter 5 focuses on the literary use of food and manners as signifiers in a social context, this final chapter moves towards a more uncertain, expansive and perhaps challenging view, exploring how eating might be deemed to relate to society as a whole, to social function and to some conception of community. Whether 'community' is more than an ideal remains to be seen. How eating is involved depends upon the play of relationships within and between social groups of various sizes, from family, work and friendship clusters to class, ethnicity or society at large.

Given the scale of such a canvas, probably the best way to construct a general or societal perspective is by looking at particular, representative examples of what might constitute social eating. How, for example, do food and eating relate to the identity or cohesion of a certain group and the links between that group and its society? How are food and eating instrumental in the formation of identity in a particular society and what role do they play in socialisation? What is the cultural place of ritual or the social implication of cooking? And are such questions answerable in other than relative terms, given that food and behaviour depend very much on contexts of period, ethnicity, gender, religion, ideology, nationality and cultural systems? This chapter will respond to some of these questions in the light of texts – both realist and non-realist – by Doris Lessing and Angela Carter, texts in which concepts of community and communion are in varying degrees put to the test through food and eating.

One way of approaching the subject is to look at a fictional group in relation to the actual society in which it is located. Such a contextual view can be peculiarly revealing; for example, Angela Carter's so-called Bristol novels (*Shadow Dance*, *Several Perceptions* and *Love*), though often considered as fables or romances, can, as Marc O'Day points out, be quite specifically related to the time they were written, the 1960s.[1] Not only is there the circumstantial detail of junk-shop culture, pubs and coffee bars, but the emphasis on youth, the vampiric devouring, mutual suspicion and self-destruction, the predatory hunger coupled with passivity and fear of engulfment might all be taken for metaphors of 1960s' politics and social change. Carter herself claimed both specificity and purpose and maintained that *Shadow Dance* was about 'a perfectly real area of the city in which I lived. It didn't give exactly mimetic copies of people I knew, but it was absolutely as real as the milieu I was familiar with: it was set in provincial bohemia.'[2] The city is real, the settings authentic; only the people, it seems, are inventions.

In the same interview Carter asserted that the novel should in some way help to explain experience and make the world 'comprehensible'. The world in this case is English, provincial, bohemian, early 1960s. Its strange, alienated subgroup of society, marked by a cannibalistic or vampiric culture of 'eat or be eaten', reliant on instant coffee and aspirins, sugary cakes and tea, is apparently sequestered from wider contemporary society other than its tenuous links with the largely critical Greek Chorus of similarly alienated acquaintances at the local pub. The group, such as it is, does not connect through food at all, the only social eating taking place when Emily cooks for Honeybuzzard and Morris, and this is an act of love to which Morris is incidental. The communicative aspect of eating together is even deliberately reversed at one stage, when Morris is ostracised in the pub and the café. The lack of real connection or cohesion among the characters and their anarchic marginality function to further alienate and ultimately fracture the group. Since Carter espouses the view that you are what you eat, we can assume that an infantalising diet (literal and metaphorical) saps the marrow and indulges a sense of megalomania, and that – as the metaphor itself predicts – vampiric behaviour is self-perpetuating.[3]

Like Carter, Doris Lessing holds a view of the writer as both powerful ('an instrument of change for good or bad') and having a duty to his or her society: 'If a writer accepts this responsibility, he must see himself, to use the socialist phrase, as an architect of the soul . . . one must have a vision to build towards, and that vision must spring from the nature of the world we live in.'[4] As with Carter's fiction, illumination, explanation and informing vision do not rely on literal realism, even if many realist devices are employed. The dystopian scenario of Lessing's *The Memoirs of a Survivor*, written in 1974 and set in an indeterminate future, outlines a society progressively fragmenting into (often literally) cannibalistic groups. The dynamic within and the interaction between some of these groups are indicative both of progressive social collapse and of the importance and strength of residual (and future) socialisation.

The unnamed, rather detached narrator, apparently an erstwhile member of the bourgeoisie, chronicles what happens in the street outside her window, inside her flat and in the symbolic metaphysical realm beyond its walls, encompassing both psychoanalytic and visionary projections. Her narration implies that she embodies much in the way of 'old' values, particularly a proper sense of individual and social responsibility which seems to have disappeared in this disintegrating world. Thus when Emily is brought to her by a stranger, without explanation, she takes on the responsibility for this young girl and her cat-dog companion, feeling she has no alternative. (As discussed in chapter 1, the responsibility is enacted maternally, but its acceptance seems to be a manifestation of social duty rather than maternal desire.)

Outside in the street, the narrator sees tribal groups form and reform, gather and leave; the travellers are distinctive because they have given up their individuality, or at least 'individual judgement and responsibility' (33). The groups of young show the way to their more isolated elders, devising new ways of behaving in the face of a disintegrating society. They learn how to forage for supplies, they connect in experimental and shifting alliances, burn fires on the pavements and roast meat of dubious origin. New rituals are evolved, new tastes formed and incorporated by the shifting groups of the changed society; the narrator points out that some of the children even seem to prefer what to her are unappetising meat substitutes, and she comments stoically, 'we learn to like what we get' (90). The tribes or gangs or groups are larger than the sum of their members. When it comes to moving on, it does not matter which individuals join the leaving tribe; those remaining on the pavement simply accumulate another crowd to replace them and subgroups continue to assemble and depart, with a trolley or cart of root vegetables and grain, and perhaps a last-minute bleeding parcel brought by some self-conscious youths.

Inside the flat, Emily's passage through the phases of adolescence is connected with the development of the groups outside, and the narrator speculates about peer influence, surmising that gangs arise from the desire to be similar. Slowly but surely, Emily reinvents herself to join the pavement society, as life in the city worsens, services disintegrate, food becomes more scarce and law and order must increasingly be self-imposed. These groups become, in effect, primary social units, their communality superseding accustomed modes of interaction:

any individual consummations were nothing beside this act of mingling constantly with others, as if some giant rite of eating were taking place, everyone tasting and licking and regurgitating everyone else, making themselves known to others and others known to them in this tasting and sampling – eyeing each other, rubbing shoulders and bodies, talking, exchanging emanations. (74)

The suggested cannibalism of this 'communal feast' hints at the savagery of society, but the universality and equality of reciprocal eating – or rather tasting and regurgitation – indicates mutuality rather than exploitation. This mutuality lies somewhere between the deathly spirit of cannibalism (outlined in chapter 2), which is certainly evident in the disintegrating society of *Memoirs*, and the lover's desire for total union with the beloved proposed by Freud.[5] In *Memoirs*, any such personal desire is tempered with suspicion; experiences occur not as individual and private sensations, but are writ large onto a collective psyche. Against this ethos, Emily's wanting time alone with Gerald is an anachronism, retrogressive, possessive, individualistic. Yet they do come together, in a large, family-like group, when Emily joins Gerald after he gathers children from the streets and installs them in a house. For a while at least, Gerald and Emily are the household's parent figures. This household, or organised commune, is portrayed as of a piece with pockets of life all over the city: reverting to the pre-industrial, reinstating privies in gardens, composting sewage for growing vegetables, keeping pigs, setting up workshops for making household goods and furniture – communities that draw on the utopian ideal of self-sufficient hippy communities of the late 1960s and 1970s (their effortful self-sufficiency setting them apart from the more expectant benefits-supported squatters of *The Good Terrorist*).

The narrator's visit to the household reveals much about this small community, its focus on food and self-sufficiency and its relation to the environment. As the narrator, Emily and June make their way to the house, some young men with guns call out to June and give her a dozen pigeons. These young men, like June and the 'hugger-mugger' Ryans, are more easily able to adapt to an unpredictable, inconsequential lifestyle than the middle classes who, as Lessing acerbically puts it, cannot accept that 'respectability, property and gain' are no longer the measure of personal worth. Further on, Emily pulls up plants from old railway lines for use as herbs in the commune's kitchen. These two incidents suggest a vital connection with both physical environment and other groups in the area.

Running like a counterpoint to what goes on in the household and the public domain is the narrative of the 'personal' realm which the narrator discovers beyond the wall of the flat. Here there is both explanation and possibility. Something like rebirth is suggested for, despite the dilapidation and degradation of the house, the gardens are full of the promise of peace and fruitfulness, and the symbolic egg suggests futurity. It is indicative of the narrator's social conscience that she sets herself to do what she can to clean, restore, repaint, reorder the decaying house. As a solution patching up is inadequate, as the accelerating degradation behind the wall and Emily's battles to sweep up against a swamping tide of leaves suggest. The real possibility the novel offers is that of beginning again with new ways of thinking and being.

The beyond-the-wall childhood scenes, located, as Kate Fullbrook notes, right in the period during which Freud was putting forward his theories of infant sexuality and psychic development, contain clear allusions to Freudian psychology, suggesting links between upbringing and nurturing (or their lack) and the disintegrating world outside.[6] Repressive factors in the development of a 'good baby' are sketched, including the reinscription of frustration and inhibition on generation after generation.[7] The maternal disgust at the excrement-eating baby may be compared with Gerald's despair at the casting of a first murderous stone by a four-year-old member of his gang of small savages. The crying of the punished baby goes on echoing, not only in the dreamlike world behind the wall, but bleeding into the narrator's everyday life as well. The stifling of a natural human impulse towards epistemological omnivorousness and the cruel denial of a need for emotional nourishment have social consequences; the traumatising effect of the baby's treatment is tellingly juxtaposed with evidence of social breakdown. We are effectively shown two opposing explanations for social dysfunction: at one extreme an infant traumatised by excessive discipline, at the other a gang of children brutalised by a complete *lack* of socialisation.

The fact of general social breakdown is not to say that the 'savages' do not have a group identity, however, even if it is solely based – dedicated as they are to sheer physical survival – on fighting and eating. Though defined almost entirely in terms of negatives, the children do have characteristics in common (youth, desperation, fierceness, amorality and so on) through which a group identity and even a rudimentary sense of solidarity emerge, suggesting at least residual (if parodic) socialisation. When the children are first introduced they are shown without parents, family or civilising influences, living in the (literal and metaphorical) underground, surviving by stealing and fighting, united only by the need for protection in numbers. An emblematic do-gooder who offers them food has to run for her life. Their entry into Gerald's and Emily's smooth-running community is wholly destructive. The child gang has no structure, is simply a collection of individuals with no common purpose save personal survival and primitive dominance; they snatch at the food, rampage and destroy, drive everybody out and colonise the place overnight, so that they are discovered in possession in the morning, scratching among the half-cooked rats that they resemble. The commune, with its principles of cooperative feeding and mutuality, is destroyed. Their trashing of Gerald's house is described as an irreversible destruction of the organic.

Gerald's and Emily's ameliorative attempt to impose discipline on the rampaging small children is met only with fierce attack. Gerald, who will not relinquish responsibility, seeks them out after they have fled, insisting that not saving them would be tantamount to blaming them for what is clearly society's failure. The problem is that he surrenders himself to their mores and when he and two children who bring supplies to Emily and the narrator stay to eat a meal, it is evident that Gerald has given up attempting to 'correct' their manners; his mute appeal to Emily claims that she could help to civilise them, but she recognises the compelling force of the group that has incorporated Gerald; there is no doubt that the group is more powerful than the individual. Lessing is quite unsentimental concerning both the limitations of the individual and the (in)effectiveness of liberal humanist ideals in the face of social, political and psychological realities. Eventually, for all his sacrifice, Gerald is shown to be as vulnerable to attack by the group as anyone, insider or public at large; his despair renders him 'different' and the volatile gang pelt him with stones. Finally coming to share Emily's apprehension of the danger of getting sucked into amorality and cannibalism, Gerald abandons the gang and suspends his idealistic struggle.

Yet the children are not ultimately condemned, either by Gerald or the narration. These children of anarchy who have not been 'good babies' or learned a place in the social hierarchy are as much victims as wreckers, and notions of original sin or inherent evil are as inappropriate as Rousseauesque ideas of essential innocence (a point that applies equally to the amoral Ben in *The Fifth Child*). Yet it is a kind of innocence, or at least potential, that remains; at the transfiguring end of the novel, Gerald's hesitation on the brink of 'another order of world' is resolved, as he stands hand-in-hand with the four-year-old criminal, by the arrival of 'his' children at the last moment, running after him and with him, into the future.

To summarise the social action of the novel, the breakdown of society at large is mirrored in the breakup of family (Gerald's first household), directly attributable to a release of savagery (Gerald's second gang of children) occasioned by society's failures and characterised by a lack of group coherence and mutual care or cooperation. This is a logical development from the burglary of the narrator's flat by June and others of the first household; as Emily explains, this robbery is a kind of compliment, attributing to the narrator the generosity of non-attachment. The child gang, by contrast, despite accompanying Gerald on pleasant visits to the flat, could as easily kill and eat Hugo, or even Emily, as bring presents: there is no behavioural norm.

It is worth pointing out that the children's cannibalistic behaviour should be seen as dystopian rather than primitive. Almost all anthropological studies suggest the most precise and rule-bound rituals for 'primitive' cannibalism.[8] The whole point is that this group is the product of post-civilized, negative socialisation. This is why the children are portrayed as so young; like so-called wolf-children, they have been taught nothing, have learned only how to survive.[9] The fundamental interpersonal and social act has been withheld from them: they have not been fed. The children are deprived and unnourished, physically, psychically and socially, to the extent that they are unable to accept food (attacking the do-gooder who tries to feed them) or to function as social beings. The 'old' society has its faults, but its representatives and descendants care for others: the narrator and Emily look after and cook for each other and feed and care for Hugo; Gerald has a deep sense of commitment; even the rigid and unloving mother-figure behind the wall provides the minimum to instil a sense of responsibility. This is why the moving on from this 'collapsed' world at the ending of the novel includes all these representative figures as well as the children yet to be socialised; the glimpsed scene towards which they move may be something like the earlier behind-the-wall image of people working together to bring a dull carpet to life, a vision of social harmony where there is no competition but only high-minded and loving cooperation.

Lessing develops her interest in the metaphysical in two further novels whose endings see characters transcending their physical selves: *The Marriages Between Zones Three, Four and Five* and *The Making of the Representative for Planet 8*.[10] In these 'space-fiction' novels the idea of social eating has implications that link the interpersonal and societal perspectives outlined here with a desired advancement towards transcendence of the physical as a means to communion, as discussed earlier in chapter 3. As Kate Fullbrook points out, whereas the orientation of modern world is towards individual experience, Lessing's interest tends rather towards collectivity and a communion the central character in *The Sirian Experiments* articulates as 'the group mind, the collective minds we are all part of'.[11]

The inculcation of individuals into some sort of collectivity constitutes the process of socialisation (so truncated in *Memoirs*), part of which – as the previous chapter's discussion of taste indicates – involves the social construction of appetites and preferences. Whether people eat a main meal at ten o'clock in the morning or four in the afternoon or simply eat whenever the need is felt, and whether the meal consists of raw flesh or cooked porridge, is entirely a matter of convention. For people within a particular social group its conventions seem to be natural or normal; it is only in comparison with those of different societies that specific customs begin to appear peculiar. We habitually define ourselves in relation to what is other and this is nowhere more evident than in questions of food (as both Visser and Farb and Armelagos illustrate). In *The Marriages Between Zones Three, Four and Five* Lessing sets up three different sets of convention concerning food, to reflect the differences between the societies of each Zone. Indeed, the food itself is different. The people of the matriarchal Zone Three, peaceful and telepathic, eat little of a light, almost wholly vegetarian diet; their regime where possible consists only of fruits and grains and does not involve even the killing or uprooting of plants: this is empathetic and ideological eating. Zone Four, being a military society, features mess catering, heavy drinking and meat-eating. The nomadic fighting tribes of Zone Five live on dried food and the milk of their mares. Whereas Lessing creates no evident demarcations within each zone as to who eats what, the contrasts between zones reinforce each zone's separate identity.

The mores of the zones vary along with their kinds of food. Zone Five is the most unsocialised, anarchistic, immediate in the satisfaction of physical appetites, without sexual ceremony or communal meals; Vahshi and her Zone Five warriors are impulsive and they childishly indulge their desires, characteristics graphically reflected in Vahshi's 'dismantling' of two chickens and the description of her 'rummaging in her chicken carcasses for titbits and licking her fingers in a way which both shocked and tantalized her bridegroom' (255). An energetic spirit of excess is manifest; the wedding feast lasts for a week, with great platters of whole sheep and calves. Such eating is more a matter of ritual than the satisfaction of hunger; the purpose of feasting and sacrifice is for the occasion to be magnificent and unforgettable, a ceremonial to establish precedents and recall the grandeur of similar events in history.

By comparison with such brio the disciplined eating of Zone Four appears without spirit or imagination, the deadening victory of an aggressive rationalism; Zone Four controls passions and animality with laws and regulations, military routines (camp kitchens) and the force of internalised custom, something Al·Ith discovers in her surprised desire to lick her baby. The heavy food, patriarchal authority and emphasis on the passions in Zone Four are seen as primitive, undeveloped and boorish by the Buddhistic society of Zone Three, where the ascetic, the aesthetic and the empathetic are combined in both eating and social behaviour. By comparison with Vahshi's immoderate wedding, the marriage of Al·Ith, 'Queen' of Zone Three, to Ben Ata is heralded by no feast or celebration, and it is only after a period of mutual suspicion and strife that they eat together. In Zone Three there is great sympathy with the natural world (they commune with their animals and send messages by tree) and an automatic hospitality born of a detachment from desire that goes hand in hand with their asceticism. Zone Two is peopled, if that is the right word, by the wholly disembodied.

Just as the stifling of omnivorousness in *Memoirs* is shown to be crippling, so closed frontiers – geographical, cultural and culinary – encourage a sense of absolutism in the zones about what should truly be seen as conventional. The project of breaking down the borders, set in motion by the Providers, is a momentous one, characterised in the realized idiom that they do not even breathe the same air. It is indicative that Ben Ata and Al·Ith do not eat together for such a long time, and that it is not until Al·Ith is pregnant that they eat the same food. Furthermore, when Ben Ata tastes the honey and nut dish Al·Ith has desired, he rolls his eyes in disbelief at the idea of its doing her and his future son any good. As Margaret Visser points out, it is often the small ethnic differences (tea poured until it overflows into the saucer rather than eating sheep's eyes) that are most disturbing, perhaps because we are unprepared for them. So, for example, the visiting women of Zone Four are nonplussed by the fact of breakfast in Zone Three. It is not until Al·Ith and Ben Ata have reached a considerable degree of intimacy, figured in almost perpetual mutual nakedness, that they find they can no longer conjure separate foods and are supplied with stewed beans and bread from the officers' mess – a suitable compromise between the light fruits and grains of Zone Three and the heavy meats and proteins of Zone Four – which they eat together with hungry relish.

The boundary-breaking union is not easy, however, and – taking place as it does entirely *within* Zone Four – neither does it effect a wholesale transformation in the relations between the zones. Indeed, Al·Ith is effectively made a scapegoat by Zone Three, being blamed for the malaise that is to be cured by the marriage, and she is marginalised once the marriage is effected and is ultimately exiled. She is herself changed by entry into Zone Four: 'Do you know that as soon as I cross into your land I cease to be my real self? Everything I say comes out distorted and different. Or if I manage to *be* as I *am*, then it is so hard, that in itself makes everything different' (125). What she identifies is evolution rather than revolution; just as small differences may be more disturbing than large ones, so apparently marginal shifts begin to dislodge the stasis that produced sterility. Al·Ith's comment when she learns of the Zone Four punishment for gazing towards Zone Three is revealingly ambiguous; telling Ben Ata that it never occurs to the people in Zone Three to look beyond their borders, she says 'We are too prosperous, too happy, everything is so comfortable and pleasant with us' (95). It is precisely her unexpected apprehension of the cosiness and complacency of her own people that drives Al·Ith to explore the borders with Zone Two. Without her initially unwilling sojourn in Zone Four, she would not be able to realize her yearning for Zone Two, eventually paving the way for like-minded followers.

As might be expected, Zone Two is at the furthest point of the scale from animality, representing an ideal for those who feel an inadequacy in Zone Three. Interestingly, though, it is not reaching the summit of entry to Zone Two that is shown to be the triumph, but the opening up of the possibility to do so. Al·Ith is, in this sense, representative. The reformation wrought through her acceptance of responsibility and the sacrifice of one group's contentment to the higher good of growth and change result in a metaphorical airing: 'a lightness, a freshness, and an enquiry and a remaking and an inspiration where there had been only stagnation' (299).

The gradual retreat from physical embodiment illustrated by increasing references to Al·Ith as thin, worn, burnt out, dried up, is repeated in *The Making of the Representative for Planet 8*, only here it is more overt, radical and inevitable, since there is no alternative but death. Restraint from eating for a higher social purpose, connected with the acquisition of telepathic abilities in *The Four Gated City* and *The Golden Notebook*, is in these books developed into a transcendence of the physical body itself. Just as Al·Ith's culminating disembodiment can only be achieved after she has forged a communion with another society – suggested most intimately in her eating with Ben Ata – so the transfiguration of Planet 8's representatives, again enacted through food and its lack, results from the exhaustion of resources and their combined efforts to provide for the dying inhabitants.

It is worth adding a word about the status of the representative and its relation to social eating. Social eating is not simply a question of group function, but is linked with the (political) relation of individuals or groups to bigger groups and thus to society at large, and this must almost inevitably be by way of representative figures. While it might be argued that many if not all of Lessing's characters are in some sense 'representative', in her space-fiction novels the individuals bear a notably public or social burden. The metaphorical or even mythical dimension of these narratives confirms the importance of characters' roles in and on behalf of their society. In *The Making of the Representative for Planet 8* in particular, there is an almost total lack of individual characterisation, the inhabitants being named according to whichever function gives them their identity at the time: Masson the Builder, Pedug the Teacher, Marl the Keeper of Herds (so that a change of function, e.g. from builder to teacher, would entail a change of name from Masson to Pedug). Even the narrator, Doeg, 'Memory Maker and Keeper of Records', is undifferentiated in terms of sex, family or age; individualism is subordinated to the importance of the person's role in society. The 'representative' of the title is an extension of this social function: a compound social being.

This social or group being is only achieved through the most extreme circumstances detailed in the novel. (The extremity of the circumstances is of the essence; in her 'Afterword' to the novel, Lessing ascribes her interest in Scott's expeditions to Antarctica in part to the expedition's engagement with extreme conditions which she sees as 'an attempt to transcend themselves' (176)). As in the *Marriages'* zones, the inhabitants of Planet 8 are forced by external circumstances to abandon their perceptions of life as fixed, immutable; as Canopus says, there is too much 'earth' in their conception and they need to learn that everything is subject to change. As the ice comes and the crops fail, so their diet and way of life are forced to adjust, and they crowd hungrily together. The light diet of fruit and cereals and vegetables so reminiscent of Zone

Three gives way to cheeses and fatty meat; their bright clothes are replaced by heavy coats and skins; slowly the people become coarsened, thickset and greasy, as grey as their surroundings.

The social harmony of their once stable and egalitarian planet is subjected to severe strain. Initial cooperation in the face of crisis (the building of the wall, the breeding of new animals) gives way to a sense of alienation:

we were not at ease with even the smallest and most ordinary and often-repeated things in our daily lives, from the putting on of the heavy coats to the preparing of the fatty meat which was our staple food . . . There seemed to be nothing left to us that was instinctive and therefore joyful, or ordinarily pleasurable. We were foreign to ourselves as much as to our surroundings. And therefore groups, and crowds, sank easily and often into silences. (49)

The alienation is social; 'groups' and 'crowds' fall silent, feel uneasy in their skins, are sapped of joy. The bemoaning of a lack of 'instinctive' joyful or pleasurable behaviour suggests that learned social responses have become inappropriate, that a change is necessary to adapt to the altered circumstances. The shift in behaviour over the society as a whole is a predictably negative one.[12] Sharp increases in crime and violence are reported from various parts of the planet: casual looting, murder, battles over shelter and food riots become commonplace, and Doeg horrifies himself by his 'instinctive' (though recalled) gesture in snatching Johor's red fruits. Along with the violence goes a decrease in caring, because of the cold and misery and the fact that death seems almost welcome. The stasis of Zone Three recurs with depressive interest.

The extremity of the circumstances and the poverty of social response expose the society's cherished beliefs. According to Jeannette King, it is the 'deification' of Canopus that is revealed as faulty. The people regard Canopus not only as their 'maker' for having brought them to the planet, but as their rescuer in promised removal to Rohanda; in awaiting rescue they become passive and fail to help themselves, taking refuge in dreams of heaven.[13] Their reliance on deliverance is mistaken, for Canopus only sends food and shelter, and in the end, with the greatest reluctance, they are forced to abandon their expectations. The sacred, inviolate ocean is eventually harvested for the sake of the starving. Just as their eating practices are adaptive, so in the end is their ideology, and the sense of 'solidity', 'immobility' and 'permanence' which had prevailed when the planet seemed stable is revealed as chimerical. Slowly, the representatives, at least, begin to feel perceptual movement: on their journey around the planet they huddle together to eat their 'tasteless and disagreeable' dried meat and half-frozen roots and to doze, 'as if we were one organism, not many – as if our separate unique individualities had become another burden that had to be shed, like unnecessary movement. Yet we *were* in movement . . . alone of our peoples we felt some kind of restlessness . . .' (64).

It is these representative figures with their first flickering of understanding who are able to carry the spirit of Planet 8 forward into the future. But first they have much to learn, which they do in long slow conversations with Johor, through wordless communication with each other as a group and through feeding their fellows and helping them not to die. Their struggles change them all, and the Representatives come to understand that they are none of them alone but form part of the whole, just as each individual is a collection of atoms. Notwithstanding the inevitability of death they feel there is no choice but to go on pulling the last creatures from the lake and chasing the blue plants of the summer to feed life into the starving. The sense of personal submission to a greater good is acutely and empathetically evoked through the lust for food:

I felt myself being drawn across the ice to the edges of the pond, my hands out, my mouth filled with need, already tasting the crunching salty freshness – but I was brought to a halt before I took one up off the ice and bit into it. And others too, like myself, stumbled towards the food, but stopped, and we were all thinking of those starving in their ice houses, or going about their work, starving. (138–9)

It is only when they face what they know is the end of the planet and realise that they have gone beyond the need to eat that they wait and watch and begin to understand what Doeg had long ago known would be 'some new possibilities of growth' (73). Social eating was the busy enactment of social being, an ideal condition depicted ultimately in the metaphysical transformation of the Representatives into the Representative: 'like a shoal of fishes or a flock of birds; one, but a conglomerate of individuals – each with its little thoughts and feelings, but these shared with the others, tides of thought, of feeling, moving in and out and around, making the several one' (159). What Lessing explicitly sets up in her Canopean empire is something she undertakes again and again: an exploration of what it means – for the individual, the group and society – to be a social being. Whether in fantastic, mythical or realist settings, cooking, feeding and eating are in Lessing's writing connected with questions of social behaviour. Providing or sharing food could even be said to be the principal enactment of social responsibility.

When Lessing returns to a solidly realist mode, in *The Diaries of Jane*

Somers (published just after *The Making of the Representative*, in 1983 and 1984), the provision of food indicates an assumption of responsibility. As outlined earlier in chapter 3, the first triumph of the *Diaries'* protagonist, Janna, is to overcome the reluctance and even repulsion she experiences when faced with the aged and sick, through her unlikely friendship with the lonely, poor and irascible old Maudie Fowler. Janna's relationship with Maudie is contrasted to philanthropic initiatives; before Janna meets Maudie she has tried and rejected visiting the old on Sundays with 'cake and sympathy', and later several times resents the suggestion that she is a 'Good Neighbour'. As a friend, she is set against all the perceived enemies who have official functions: 'Council Women', Home Helps, doctors, District Nurses, people who might put Maudie into a Home – the idea of which reverberates throughout the book as both a threat (for the old) and a tempting solution (for the young and the hard-pressed). The spectre of old people's homes in particular provokes reflection about how a society values its members, if social perceptions of the old revolve around criteria of usefulness/uselessness.

It is through her friendship with Maudie that Janna becomes aware of other old ladies, begins to look after, visit and buy food for them too and is drawn into dealing with the Social Services on their behalf. Both Janna and the old ladies are in some sense representative, at least of their time and class. Janna's actions, specifically distanced from institutional-ised middle-class do-gooding (generally given a hard time by Lessing), raise some doubts as to the effectiveness of public services in catering to personal needs; Meals on Wheels and Thermos tea are contrasted to cakes and conversation, a nice piece of fish, a companionable glass of scotch. Notwithstanding Janna's empathy and goodwill, these are not easy relationships; differences in age, fitness, class and money make for unbridgeable inequalities and minefields of potential offence. Janna rec-ognises this: 'To involve oneself with the infinitely deprived means you take on a weight of guilt. They need so much: you can give so little' (229). The little is incremental, however and Janna is shown to give more than she thinks; she continues to visit and care for each of her old women right up to the time they die, which in the case of Annie Reeves spans a period of more than five years.

In *The Good Terrorist* the connection between the provision of food and responsibility is more complex and more difficult as Lessing explicitly examines relationships within and between a highly marginal social group and its society. To refer to the squatters as a group is even slightly misleading, since much of the novel has to do with the problematic nature of the collective and its boundaries; it is difficult to reconcile aspirations for cohesion with behaviour that is essentially antisocial, disruptive. What defines the constitution of this group is an open question: does it consist solely of the revolutionaries, in which case Jim (the squat's original resident), Philip the builder, and the more conventional Mary and Reggie never really belong, or does participation in the domestic arrangements of the house constitute the unifying factor, in which case the passive Bert, Jasper and Faye become marginal? Or, should they simply be defined by who eats together? Alice, who with her overwhelming desire for a family is the driving force behind the development of the squat and the coming together of the inhabitants, is the only one with an ideal of coherence.

The group's difficulty in cohering is vividly illustrated in the conflict over take-away food, which rapidly becomes the focus of discussions about regularising the squat. Alice argues that the additional cost of rates and services could be offset by cheap communal cooking and eating instead of buying take-aways and eating out, which as Pat points out is expensive. The problem is that such a shift in living patterns involves a potential infringement of autonomy that strikes at the heart of the deliberately uncommitted relationships of the group. Faye's barely controlled response to the proposal, asserting a childish resistance to any kind of incorporation, voices a profound if unacknowledged truth about all the members of the group: '"Just a minute, comrades," said she. "Suppose I like take-away? I like take-away, see? Suppose I like eating out, when the fancy takes me? How about that, then?"'[14] 'When the fancy takes me' is all important: not only do the individual squat members jealously guard their personal freedoms, they act, by and large, according to whim. Like the rest of the group, Faye is split: even as she asserts resistance and autonomy she is wholly dependent on the motherly Roberta. Each member of the group displays a profoundly childish, egocentric refusal to submit herself or himself to a common good, in fact to take proper responsibility, preoccupied as they are with their own agendas.

Alice's cost-effective view prevails, endorsed by Pat's confirmation from her previous experience and by the unusually and minimally expressed loyalty of Alice's homosexual companion Jasper: ' "Alice is good at feeding people cheap" ' (31). But Alice too has hidden motivation. Driven by childhood rage and misery, she seeks to (re)create the family she feels she was denied; now placing herself in the powerful maternal position, she mothers not only Jasper but Jim, Philip, even the stray cat, attempting to quiet her own doubts and misgivings:

Oh yes, all this love and harmony was precarious enough, Alice was thinking as she sat and smiled; just one little thing, puff! and it would be gone. Meanwhile, she put both hands around her mug of coffee, feeling how its warmth fed her, and thought: It is like a family, it *is*. (248–9)

The shift she engineers has not only economic and emotional dimensions, but class ones too. As Faye points out, Alice's domestic standards are distinctly bourgeois, and her dealings with the authorities demonstrate a confident manipulation of middle-class discourses. She is nutritionally and hygienically well-educated, worrying about cholesterol and health hazards, and opting always for the healthy, 'good' alternative.

Ironically, her fastidiousness distances her from the very people with whom in theory she wishes to identify, as when, for example, she sits in Fred's Caff, saying 'dutifully' to herself that the customers are the salt of the earth, for she is repelled by the fact that they eat cholesterol-laden food, look pallid and greasy and read the *Sun* or the *Daily Mirror*. In the end she takes comfort in the notion that they are 'only lumpens', labourers, perhaps even self-employed and thus not the men who would rescue Britain – a rationalisation that points up the gap between revolutionary theory and (self-deceiving) practice. Her middle-class fastidiousness is echoed and parodied when she and Jasper, Pat and Bert, after a visit next door, return to the kitchen where they have recently eaten their different take-aways and come upon Mary and Reggie in the kitchen: 'eating properly off plates. The mess of pizza fragments, uneaten chips, beercans, papers, had been swept into the litter bin' (188).

Just as the cohesion and identity of the group is never properly effected, so its relationship with the world of authority – establishment and revolutionary – is woolly and ill-defined, an irresolution equally reflected in their eating practices. Unlike the truly resourceful group surrounding Emily and Gerald in *Memoirs*, these petty anarchists establish no counter-capitalist or alternative system; far from becoming the norm, cheap nourishing food is obstinately associated solely with Alice: 'her' soups. It is only when Roberta is away that Faye shows Alice how to make a vegetable stew that they all enjoy, though even here Faye does not take responsibility for cooking the meal. When, eventually, someone other than Alice brings in 'real' food, it is Caroline, 'good daughter of the middle classes' (309), who cooks for Alice with secret and almost professional relish; this, along with her brisk taking of sugar in her tea ('a gesture that announced self-determination' (269)), suggests a distance from the group as a whole which is borne out in her decisive rejection of the bombing plan when she realises the others are careless of casualties.

Despite Alice's efforts, the group only temporarily holds together, since the private needs of its individual members – even when acting in the name of ideology – are privileged over its collectivity. Eating out and the bringing in of take-away food continue alongside the provision of Alice's soups. Alice too eats elsewhere: she scrounges from her mother, raids the fridge at her Aunt Theresa's, takes Jim out to celebrate his job with fish and chips, takes tea at the Savoy on a spree with Pat, follows breakfast at Fred's Caff with a move to another café where she feels more at home eating wholemeal buns and honey. Indeed, it is Alice who suggests going to a café when it becomes difficult to talk in the house and happily agrees to go out for a cheering-up meal with Jasper when they have run out of money. Each foray against 'society' is marked or celebrated by eating commercially prepared food. Towards the climax of the book, when the bombing is being planned and executed, the 'comrades' celebrate their choice of target by going to the local Indian restaurant. Then they go out for tea and to the cinema after reconnoitring the target, and they wind up for supper again at 'their' Indian restaurant. And when they have installed the explosives in the car they go, despite the recognition that they are noisy and noticeable, to an all-night café for a meal together: ' "To hell with it," had said Jocelin, and "Fuck that," had said Bert' (369).

How, then, do the group's eating practices characterise them and reflect their connection with society at large? This 'Communist' anarchistic opportunist group, themselves rejected in many ways, both reject and exploit what they reject; they consume the edible products of the society they condemn with only sporadic and ineffectual efforts at a culinary separatism that might express independence and solidarity. Their heedless inconsistency, their failure to assume responsibility and think through what they are about, is consonant with Dorothy Mellings's disillusioned view of them as spoiled children, 'running about playing at revolutions, playing little games, thinking you're important' (354), and Caroline's dismissal of their action and analysis as 'amateur'. What the house offers as a symbol of the social body is never developed; only Alice, Pat (who leaves) and Philip (who is not of the group, and dies anyway) strive to make it functional. Social eating, the group currency, is either a one-way transaction, in which Alice cooks and the others eat, or a value-free commercial purchase which does nothing to reinforce a sense of working together towards something they all believe in.

There is, it must be said, nothing 'natural' about social eating, for, like taste and appetite, consideration for others is a social, even political, construction. The commune's heedless impulse towards personal satisfaction is indicative of the unevolved state of their consciousnesses, whether seen from a political, social, psychological or mystical point of view. Utopian communion is not really in question, however, and any 'ideal' model of social eating would be prescriptive, probably bland and unrealistic. Lessing, more comprehensively, displays a robust recognition of social struggle, of deprivation, intractability and that in humans which is inimical to society.

This hard nub of the unsocialisable is explored in *The Fifth Child*, when a harmonious and smoothly functioning social group is disrupted by the unsocialisable Ben, the fifth child, who destroys Harriet's and David's romantic notion of a (natural) happy family. There are numerous indications of Ben's otherness even before his birth: the 'impossibility' of his conception, the violence of his inter-uterine movements, the listless irritability and distress of Harriet and her appetite: 'enormous, insatiable – so bad she was ashamed and raided the fridge when no one could see her. She would interrupt her nocturnal peregrinations to stuff into herself anything she could find to eat. She even had secret caches like an alcoholic's hoards, only it was food: chocolate, bread, pies' (54). In this family of plenty (albeit sustained by the grandparents), where it is characteristic for everyone, together around the large table, to be supplied with liberal helpings of food, such secrecy and gorging are uncharacteristically antisocial, suggesting alienation, even perversion.

An appetite that is socially shameful and yet which may not be denied foreshadows Ben's resistance to socialisation through the training of eating habits. Ben resists from the first: like a monstrous inversion of Melanie Klein's infant, he sucks his mother's breast dry; he roars for food; he bites with intent. Significantly, his first words are not 'Mummy' or 'Daddy', but 'I want cake'.[15] As he grows he acquires a facade of normality, learning through imitating his siblings not to talk with his mouth full or eat with his mouth open, but this can barely conceal his fierce animal energy. Ben's superficial conformity does not extend to the absorption of socially endorsed food preferences and eating practices instrumental in the construction of social identity. This is startlingly revealed when his mother finds him squatting on the kitchen table over a dismembered raw chicken. His Shakespearean response to her scolding is merely 'Poor Ben hungry.'[16]

Ben is constitutionally unable to join and share, as his uncompromising 'I want cake', 'I want milk' suggest; he has strong, competitive, individualistic survival instincts that make no connection with others. This

is mirrored in his inability to perceive narrative (that fundamental communicative act by means of which we construct identities, both social
and individual) and provides a vivid indication of his incapacity to
become socialised. Though Ben's siblings try at first to help him they
progressively withdraw until the family splits apart. The causal connection is unmistakable: it is precisely because Ben is not incorporated by
the family group that it is destroyed by him.

Yet Ben does achieve an enculturation of sorts. The first group to offer
him some kind of acceptance do so for money. Unemployed, hanging
out at 'Betty's Caff' and devoting themselves to motor bikes, they form
a marginalised and alienated subgroup of working-class culture, and
though they treat him as a pet and call him names, he does, through
them, acquire some skills: 'Half a plate of chips, half price big plate of
chips . . . Shut the door, because it is cold . . . Eat with a spoon, not with
fingers . . . Hold on tight going around corners' (118). Their recognition
of him and their tolerance exist precisely because they are themselves
marginal; as Harriet acknowledges to herself, it is the experts and
doctors who fail to understand, for such experts cannot and will not
accept that Ben lies outside their terms of reference.

In due course, a collection of educational and social rejects gravitate
towards Ben. As with the children of *Memoirs*, a group identity is constituted by the negatives or absences they hold in common. They all play
truant, watching television for hours, raiding the fridge, bringing in fast
food or roaming off as a gang in the town or to the seaside. Not merely
unemployed and marginalised, this group is unemployable, and probably criminal, living only for their own thrills and pleasures and quite
outside the norms and strictures of their society. As their antisocial behaviour grows bolder, so their taste expands to encompass wider areas:
'foodstuffs that originated in a dozen countries. Pizzas, and quiches;
Chinese food, and Indian; pita bread filled with salad; tacos, tortillas,
samosas, chili con carne; pies and pasties and sandwiches' (154).
Through their eating, they are metaphorically drawn towards the only
society they could belong to, a nomadic, polyglot underworld, peopled
by the unassimilable and overlooked, those whom society can neither
label nor incorporate, who can eat ('Give me cake.' 'Bring me Coke.')
but never share, never cook.

Like Gerald's gang of children in *Memoirs* (to whom, with Gerald,
Emily, Hugo and the narrator, the future belongs), these social misfits do
form a social group, even if it is defined by negatives. But equally,
like that of the chaotic squatters of *The Good Terrorist*, their eating never

realises what might be seen as its radical potential, except inasmuch as it cuts across boundaries, subverts custom and contributes to the collapse of order. In both cases, the social or political import lies not so much in what these subgroups establish as in what they subvert. Neither the inhabitants of Alice's squat nor Ben's gang can offer a cohesive, let alone coherent, alternative to the established, habitual social patterns of consuming against which (among other things) they rebel. Instead, their peculiar, antisocial versions of social eating exert a disruptive, iconoclastic pressure. Social eating here becomes so, and becomes political, not by dint of communion and solidarity, but by refusal and rejection.

Ben's case is further complicated by the fact that it is his refusal or failure to be a social being that leads to his being incarcerated, drugged and starved, as a result of which he becomes both more malleable, since he can now be threatened, and more alienated. The situation is a little different for the characters in *Memoirs*. The very real possibility of starvation itself acts as a radicalising force; the gang of small children, whose lives are filled with hunger and fighting, come together simply for protection in numbers, but their collectivity grants them visibility. Their subsequent actions against the 'haves' are unsuccessful inasmuch as they confirm their own exclusion and deprivation, but they serve to further strengthen the identity of the gang, and ultimately gain them the care if not the control proffered by Gerald.

An assumption implicit in much of this argument, especially concerning *The Good Terrorist*, is that when people come together for the collective purpose of eating there is potential for some sort of radicalisation. The juxtaposition of shifts and changes with social eating in *The Marriages* (especially the all-women ceremonies) and the frequency with which the comrades eat together in the 'Children of Violence' novels suggest as much. Radical potential must nevertheless depend to some extent on circumstances; the quip 'let them eat cake' would hardly be likely to inflame a mob with full bellies, and the actual effects of eating are frequently soporific. Equally, the traditions, rituals and celebratory nature of much social eating are almost by definition conservative.

The question of radicalisation is, therefore, problematic. None the less, since Angela Carter's self-proclaimed stance is radical, if not subversive, the concluding part of this chapter will look at her final two novels as a way of exploring the political significance of social eating (not that Carter only politicises social eating, indeed her cannibalistic, vampiric and sexual eaters are highly suggestive political figures). Given her use of non-realist modes, this is by no means a straightforward matter of looking for socialist suppers, though Lizzie's communistic mutterings in *Nights at the Circus* (like the sabotaging effects of the *bombe surprise*) do offer a sort of dialectic. More comprehensively, and with varying degrees of subtlety and obliqueness, *Nights at the Circus* suggests several means by which social or communicative eating can be politicised: through the encouragement of solidarity, when the eating together leads to subversive activity or because social eating is associated with some sort of perspectival shift in time and space.

Solidarity in Carter's writing tends, on the whole, to be female, though it is not exclusively so, and neither are all women included. Ironically, the traitorous women who eschew sisterhood are often themselves cooks: Saskia in *Wise Children*, for example, or the drunken cook at Madame Schreck's house of freaks in *Nights at the Circus*. Here the 'freak' women look out for each other; the capable and loving Fanny takes responsibility for feeding Sleeping Beauty, prepares food for the other women when the drunken cook is comatose, and most notably sends Toussaint out for a piece of pork on Fevvers's last day, as well as organising the women's – and Toussaint's – flight. Though equally oppressed, Toussaint is distinguished from the women by his refusal to take part in the *tableaux vivants* and by his lack of a mouth, an absence emblematic of his silenced oppression, but which also prevents him from eating other than by means of a tube through his nose; although he is thus with the oppressed women, he is not of them.

At Nelson's brothel there is still greater expression of solidarity, though not so much in the face of occupational oppression as against the 'horrors' of the outside, including, we must assume, those of masculinity. The house is decidedly and wholly female, even down to its dog and fecund cats: 'a sub-text of fertility underwrote the glittering sterility of the pleasure of the flesh available within the academy',[17] simultaneous 'fertility' and 'sterility' offering a challenge to polarised views of female potential. Interestingly enough, there is no mention of food or eating among all the sex and industry until Ma Nelson's death; it is over the funeral baked meats that the harsh (masculine and religious) external world breaks in, in the shape of Nelson's unforgiving Nonconformist elder brother. Though he upends the pork pies and vintage port in righteous rage as he gives the women notice to leave the following morning, it is they who have the last laugh. After a valedictory bottle of port and piece of fruitcake, the women give Ma Nelson a heroic send-off by setting fire to the house.

The women's solidarity persists until the fire is burning well, at which point they disperse to their separate new lives. Thus the only occasions on which this group of women are seen to eat together are at the funeral, at which their solidarity is defensively triggered by attack from without (inflaming their grief into full-blown grievance), and the farewell snack which, echoing the previous communal eating and recalling their shared past, precipitates their collective act of reprisal. Not only does their eating as a group express communion and solidarity, it leads directly to insurgent action. Subversive solidarity is similarly generated over food in the Siberian ('House of Correction') panopticon, as first Olga Alexandrovna, touching the guard's gloved hand that holds her break-fast, and then all of the prisoners and guards breach the distinction between guard and guarded and the boundaries between prisoners. Notes and drawings are secreted in bread rolls, glances exchanged through grilles, touches and caresses sneaked in exercise periods. When the incarcerated prisoners and guards unite against the surveillant Countess, they equip themselves with bread and sausage, before setting off to found the republic of free women.

The panopticon is watched over not only by the Countess but by a clock adjusted not to local time but to Moscow time, a clock that regu-lates every minute of their imprisonment. The space and time in which the women are located are brought together under control, parcelled up like the black bread, broth and porridge the prisoners are fed, morning and evening. The united women's act of liberation results in the destruc-tion of the clock, the symbolic stopping of regulated time, so that they move from the global, regulated world of the panopticon into regional, unmarked time and the local anonymity of the taiga.

According to Anthony Giddens, modernity is characterised by a dis-connection between time and space (and place) and the 'emptying' of both. This he contrasts with pre-modern societies, in which time-reckoning required socio-spatial markers; 'when', as he puts it, was inseparable from 'where' or from things that happen regularly in the natural world. In other words, clocks permit a measuring of time unre-lated to the activities that fill it. Space is similarly emptied, the modern dislocation between space and place giving rise to depersonalised com-munication: 'foster[ing] relations between "absent" others, locationally distant from any given situation of face-to-face interaction'.[18] Thus any particular locale may be shaped by social or political influences geo-graphically far removed. The panopticon futuristically embodies pre-cisely these modern dislocations, with its emptied space and Moscow time. The breaking of the panopticon clock suggests a refilling of time, for without such a timepiece the hours will have meaning only in relation to what they contain. Space is 'refilled' by its reconnection with place, a reconnection for which food and eating form a suitable vehicle.

In the case of the panopticon escape, such a refilling is clearly and intentionally political. The appropriation, or reappropriation, of time and space inevitably represents an arrogation of power, but where this is associated with eating – a thoroughly embodied activity – something of the filled quality of pre-modern social time pertains. So, just as theorising of the body aims to resist the fragmentations of postmodernism, so food and eating might be a way of resisting the dislocations of time, space and place, for it is difficult to imagine the satisfactions of a virtual dinner – unless for a virtual stomach. Time and space, occupied with the present activities of eating, expand to accommodate comradeship, collaboration, radical discourse, sedition.

In *Nights at the Circus* Carter deliberately invokes a pre-modern time frame, describing New Year's Eve 1900 at the end of the novel as 'the cusp of the modern age', of which the Siberians (and, the narrator suggests, most of the world's inhabitants) remain blissfully ignorant: 'the whole idea of the twentieth century, or any other century at all, for that matter, was a rum notion' (265). Carter exorcises modern time in other novels too, though less overtly. Most of *Heroes and Villains* takes place in a highly localised, timeless space; various episodes in *Dr Hoffman*, such as Desiderio's living and eating with the peepshow owner or river people, take place in a space outside time, and in *The Magic Toyshop* Finn recklessly cries 'There goes the time' as he breaks the cuckoo clock during their festive final breakfast.

There are also episodes in *Nights at the Circus* in which time and space are themselves shifted, as though they somehow cannot contain their content. The Clowns' supper is one such occasion, prefiguring both Buffo's last supper and the Clowns' departure. Over the fish soup and black bread Buffo expounds on the nature of the Clown, a sermon that gives way, with the help of vodka, to a dance: 'It seemed that they were dancing the room apart. As the baboushka slept, her too, too solid kitchen fell into pieces under the blows of their disorder as if it had been, all the time, an ingenious prop, and the purple Petersburg night inserted jagged wedges into the walls' (124). The radical content of the Clowns' supper threatens the disintegration of time and space, asserting the potential to invoke the end of the world, a reminder that collectivity and subversion are not of themselves a good.

But the major section of this novel in which time, at least, is shifted or appropriated is in Fevvers's heady initial narration. As she and Lizzie and Walser sit in her dressing room, she tells her story, accompanied by champagne and tea, and punctuated first by eel pies with mash from the local pie shop and later by bacon sandwiches from the all-night cab-stand. As Lizzie makes the first cup of tea, Big Ben strikes midnight for the second time; as she brings in the bacon sandwiches and makes more tea, it strikes for the third. The tea-drinking, eating, storytelling thus take place in a piece of suspended time, somehow achieved between Fevvers and Lizzie and Ma Nelson's clock, proof in itself, according to Fevvers, that time stands still. Indeed, Fevvers originally describes the clock as:

the sign, or signifier of Ma Nelson's little private realm . . . on which the hands stood always at either midnight or noon . . . for Ma Nelson said the clock in her reception room must show the dead centre of the day or night, the shadowless hour, the hour of vision and revelation, the still hour in the centre of the storm of time. (29)

The 'sign or signifier' (deliberately lacking a signified?) is, it seems, trans-ferable to Lizzie's and Fevvers's equally special realm. Time that stands still is story time, carnival time, larger-than-life time, an occasion for unsettling Walser's innocent New World certainties, and setting in motion a train of events in which all have to revise their ideas.

Walser does not eat either the pies or the bacon sandwiches, reserv-edly describing English food as 'an acquired taste' and 'the eighth wonder of the world' (22). He is also (mildly) adversely affected by the champagne and the tea. He both withholds himself and is located by the women as marginal to Fevvers's discourse. The eating focus is on Fevvers's large and uninhibited feasting, which serves both as a state-ment of Cockney solidarity (eel pies, food of the cabbies) and as a chal-lenge to Walser. But the main significance of the episodes relates, I think, to the interplay between the storytelling, the food and drink and gender politics. Much of Fevvers's narration during this night has to do with sis-terhood and with female surmounting of adversity. Walser is inveigled or hustled into the suspension of disbelief and criticism. The two addi-tional hours of night appropriated by the two women are filled with their story. Even the space is brimming with accoutrements of femininity, or the means by which it might be constructed: frilly drawers, silk stockings, corsets, *billets doux*, pots of rouge, powder, cold cream, although it also has a political dimension in the form of Lizzie's pamphlets, and the fem-ininity is not so much personal as generic, 'notable for its anonymity' (13).

The time and space annexed by Fevvers, by the Clowns, by the whole world of shows and circus is the time of carnival. *Nights at the Circus* is a thoroughly carnivalesque novel, as many commentators have pointed out, and Fevvers herself embodies much that accords with Bakhtin's analysis of carnival: association with popular culture, the subversion or reversal of the expected, overblown bodily function and above all the play of an inclusive, 'profoundly universal laughter', most evident at the end of the novel in the 'spiralling tornado' of Fevvers's laughter which looks set to envelop the world.[19]

Wise Children is, if anything, still more inclusively carnivalesque, and there are few intimations of what happens when the carnival is over. I will come back to this point, but first it is important to consider the nature of *Wise Children*'s carnival. According to Bakhtin, carnival is essentially opposed to 'official' culture, and is located on the borderline between art and life, two characteristics evident in Carter's choice of circus and music hall. Carter's carnival, both here and elsewhere, resembles the inclusive carnival which Bakhtin ascribes to the Middle Ages and which accentuates corporeality, flux and regeneration (as opposed to what he characterises as the more limited 'aesthetics of the beautiful' of the Renaissance or the emphasis on subjectivity and alienation of Romanticism and Modernism).[20]

Bakhtin claims that laughter effects a destruction of existing false hierarchies and the creation of new connections (specifically rooted in the body) in order to embrace fundamental realities.[21] As a trope for the expression of heresies, the undermining of legitimacy and the making of radical connections it appears ideal. Carnival, says Bakhtin, has a characteristic 'peculiar logic of the "inside out" (*à l'envers*), of the "turnabout", of a continual shifting from top to bottom, from front to rear, of numerous parodies and travesties, humiliations, profanations, comic crownings and uncrownings'.[22] All the elements listed in this quotation are easily identifiable in *Wise Children*, from the alternating humiliations of Tiffany and Tristram to the crown-play between the Hazard brothers. The 'turnabout' logic equally informs the deliberate evocation of carnival – including its subversiveness and emphasis on food, drink, bodies, sex and death – manifest in *Wise Children*, with its disingenuously artless pursuit of truth through a dizzying play of oppositions, doubleness, substitutions and the transgression of boundaries.

The novel is filled with contradictions and reversals, and the set piece feasts, the formal 'social eating' organised by those at the top of the hierarchy, are always undermined: the party that culminates in the burning down of Lynde Court; the sabotaged Hollywood Elizabethan engagement celebrations; Melchior's one hundredth birthday party with its unforseen revelations. (It is not only Bakhtin who is evoked, of course, but Shakespeare, in both the narrative content and in terms of plotting, coincidences, revelations and other romance characteristics, as well as textual allusion to almost all of his plays.[23]) Other oppositions contribute to the pattern: the themes of legitimacy and illegitimacy, the putative and disputed paternities, pregnancies, the opposition between theatre and music hall and the very polarities of negation and affirmation. Theatre is in decline and music hall diminished to crude revues, yet the whole culture of show business expressed in the twins' motto, the 'joy it is to dance and sing' is associated with renewal, multiple births and continuity. This renewal combines with the decline to produce an oxymoronic combination typical of what Bakhtin describes as the 'pregnant death' of grotesque realism, 'always conceiving', the aged body in proximity to the newborn, one body emerging from another.

One character almost single-handedly embodies carnival in *Wise Children*, and this is Uncle Peregrine, encapsulated as 'not so much a man, more of a travelling carnival'.[24] Of a generous physicality, growing ever larger as the book progresses, Peregrine is associated with eating, drinking, a profligate sexuality and repeated evanescence. He blows in on a wind full of butterflies, a reverse echo of the wind called up by Buffo's Clowns; he claims that 'Life's a carnival' (222) and is described as 'the heart and soul of mirth' (92), embracing the whole cast. He is, in short, a man of limitless and generous appetite, the source of crème de menthe, Fuller's walnut cake and cream buns drawn from Grandma's cleavage on the seafront at Brighton. His gargantuan size is not only a product of Dora's desire, but an indication of largeness of function. The erotic force of Uncle Peregrine offsets all the negating and entropic influences at work in the novel, including physical decline, so that he remains a potent redhead at a hundred years of age. This towering, Falstaffian figure stands for and emphasises the comprehensiveness of carnival, which through him encompasses all appetites – murder, incest, poisoning, cruelty, gourmandism, as well as 'laughter, forgiveness, generosity, reconciliation' (227).

Carter follows Bakhtin in embracing both negation and affirmation: 'Combined in the act of carnival laughter are death and rebirth, negation (a smirk) and affirmation (rejoicing laughter). This is a profoundly universal laughter, a laughter that contains a whole outlook on the world.'[25] Carnival is thus inclusive, and its subversive, democratising and regenerative functions are irresistible:

While carnival lasts, there is no other life outside it. During carnival time life is subject only to its laws, that is, the laws of its own freedom. It has a universal spirit; it is a special condition of the entire world, of the world's revival and renewal, in which all take part.[26]

However, Bakhtin states that this is only true *during* the carnival. Carter herself insists on the limitations of carnival, puncturing her romp through 'Pantoland' with the reminder that the essence of carnival is transience, that it offers release not revolution.[27] She makes much the same point in an interview, even to criticising a popularising of Bakhtin that (over)emphasises the subversive:

It's interesting that Bakhtin became very fashionable in the 1980s, during the demise of the particular kind of theory that would have put all kinds of question marks around the whole idea of the carnivalesque. I'm thinking about Marcuse and repressive desublimation, which tells you exactly what carnivals are for. The carnival has to stop. The whole point about the feast of fools is that things went on as they did before, after it stopped.[28]

Carter does not allow that anything might be changed by the carnival; on the contrary, in her view things go back to being exactly as they were. From this seemingly conservative perspective, the carnivalesque in Carter may be seen as in fact *less* subversive than her other writing, for the sting of the aberrant is drawn by legitimation or acceptance by the powers that be, and a sanctioned feast of fools has no real potency.[29] By this token, carnival's embracing of plurality, its very inclusiveness, is ultimately affirmatory rather than subversive. Marina Warner argues that Carter's 'comic disguise' constituted a kind of defeat in the face of Thatcherism, despite what she calls the 'heroic optimism' in the assertion of joy in *Wise Children*.[30] Persuasive as Warner may be, her argument depends on a particular view of humour and its function. Cast a more Carterish eye over the novel, loosen a little the totalising tendency of carnival, translate 'heroic optimism' into heroic defiance and the comedy – satirical, puncturing and rebellious as it is – takes a harder edge.

For, despite its prevalence, carnival is not the only frame within which food and eating may be examined, and it is worth considering finally whether the novel's overall championing of the illegitimate is politically relevant and whether whatever might be called social eating in *Wise*

Children in any way radicalises the spurned and marginalised. The eating habits of the 'illegitimate' branch of the family certainly seem to be endorsed as a traditional, potentially nostalgia-inducing diet of the impoverished: the Chance twins ingest bread and dripping and jam, Grandma's odorous cabbage, crumpets, poached eggs at Joe Lyons, sausage rolls and Scotch eggs as young hoofers, bacon and bacon sandwiches as adults – and they drink cup after cup of tea, as well as gin.

When Uncle Peregrine swoops into the picture, the food takes an extravagant turn, as it does on the Brighton beach picnic, with ham and chicken and foie gras and champagne. But when the eating occasion takes place in a highly 'legitimate' and public space, an element of discomfort is introduced, for example at the Chance twins' birthday meal at the Savoy Grill:

> there we were, us girls, done up to the nines, little navy suits, gloves to match, red hats with big brims down over one eye, nice shoes, nice handbags, trying to look as if [Grandma] didn't belong to us, and Peregrine, at ease, as ever, enjoying every minute, the bastard.
>
> The waiter hovered: 'For the first course may I suggest oysters, caviar, smoked salmon . . . ' 'That sounds quayte nayce, thanks very much,' she said so she had all three, washing them festively down with crème de menthe, lifting her pinky like a dog lifts its leg as she raised her glass . . . We could have dropped through the floor. (93–4)

There is a certain deflating of waiterly unctuousness, but it occurs at the expense of a poignant lack of solidarity. This is, it seems, part of the point. As suggested earlier, the big 'legitimate' public eating occasions are without exception subverted: the swan-centred party at Lynde Court is subverted by the building's immolation; the birthday party for the 'Darling Buds' (bloody duck, syllabub, Harrods' birthday cake) by the cake-destroying tantrum of the spurned Saskia and Imogen; the 'Elizabethan' wedding feast in Hollywood by many factors, including an excess of garlic in the marinara sauce. Even the final birthday party does not run as planned by Melchior and his third wife, subverted both by Saskia's catering and by the series of comic revelations and resolutions.

Indeed, the only group that seems to establish or confirm its sense of coherence in eating together is the English colony in Hollywood, who have tea parties instead of sex, and calmly eat their kippers and toast with Cooper's Oxford marmalade when Daisy Duck arrives to drop her bombshell. Since this is a largely upper-middle-class group, there is no question of radicalisation here. Social eating, it seems, is political in this novel specifically through its celebration of the illegitimate, at home in their own (impoverished, South London, working-class) sphere, or when its effect is subversive, puncturing the intended patronage or power-wielding of the rich and privileged and going some way to reducing the odds of material inequality. As with Lessing's misfits, the implication is of a politics of refusal.

Conclusion

In some ways, the discussion in this book has taken a fairly conservative line. Attempting to relate fictional representations of food and eating to pre-existing explanations of human behaviour – whether in terms of psychoanalytic theory, the history of manners or socio-political analyses – almost inescapably privileges continuity over change, even when context is taken into account. The more essentialist theories (such as the psychoanalytic) produce their own difficulties, not least the temptation to make sweeping generalisations about people's fundamental relationship to eating. But even the more dynamic theories invoked (Foucault's unstable power relations, for example) serve to endorse the idea of food as a language, eating an exchange.

A large part of the book's argument has been devoted to suggesting just this, for it seems to me most of the novelists considered use food and eating as communication in one way or another. Implicit throughout the discussion has been the suggestion that, when it comes to food, conventions, traditions and rituals, nostalgia and sheer human insecurity serve to reinforce existing patterns. By the same token, 'aberrant' appetites are measured against what is generally taken to be a social norm, whether they are predatory or insatiable or severely repressed. Both the food that is consumed and the behaviour surrounding its provision, preparation and eating, relate sufficiently to what is known, understood and expected for us to decode what is significant about them or about any and many deviations from the norm.

In this way (as well as providing 'conversation' within fiction) food and eating become a specific mode of communication to the reader. There is, however, a problem with contemporary life and those who write of it: radical change. Though Margaret Atwood reflects shifts towards snacking and fast foods, Doris Lessing is effectively the only writer considered here to write explicitly about the massive cultural changes currently involving food and eating, to have characterised what Anthony Giddens refers to as the 'discontinuities' of modernity. Giddens suggests not only that the sheer pace and scope of change have produced a different kind of social order, but that such change is constant, our knowledge of instability itself contributing to the world's 'mutable character'.[1] Lessing's characterisation of Ben's gang towards the end of *The Fifth Child* focuses precisely on this element of rapid change, instability and uncertainty in the modern world. Her depiction centres not only on the gang's 'hanging out' in parks and cafés and cinemas and their indiscriminate consumption of television, but on their eating habits, which enact the late twentieth-century shift from more or less formal meal times to 'grazing'. Ben's gang eat, simply, when they feel like it, drinking beer from the can and consuming 'take-away' straight from the paper or the cartons, with no concern for mealtimes or any idea of conventional 'good' manners. Their eating is – in Giddens's terms – marked by its lack of differentiation, in time, place and content. Part of the point Lessing is making has to do with Ben's belonging not to his family but to an unnamed, even unrecognised underworld of the unassimilable that is truly international – and this too is a feature of modernity as portrayed by Giddens. But on a more general and mundane level, Lessing characterises what have been profound changes in our eating habits in the last few years: the attrition of family mealtimes and the effective disappearance of the dining table, shifts in gender roles related to food, the increased tendency to eat at different hours and in different places, the prevalence of snacks and 'fast food' and the rise of what in marketing parlance is referred to as 'leisure eating'.

Clearly this poses problems for the notion of food as a currency or language and eating as an exchange. Once food is internationalised it begins to lose many of its specific ethnic or cultural connotations, such as those discussed in chapter 4. Similarly, more or less constant eating, without form or ceremony, allows none of the complex and subtle interactions and power plays that are possible in situations of shared cultural training and expectations. Women's roles as cooks and carers – with their attendant power and responsibility to shape and influence – are threatened. The logical progression of such globalising changes in food content and eating habits is on the one hand homogeneity of choice and on the other progress – or reversion – to 'uncivilized', unsocialised manners with the expectation of instant gratification.

Only the future can tell whether food and eating generally will move in this direction, or exactly what writers will do with it. Given the developments of the past (the comparatively recent invention of the fork, for example, or the emergence and then demise of afternoon tea), it seems highly likely that whatever new forms of eating emerge, they will soon develop their own sets of customs. A hierarchy of fast foods will perhaps emerge (and fluctuate) and fashionable people will appear at the most chic outlets. Neologisms and arcane rituals will be devised by fast food devotees and patterns in New Eating behaviour will be documented by sociologists and anthropologists. Or, prompted by ecological pressures and the bland sameness of genetically modified, irradiated, ready-made foods, a massive organic revival will transfigure the domestic arts; families will regroup in the kitchen and cooking mothers will become revered; the ability to transform humble ingredients into delicious food will be the most sought-after skill and an educational priority. Or . . .

Whatever happens, it is likely – unless by some strange chance social behaviour should fundamentally change – that the discourses of food and eating will become modified, will shift to incorporate global foods and the New Eating or to revalue mundane home cookery. As for power relations, they will simply and swiftly adapt, slippery and implacable as they are.

And women writers? In this culture at least, they will no doubt continue to use food and eating to explore and convey philosophical, psychological, moral and political concerns probably not so very different from those outlined in these chapters. Whatever the scale and scope of future lives, there is little doubt that people will continue to hunger, to struggle for control, to eat, to feed each other or to starve, that nourishment, however different, will remain essential in people's lives. If for this reason alone, food and eating will continue to be of major interest to writers.

Such, in effect, is the import of this book: food and eating are at the core of lives, inscribed in psyches, embedded in culture, vehicle and substance of social interaction, enmeshed with the relationship of the self to the world. For writers and readers alike, such a resource is almost immeasurable.

Notes

INTRODUCTION

1. Angela Carter, *The Sadeian Woman* (London: Virago, 1979), 11.
2. See Edwin M. Schur, *Labeling Women Deviant: Gender, Stigma and Social Control* (New York, NY: Random House, 1984), and Mike Featherstone, 'The Body in Consumer Culture' in Mike Featherstone, Mike Hepworth and Bryan S. Turner, eds., *The Body: Social Process and Cultural Theory* (London: Sage, 1991).
3. 'Angela Carter's Curious Room', *Omnibus*, dir. Kim Evans, BBC Television (15 September 1992). See also Angela Carter, 'Notes from the Front Line' in Michelene Wandor, ed., *On Gender and Writing* (London: Pandora 1983), 70; John Haffenden, *Novelists in Interview* (London: Methuen, 1985) and [Lorna Sage], 'Angela Carter interviewed by Lorna Sage' in Malcolm Bradbury and Judy Cooke, ed., *New Writing* (London: Minerva, 1992), 185–93.
4. Haffenden, *Novelists in Interview*, 80, 87.
5. [Lorna Sage], 'Angela Carter interviewed by Lorna Sage', 193, and Angela Carter, 'Notes from the Front Line', 73.
6. Interview with Linda Sandler, 'A Question of Metamorphosis' in Earl G. Ingersoll, ed., *Margaret Atwood: Conversations* (London: Virago, 1992), 53.

I   THE FOOD OF LOVE: MOTHERING, FEEDING, EATING AND DESIRE

1. See Margaret Visser, *The Rituals of Dinner: The Origins, Evolution, Eccentricities, and Meaning of Table Manners* (London: Penguin, 1993), especially the section 'Bringing Children Up', 40–56, and Deborah Lupton, *Food, the Body and the Self* (London: Sage, 1996), in particular chapter 2, 'Food, the Family and Childhood'.
2. Michèle Roberts, *A Piece of the Night* (London: The Women's Press, 1978), 47.
3. See Sigmund Freud, 'Female Sexuality' in *The Standard Edition of the Complete Psychological Works of Sigmund Freud*, vol. VII (1931; London: Hogarth Press and The Institute of Psycho-Analysis, 1961). Further references to the works of Freud will be abbreviated to *SE* followed by the volume number. Full details are in the bibliography.
4. Michèle Roberts, *The Visitation* (1983; London: The Women's Press, 1986), 153.

5. Michèle Roberts, *The Wild Girl* (1984; London: Minerva, 1991), 111.
6. Michèle Roberts, *In The Red Kitchen* (1990; London: Minerva, 1991), 118.
7. Margaret Atwood, *The Robber Bride* (1993; London: Virago, 1994), 241.
8. Nicole Ward Jouve, 'Mother is a Figure of Speech . . .' in Lorna Sage, ed., *Flesh and the Mirror* (London: Virago, 1994), 136–70.
9. Angela Carter, *The Magic Toyshop* (1967; London: Virago, 1981), 47.
10. Doris Lessing, *The Memoirs of a Survivor* (1974; London: Flamingo, 1995), 47.
11. And indeed Lessing's own. See Doris Lessing, *Under My Skin: Volume One of my Autobiography* (1994; London: Flamingo 1995), especially 28–39.
12. Nancy Chodorow, *The Reproduction of Mothering: Psychoanalysis and the Sociology of Gender* (Berkeley, CA: University of California Press, 1978), 7.
13. Ibid., especially chapters 5, 6 and 12.
14. For a discussion of the failure of maternal separation as a contributory factor in eating disorders, see Joan Jacobs Brumberg, *Fasting Girls: The Emergence of Anorexia Nervosa as a Modern Disease* (Cambridge, MA: Harvard University Press, 1988).
15. Alice Thomas Ellis, *The Clothes in the Wardrobe* (1987; London: Penguin, 1989), *The Skeleton in the Cupboard* (1988; London: Penguin, 1989) and *The Fly in the Ointment* (1989; London: Penguin, 1990).
16. Stephanie Demetrakopoulos, 'The Nursing Mother and Feminine Metaphysics: An Essay on Embodiment' in *Soundings: an Interdisciplinary Journal*, 65, 4 (1982), 430–43, 432–3.
17. Angela Carter, *Wise Children* (1991; London: Vintage, 1992), 123, 142 and 159.
18. Alice Thomas Ellis, *The Other Side of the Fire* (1983; London: Penguin, 1985).
19. Ella Freeman Sharpe, 'Psycho-Physical Problems revealed in Language: an Examination of Metaphor' (1940) in Marjorie Brierley, ed., *Collected Papers on Psycho-Analysis* (London: Hogarth Press Ltd and The Institute of Psycho-Analysis, 1950), 155–69, 168.
20. Ibid., 159, 164, 166–7.
21. Philip Roth, *Portnoy's Complaint* (London: Jonathan Cape, 1969).
22. *Tampopo*, writer/dir. Juzo Itami (Itami Productions/New Century Producers, 1986).
23. For discussion of Klein see chapter 2.
24. Freud, 'Three Essays on the Theory of Sexuality', *SE*, vol. VII, 181–2.
25. Maud Ellmann, *The Hunger Artists: Starving, Writing and Imprisonment* (London: Virago Press, 1993), 36.
26. For further exploration of the significance of Ellmann's approach and her use of the word 'catastrophe', see chapter 3.
27. Angela Carter, 'Noovs' Hoovs in the Trough', *London Review of Books* (24 January 1985), 22–3.
28. Helen Simpson, 'Sugar and Spice' in Joan Smith, ed., *Femmes de Siècle (Stories from the '90s: Women Writing at the End of Two Centuries)* (London: Chatto & Windus, 1992), 26–32.
29. Angela Carter, 'The Kitchen Child' in *Black Venus* (1985; London: Pan Books, 1986), 89–99.

30. Sigmund Freud, 'Three Essays' in *SE*, vol. VII, 149–50.
31. Ibid., 191.
32. Michèle Roberts, *Daughters of the House* (London: Virago Press, 1992), 67.
33. Angela Carter, *Nights at the Circus* (1984; London: Pan Books 1985), 10; *The Passion of New Eve* (1977; London: Virago, 1982).
34. David Punter, 'Angela Carter: Supersessions of the Masculine', *Critique*, 25, 4 (Summer 1984), 211.
35. Angela Carter, *The Sadeian Woman: an Exercise in Cultural History* (London: Virago Press, 1979), 27.
36. Angela Carter, *Wise Children*, 173.

2   CANNIBALISM AND CARTER: FANTASIES OF OMNIPOTENCE

1. Margaret Atwood, *The CanLit Foodbook: from Pen to Palate – a Collection of Tasty Fare* (Toronto: Totem Books, 1987), 2.
2. *Collins English Dictionary*, ed., Patrick Hanks, (London & Glasgow: Collins, 1979).
3. See above, chapter 1 and note 19.
4. Piers Paul Read, *Alive! the Story of the Andes Survivors* (London: Pan Books, 1975).
5. See for example Peggy Reeves Sanday, *Divine Hunger: Cannibalism as a Cultural System* (Cambridge University Press, 1986).
6. See Freud, 'Civilisation and its Discontents' in *SE*, vol. XXI, 59–145.
7. Italo Calvino, *Under the Jaguar Sun* (1986; London: Jonathan Cape, 1992).
8. Michèle Roberts, *Impossible Saints* (London: Virago, 1998), 14.
9. Angela Carter, *Black Venus* (1985; London: Pan Books, 1986), 101–21.
10. Freud plays with the same myth, but in his cultural narrative it is the primal sons who eat the father, then realising they have internalised his power against them (ego and superego) – but in both myths the result is a complexity of conflict, an intestine war rather than the desired subsuming through incorporation. See Freud, 'Totem and Taboo' (1912–13) in *SE*, vol. XIII, 1953, and 'Moses and Monotheism', *SE*, vol. XXIII.
11. Introjection is the process whereby a person, in fantasy, transposes objects and their qualities from outside him- or herself. See J. Laplanche and J. B. Pontalis, *The Language of Psychoanalysis*, trans. Donald Nicholson-Smith (London: Karnac Books and The Institute of Psycho-analysis, 1988), 229–30. Nicolas Abraham and Maria Torok, 'Introjection–Incorporation, Mourning or Melancholia' in Serge Lebovici and D. Widlocher, eds., *Psychoanalysis in France* (New York, NY: International Universities Press, 1980).
12. See Juliet Mitchell, ed., *The Selected Melanie Klein* (London: Penguin Books, 1991), and Laplanche and Pontalis, *The Language of Psychoanalysis*.
13. See Karl Abraham, 'A Short Study of the Development of the Libido, Viewed in the Light of Mental Disorders' (1924) in *Selected Papers* (London: Hogarth Press, 1927), 442–53, and Melanie Klein, 'Some Theoretical

Conclusions regarding the Emotional Life of the Infant' (1952) in *Envy and Gratitude and Other Works 1946–1963* (London: Hogarth Press, 1975), 61–93.

14. Freud, 'Negation' in *SE*, vol. XIX, 237.
15. Maggie Kilgour, *From Communion to Cannibalism: an Anatomy of Metaphors of Incorporation* (Princeton University Press, 1990), 5.
16. John Haffenden, *Novelists in Interview* (London: Methuen, 1985), 87.
17. Michel Foucault, *Madness and Civilisation: a History of Insanity in the Age of Reason* (London: Tavistock Publications, 1965), 210.
18. Angela Carter, *The Sadeian Woman*, 32.
19. Angela Carter, *Love*, rev. edn (1987; London: Picador, 1988).
20. Lorna Sage, *Women in the House of Fiction: Post-War Women Novelists* (London: Macmillan, 1992), 171.
21. Angela Carter, 'Afterword' in *Love*, 113.
22. Angela Carter, *Several Perceptions* (1968; London: Virago, 1995), 72.
23. Angela Carter, *The Sadeian Woman*, 58.
24. Beulah is used by Blake to refer to a land of retreat, restfulness and sensual pleasures.
25. Angela Carter, *Heroes and Villains* (1969; London: Penguin Books, 1981), 35.
26. Alina Reyes, *The Butcher* (London: Minerva, 1992), 3.
27. Angela Carter, *The Bloody Chamber and other Stories* (1979; London: Penguin Books, 1981).
28. The radio play *Vampirella* is in Angela Carter, *Come unto these Yellow Sands* (Newcastle: Bloodaxe Books, 1985) (four radio plays first broadcast by BBC Radio 3); 'The Lady of the House of Love' in *The Bloody Chamber*.
29. See note 11.
30. John Haffenden, *Novelists in Interview*, 79; 'Angela Carter's Curious Room', *Omnibus*, dir. Kim Evans, BBC Television (15 September 1992).
31. David Punter, 'Angela Carter: Supersessions of the Masculine', 209 *Critique*, 25, no. 4 (June 1984).
32. Freud, 'Beyond the Pleasure Principle' in *SE*, vol. XVIII. Freud himself did not use the term 'Thanatos' in his writing, though occasionally in conversation. The term was introduced into the literature by Federn. For an account of the genesis of Freud's thinking, see E. Jones, *The Life and Work of Sigmund Freud*, eds. Lionel Trilling and Steven Marcus (Harmondsworth: Penguin Books, 1964), esp. 503–11.
33. Angela Carter, *The Infernal Desire Machines of Doctor Hoffman* (1972; London: Penguin Books, 1982), 24.
34. Kilgour, *From Communion to Cannibalism*, 5.
35. See Punter, 'Angela Carter: Supersessions'.
36. David Punter again: '"Desiderio," the desired *one*, is also anagrammatically ambivalent: the name contains the "desired I," but also the "desired O," and this encapsulates the problems of subjectivity which the text explores' (213).
37. See Carter's comments on the construction of femininity in 'Angela Carter's Curious Room', *Omnibus*.

38. Jacques Lacan, 'The Mirror Stage as Formative of the Function of the I', *Ecrits: a Selection*, trans. Alan Sheridan (London: Tavistock, 1980), 1–7. Although Lacan focuses on desire and lack, his emphasis is on language rather than the body or consuming.

39. Angela Carter, 'Notes from the frontline' in *On Gender and Writing*, ed. Michelene Wandor (London: Pandora, 1983), 70.

40. See also Haffenden, *Novelists in Interview*, on Walser's becoming a 'serious person' (89).

3 EATING, STARVING AND THE BODY: DORIS LESSING AND OTHERS

1. In Charles Dickens, *Great Expectations*; Virginia Woolf, *To the Lighthouse* and Marcel Proust, *A la recherche du temps perdu*.

2. Roy Porter (and U. A. Fanthorpe), *Body and Mind* in the *Parallel Lines* series at the Voice Box, Royal Festival Hall (11 February 1992). Porter draws heavily on the work of Foucault here (see note 5 below).

3. Kim Chernin, *Womansize: the Tyranny of Slenderness* (London: The Women's Press, 1983), 56.

4. Bryan S. Turner gives an informative summary of anthropological, sociological and socio-cultural thinking about the body in 'Recent Developments in the Theory of the Body' in Mike Featherstone, Mike Hepworth and Bryan S. Turner, eds., *The Body: Social Process and Cultural Theory* (London: Sage, 1991), 1–35, 17.

5. See Michel Foucault, *Discipline and Punish: the Birth of the Prison* (Harmondsworth: Penguin Books, 1979), and *The History of Sexuality*, vol. 1, *An Introduction*, trans. Robert Hurley (London: Penguin, 1979), esp. the final chapter.

6. See Hillel Schwartz, *Never Satisfied: a Cultural History of Diets, Fantasies and Fat* (London: Collier Macmillan Publishers, 1986).

7. Arthur W. Frank, 'For a Sociology of the Body: An Analytical Review' in Featherstone et al., *The Body: Social Process and Cultural Theory*, 36–102.

8. Jacqueline Rose, *The Haunting of Sylvia Plath* (London: Virago Press, 1991), 27.

9. See, chapter 1, note 12.

10. Kim Chernin, *The Hungry Self: Women, Eating and Identity* (London: Virago Press, 1986), 53. Doris Lessing invents a society with something like such guides in *The Marriages Between Zones Three, Four and Five*.

11. Kim Chernin, *The Hungry Self*, 101.

12. See above, chapter 1 and note 25.

13. See Susie Orbach, *Hunger Strike: the Anorexic's Struggle as a Metaphor for our Age* (London and Boston: Faber & Faber, 1986) and Nigella Lawson, 'The Women Who Think this Perfect Body is the Wrong Shape', *Evening Standard*, (23 January 1992) on Naomi Campbell.

14. Susan Bordo, *Unbearable Weight: Feminism, Western Culture, and the Body* (Berkeley and London: University of California Press, 1993), 57.

15. Hilde Bruch, *The Golden Cage: the Enigma of Anorexia Nervosa* (London: Open Books, 1978).

16. Joan Jacobs Brumberg, *Fasting Girls: the Emergence of Anorexia Nervosa as a Modern Disease* (Cambridge, MA: and London: Harvard University Press, 1988), 164.

17. Jenny Turner, 'Consumed by anorexia', *The Guardian* (6 August 1992), 25. See also Diana Hume George, 'Sister survivors', *The Women's Review of Books*, 9 (12) (September 1992), 9–11.

18. Jenefer Shute, *Life-Size* (London: Mandarin, 1993), 64–5.

19. John Berger, *Ways of Seeing* (London: BBC and Penguin Books 1972); Susie Orbach, *Hunger Strike*.

20. Brumberg, *Fasting Girls*, 7.

21. Orbach, *Hunger Strike*, 14.

22. Julia Kristeva, *Powers of Horror: an Essay on Abjection* trans. Leon S. Roudiez (New York, NY: Columbia University Press, 1982), 1.

23. Elizabeth Gross, 'The Body of Signification' in John Fletcher and Andrew Benjamin, eds., *Abjection, Melancholia, and Love: the Work of Julia Kristeva* (London and New York, NY, Routledge, 1990), 94.

24. Julia Kristeva, *Powers of Horror*, 4.

25. Jenefer Shute, *Life-Size*, 39 and 209.

26. See, for example: Susie Orbach, *Hunger Strike*; Peter Lambley, *How to Survive Anorexia* (London: Frederick Muller, 1983); Hilde Bruch, *Eating Disorders: Obesity, Anorexia Nervosa, and the Person Within* (London: Routledge and Kegan Paul, 1974).

27. For a discussion of the 'hunger artist', and a comparison of hunger strikes with anorexia, see Maud Ellmann, *The Hunger Artists: Starving, Writing and Imprisonment* (London: Virago Press, 1993). By contrast, Joan Jacobs Brumberg notes a romanticising of anorexia nervosa, deploring popular comparisons of anorectics with suffragists, given the difference between 'conscious political strategies' and destructive obsession with self (*Fasting Girls*, p. 289, n. 67).

28. Doris Lessing, *The Grass is Singing* (1950; St. Albans: Granada, 1980), 100.

29. See note 7 and above.

30. Kim Chernin, *The Hungry Self*, 167.

31. Doris Lessing, *Martha Quest* (1952; London: Paladin, 1990), 51.

32. Doris Lessing, *A Proper Marriage* (1954; London: Hart-Davis, MacGibbon, 1977), part 4, end of chapter 1, and *A Ripple from the Storm* (1965; London: Paladin 1990), 294.

33. Susan Bordo, *Unbearable Weight*, 57; Doris Lessing, *Martha Quest*, 134.

34. Several critics note the existence of a 'divided self' in Martha: the conformist and the visionary. See Jeanette King, *Doris Lessing*, Modern Fiction Series (London: Edward Arnold, 1989); Lorna Sage, *Doris Lessing* (London: Methuen, Contemporary Writers Series, 1983); the 'Critical Studies' collection edited by Annis Pratt and L. S. Dembo: *Doris Lessing* (University of Wisconsin Press, 1974), especially Dagmar Barnouw, 'Disorderly Company:

From *The Golden Notebook* to *The Four-Gated City*. The 'division' is by no means a simple polar opposition, since both conforming and visionary selves are powered by a desire for community and belonging – a theme explored further in chapter 6.

35. See note 11 and above for Kim Chernin's comments on food battles.
36. Sage, *Doris Lessing*, 37.
37. Doris Lessing, *Landlocked* (1965; London: Paladin, 1990), 97.
38. Doris Lessing, *The Golden Notebook* (1962; London, Flamingo, 1993), 33–4.
39. Ibid., 303 and 323–4.
40. Maggie Kilgour, *From Communion to Cannibalism: an Anatomy of Metaphors of Incorporation* (Princeton University Press, 1990), 244.
41. Cf. Angela Carter's claim about the distinctiveness of experience as a contemporary woman (Introduction, note 3 and above).
42. See Jacqueline Rose, *The Haunting of Sylvia Plath* (London: Virago Press, 1991), 27.
43. Doris Lessing, *The Diary of a Good Neighbour* (1983) and *If the Old Could . . .* (1984), published as *The Diaries of Jane Somers* (London: Michael Joseph, 1984).
44. Bunny Epstein, 'Women's Anger and Compulsive Eating' in Marylin Lawrence, ed., *Fed up and Hungry* (London: The Women's Press, 1987), 39, 43.
45. Mary Russo, *The Female Grotesque: Risk, Excess and Modernity* (London and New York, NY: Routledge, 1994), 24. Russo draws on Ellmann's *Hunger Artists* here.
46. See, for example: Susan Bordo, 'Reading the Slender Body' in Mary Jacobus, Evelyn Fox Keller and Sally Shuttleworth, eds., *Body/Politics: Women and the Discourses of Science* (London: Routledge, 1990), 83–112; Annie Fursland, 'Eve was Framed: Food and Sex and Women's Shame' in Lawrence, ed., *Fed Up and Hungry*; Mike Featherstone, 'The Body in Consumer Culture' in Featherstone et al., eds., *The Body*; Edwin M. Schur, *Labeling Women Deviant: Gender, Stigma and Social Control* (New York, NY: Random House, 1984); Hillel Schwartz, *Never Satisfied: a Cultural History of Diets, Fantasies and Fat* (New York, NY, and London: Collier Macmillan Publishers, 1986).
47. Sherry Ashworth, *A Matter of Fat* (Manchester: Crocus, 1991).
48. Schur, *Labeling Women Deviant*.
49. Molly Keane, *Good Behaviour* (London: Sphere Books Ltd., 1982), 9.
50. Hillel Schwartz, *Never Satisfied*, 327.
51. Margaret Atwood, 'Spring Song of the Frogs', *Bluebeard's Egg and other Stories* (London: Jonathan Cape, 1987) 165–78.

4   SHARP APPETITES: MARGARET ATWOOD'S CONSUMING POLITICS

1. Interview with Jo Brans, 'Using What You're Given', *Southwest Review* (1982), collected in Earl G. Ingersoll, ed., *Margaret Atwood: Conversations* (London: Virago, 1992), 149.

2. See Ingersoll, ed., *Margaret Atwood: Conversations* (London, Virago, 1992), especially 137.
3. Margaret Atwood, *The CanLit Foodbook: from Pen to Palate – a Collection of Tasty Fare* (Toronto: Totem Books, 1987), 2.
4. Margaret Atwood, *The Edible Woman* (1969; London: Virago, 1994), 19.
5. Betty Friedan, *The Feminine Mystique* (London: Victor Gollancz, 1963).
6. *The Edible Woman*, 152,161, 173, 176, 178.
7. Simone de Beauvoir, *The Second Sex* (1949; London: Four Square Books, 1960), 8.
8. Margaret Atwood, *Lady Oracle* (London: Virago, 1994), 66.
9. Ingersoll, ed., *Margaret Atwood: Conversations*, 13.
10. Margaret Atwood, *Life Before Man* (1979; London: Vintage, 1996), 30.
11. Margaret Atwood, *Bodily Harm* (1981; London: Vintage, 1996), 34.
12. Margaret Atwood, *The Handmaid's Tale* (1985; London: Virago, 1987), 135.
13. Lorna Sage, *Women in the House of Fiction: Post-War Women Novelists* (London: Macmillan, 1992), 167.
14. Margaret Atwood, *Cat's Eye* (1988; London: Virago, 1990), 119.
15. Margaret Atwood, 'Spotty-Handed Villainesses: Problems of Female Bad Behaviour in the Creation of Literature', http://www.web.net/owtoad/vlness.htm, 27/03/98.
16. Margaret Atwood, *The Robber Bride* (1993; London: Virago, 1994), 281.
17. Ingersoll, ed., *Margaret Atwood: Conversations*, passim.
18. See, for example, Margaret L. Carter ed., *Dracula: The Vampire and the Critics* (Ann Arbor/London: UMI Research Press, 1988), or Christopher Craft, 'Kiss me with those red lips' in Elaine Showalter, ed., *Speaking of Gender* (London: Routledge, 1989), 216–42.
19. Lorna Sage, *Women in the House of Fiction*, 162. Coral Ann Howells, *Margaret Atwood*, Macmillan Modern Novelists Series (Basingstoke: Macmillan 1996), 83.
20. Howells, *Margaret Atwood*, 83.
21. Margaret Atwood, *Alias Grace* (1996; London: Virago, 1997), 38, 72.

5   FOOD AND MANNERS: ROBERTS AND ELLIS

1. See Peter Farb and George Armelagos, *Consuming Passions: the Anthropology of Eating* (Boston: Houghton Mifflin, 1980).
2. Ibid.
3. Toni Morrison, *Beloved* (London: Picador, 1988), 137, and *Sula* (London: Triad Grafton, 1982), 33, 104, 113.
4. 'A Terrible Privacy', interview with James Wood, *The Guardian* (April 18 1992), Weekend section, 5.
5. Alice Thomas Ellis, *The 27th Kingdom* (London: Penguin, 1982), 84.
6. Michèle Roberts, *The Wild Girl* (1984; London: Minerva, 1991), 13.
7. Michèle Roberts, *The Book of Mrs Noah* (1987; London: Minerva, 1993), 26–7.
8. Michèle Roberts, *In the Red Kitchen* (1990; London: Minerva, 1991), 115.

9. Margaret Atwood, *The CanLit Foodbook: from Pen to Palate – a Collection of Tasty Fare* (Toronto: Totem Books, 1987), 1.

10. Michèle Roberts, *The Visitation* (1983; London: The Women's Press, 1986) 24.

11. Michèle Roberts, *Daughters of the House* (London: Virago Press, 1992), 170. French bread is apparently more comforting than English.

12. Cf. Josie in Jenefer Shute's *Life-Size* (London: Mandarin, 1993), 209.

13. Michèle Roberts, *A Piece of the Night* (London: The Women's Press, 1978), 29

14. Margaret Visser describes the Mass as crossing all boundaries and spanning all meanings, and lists many examples of both. Unlike Roberts but like the Church, the boundary between male and female is one she omits to mention. Margaret Visser, *The Rituals of Dinner: the Origins, Evolution, Eccentricities, and Meaning of Table Manners* (1991; London, Penguin, 1993), 37.

15. See Robert E. Bell, *Dictionary of Classical Mythology: Symbols, Attributes, Associations* (Santa Barbara, CA, and Oxford: ABC-Clio, 1982) and Betty Radice, *Who's Who in the Ancient World* (London: Penguin, 1973).

16. Representing the words Jesus Christ God's Son Saviour.

17. Stephen Mennell, *All Manners of Food: Eating and Taste in England and France from the Middle Ages to the Present* (Oxford: Basil Blackwell, 1985).

18. Claude Lévi-Strauss, *The Raw and the Cooked: Introduction to a Science of Mythology*, vol. I (1964; London: Jonathan Cape, 1970).

19. Michèle Roberts, 'Une Glossaire/A Glossary' in *During Mother's Absence* (London: Virago, 1993), 131–81.

20. Visser, *The Rituals of Dinner*, 90–9.

21. Michel Foucault, *The History of Sexuality:* Vol. I, *An Introduction*, trans. Robert Hurley (London: Penguin Books, 1979). See especially part 4, chapter 2, 'Method'.

22. Michel Foucault, *Discipline and Punish: the Birth of the Prison*, trans. Alan Sheridan (Harmondsworth: Penguin Books, 1979), 194. See also Alan Sheridan, *Michel Foucault: the Will to Truth* (London: Tavistock, 1980).

23. Alice Thomas Ellis, *The Sin Eater* (1977: Harmondsworth: Penguin, 1986), 101.

24. Alice Thomas Ellis, *Unexplained Laughter* (1985; London: Penguin, 1986), 138.

25. Angela Carter, *Expletives Deleted: Selected Writings* (1992; London: Vintage, 1993) 55.

26. Alice Thomas Ellis, *The Skeleton in the Cupboard* (1988; London: Penguin, 1989), 127.

27. Alice Thomas Ellis, *Unexplained Laughter* (1985; London: Penguin, 1986), 95.

6   SOCIAL EATING: IDENTITY, COMMUNION AND DIFFERENCE

1. Marc O'Day, '"Mutability is Having a Field Day": The Sixties Aura of Angela Carter's Bristol Trilogy' in Lorna Sage, ed., *Flesh and the Mirror: Essays on the Art of Angela Carter* (London: Virago, 1994), 24–59.

2. John Haffenden, *Novelists in Interview* (London: Methuen, 1985), 76–96, 80, 79.

3. 'It is to a degree true that, as we used to say in the sixties, you are what you eat', (Haffenden, *Novelists in Interview*, 80).

4. Doris Lessing, *A Small Personal Voice* (1974; London: Flamingo, 1994), 10–11.

5. Deathly cannibalism appears also in Lessing's own *Briefing for a Descent into Hell* (London: Jonathan Cape, 1971).

6. See Kate Fullbrook, *Free Women: Ethics and Aesthetics in Twentieth-Century Women's Fiction* (London: Harvester Wheatsheaf, 1990), chapter 6, 'Doris Lessing: The Limits of Liberty', 141–69.

7. The suggestions of apocalypse at the end of this novel, *The Four-Gated City* and *The Making of the Representative for Planet 8* offer possibilities of breaking the cycle.

8. See, for example, Reay Tannahill, *Flesh and Blood: a History of the Cannibal Complex* (New York, NY: Dorset Press, 1975), or Peggy Reeves Sanday, *Divine Hunger: Cannibalism as a Cultural System* (Cambridge University Press, 1986).

9. See Lucien Malson, *Wolf Children* and Jean Itard, *The Wild Boy of Aveyron*, ed. Lucien Malson, trans. Edmund Fawcett, Peter Ayrton and Joan White (London: NLB, 1972) (*Les Enfants sauvages*, 1964).

10. Doris Lessing, *The Marriages Between Zones Three, Four and Five* (1980; London: Flamingo, 1994) and *The Making of the Representative for Planet 8* (1982; London: Flamingo, 1994).

11. Kate Fullbrook, 'Doris Lessing: the Limits of Liberty' in *Free Women: Ethics and Aesthetics in Twentieth-Century Women's Fiction* (London: Harvester Wheatsheaf, 1990), 165.

12. See Peter Farb and George Armelagos, *Consuming Passions: the Anthropology of Eating* (Boston: Houghton Mifflin, 1980), for an account of how normal social fabric is disrupted in time of famine.

13. Jeannette King, *Doris Lessing*, Modern Fiction Series (London: Edward Arnold, 1989), 86.

14. Doris Lessing, *The Good Terrorist* (1985; London: Paladin, 1990), 31.

15. Doris Lessing, *The Fifth Child* (1988; London: Paladin, 1989), 83.

16. In *King Lear*, III.4, Edgar, in his guise as a madman, repeatedly apostrophises himself as 'poor Tom', as in 'Poor Tom's a-cold.'

17. Angela Carter, *Nights at the Circus* (1984; London: Picador, 1985), 39.

18. Anthony Giddens, *The Consequences of Modernity* (Cambridge and Oxford: Polity Press in association with Basil Blackwell, 1990), 17–21. These crucial changes, Giddens argues, provide the conditions for the 'disembedding' of social relations and organisations from their immediate contexts, a precondition, it seems, for the globalisation and fragmentation of contemporary life. In terms of eating, both the traditionally accepted mealtimes (however much these alter over time) and relatively local content are equally disembedded – hence, perhaps, the whole 'fast food' (empty time, any space) revolution.

19. Mikhail Bakhtin, *The Problems of Dostoevsky's Poetics* (Manchester University Press, 1984), 127.

20. Mikhail Bakhtin, *Rabelais and his World*, trans. Hélène Iswolsky (Indiana University Press, 1984).

21. Mikhail Bakhtin, 'Forms of Time and Chronotope in the Novel' in *The Dialogic Imagination: Four Essays* (Austin: University of Texas Press, 1981), especially 169–171.

22. Bakhtin, *Rabelais and his World*, 11.

23. In the *Omnibus* interview, 'Angela Carter's Curious Room' (dir. Kim Evans, BBC Television, 15 September 1992), Carter says that she wanted to include references to every Shakespeare play, but does not quite get every one in.

24. Angela Carter, *Wise Children* (1991; London: Virago, 1992).

25. Bakhtin, *The Problems of Dostoevsky's Poetics*, 127.

26. Bakhtin, *Rabelais and his World*, 7.

27. Angela Carter, 'In Pantoland' in *American Ghosts and Old World Wonders* (1993; London: Virago, 1994).

28. [Lorna Sage], 'Angela Carter interviewed by Lorna Sage' in Malcolm Bradbury and Judy Cooke, ed., *New Writing* (London: Minerva, 1992), 188.

29. This accords with Foucault's view of the defusing of dissent by inclusion, discussed in *Discipline and Punish: the Birth of the Prison*, trans. Alan Sheridan (Harmondsworth. Penguin Books, 1979), and *Madness and Civilization: a History of Insanity in the Age of Reason*, trans. Richard Howard (London: Tavistock Publications, 1965).

30. Marina Warner, 'Angela Carter: Bottle Blonde, Double Drag' in Lorna Sage, ed., *Flesh and the Mirror*, 253–4. Elaine Jordan, too, implicitly in her essay, 'The Dangerous Edge' in the same volume, and explicitly in her address to the 'Fireworks' conference on Carter (York, September 1993), takes the view that Carter's earlier, riskier fiction is more radical as well as more disturbing.

CONCLUSION

1. Anthony Giddens, *The Consequences of Modernity* (Cambridge and Oxford: Polity Press in association with Basil Blackwell, 1990), 46, 45.

Bibliography

This bibliography includes both works referred to in the text and some further suggested reading around the subject. It does not, however, include further fiction or films; this is something readers can follow up to their own delight.

Original publication dates are given in brackets for works by the four main writers, and elsewhere where there is a significant lapse of time between original publication and the edition cited.

WORKS BY MARGARET ATWOOD

Atwood, Margaret. *Alias Grace*, London: Virago, 1997 (1996).
  Bodily Harm, London: Vintage 1996 (1981).
  The CanLit Foodbook: from pen to palate – a Collection of Tasty Fare, Toronto: Totem Books, 1987.
  Cat's Eye, London: Virago, 1990 (1988).
  The Edible Woman, London: Virago Press 1980 (1969).
  The Handmaid's Tale, London: Virago, 1987 (1985).
  Lady Oracle, London: Virago, 1982 (1976).
  Life Before Man, London: Vintage, 1996 (1979).
  The Robber Bride, London: Virago, 1994 (1993).
  Second Words: Selected Critical Prose, Toronto: Anansi Press, 1982.
  'Spotty-Handed Villainesses: Problems of Female Bad Behaviour in the Creation of Literature', http://www.web.net/owtoad/vlness.htm, 27/03/98.
  'Spring Song of the Frogs' in *Bluebeard's Egg and other Stories*, London: Jonathan Cape, 1987, 165–78.

WORKS BY ANGELA CARTER

Carter, Angela. *American Ghosts and Old World Wonders*, London: Vintage, 1994 (1993).
  Black Venus, London: Pan Books, 1986 (1985).
  The Bloody Chamber and other Stories, London: Penguin Books, 1981 (1979).
  Come Unto These Yellow Sands: Four Radio Plays, Newcastle: Bloodaxe Books, 1985.

Expletives Deleted: Selected Writings, London: Vintage, 1993 (1992).
Fireworks: Nine Profane Pieces, Virago rev. edn (in association with Chatto & Windus), London: Virago, 1987 (1974).
Heroes and Villains, London: Penguin Books, 1981 (1969).
The Infernal Desire Machines of Doctor Hoffman, London: Penguin Books, 1982 (1972).
'The Kitchen Child' in *Black Venus*, London: Pan Books, 1986 (1985), 89–99.
'The Lady of the House of Love' in *The Bloody Chamber*, London: Penguin Books, 1981 (1979), 93–108.
Love, rev. edn, London: Picador, 1988 (1971, rev. 1987).
The Magic Toyshop, London: Virago Press, 1981 (1967).
Nights at the Circus, London: Picador, 1985 (1984).
'Noovs' Hoovs in the Trough', *London Review of Books* (24 January 1985), 22–3.
'Notes from the Front Line' in *On Gender and Writing*, ed. Michelene Wandor, London: Pandora, 1983, 69–77.
Nothing Sacred: Selected Writings, London: Virago Press, 1982.
The Passion of New Eve, London: Virago Press, 1982 (1977).
The Sadeian Woman: an Exercise in Cultural History, London: Virago Press, 1979.
Several Perceptions, London: Virago, 1995 (1968).
Shadow Dance, London: Virago Press 1994 (1966).
'Vampirella' in *Come unto these Yellow Sands*, Newcastle: Bloodaxe Books, 1985.
Virago Book of Fairy Tales, ed. and intro., London: Virago, 1990.
Wayward Girls and Wicked Women, ed. and intro., London: Virago, 1986.
Wise Children, London: Vintage, 1992 (1991).

WORKS BY ALICE THOMAS ELLIS

Ellis, Alice Thomas. *The 27th Kingdom*, London: Penguin, 1982 (1982)
The Birds of the Air, London: Penguin, 1983 (1980).
The Clothes in the Wardrobe, London: Penguin, 1989 (1987).
The Fly in the Ointment, London: Penguin, 1990 (1989).
Home Life, London: Flamingo, 1987 (1986).
Home Life Book Three, London: Flamingo, 1989 (1988).
More Home Life, London: Flamingo, 1988 (1987).
The Other Side of the Fire, London: Penguin, 1985 (1983).
The Sin Eater, Harmondsworth: Penguin, 1986 (1977).
The Skeleton in the Cupboard, London: Penguin, 1989 (1988).
Unexplained Laughter, London: Penguin, 1986 (1985).

WORKS BY DORIS LESSING

Lessing, Doris. *Briefing for a Descent into Hell*, London: Jonathan Cape, 1971.
The Diaries of Jane Somers, London: Michael Joseph, 1984. (Originally published as *The Diary of a Good Neighbour* (1983) and *If the Old Could . . .* (1984)).
The Fifth Child, London: Paladin, 1989 (1988).

The Four-Gated City, Children of Violence Series. London: Paladin, 1990 (1969).

The Golden Notebook, London: Flamingo, 1993 (1962).

The Good Terrorist, London: Paladin, 1990 (1985).

The Grass is Singing, St Albans: Granada, 1980 (1950).

'In Pursuit of the English' in *The Doris Lessing Reader*, London: Jonathan Cape, 1989, 433–58.

Landlocked, 'Children of Violence' series. London: Paladin, 1990. (1965).

London Observed: Stories and Sketches, London: Flamingo, 1993 (1992).

The Making of the Representative for Planet 8, 'Canopus in Argos: Archives' series, London: Flamingo, 1994 (1982).

The Marriages Between Zones Three, Four and Five, 'Canopus in Argos: Archives' series, London: Flamingo, 1994 (1980).

Martha Quest, 'Children of Violence' series. London: Paladin, 1990 (1952).

The Memoirs of a Survivor, London: Flamingo, 1995 (1974).

A Proper Marriage, 'Children of Violence' series. London: Hart-Davis, MacGibbon, 1977 (1954).

A Ripple from the Storm, 'Children of Violence' series. London: Paladin, 1990 (1965).

A Small Personal Voice, ed. Paul Schlueter. London: Flamingo, 1994 (USA, 1974).

The Summer before the Dark, Harmondsworth: Penguin Books, 1975 (1973).

Under My Skin: Volume One of my Autobiography, London: Flamingo, 1995 (1994).

WORKS BY MICHÈLE ROBERTS

Roberts, Michèle. *The Book of Mrs Noah*, London: Minerva, 1993 (1987).

Daughters of the House, London: Virago Press, 1992.

'Une Glossaire/A Glossary' in *During Mother's Absence*, London: Virago, 1993, 131–81.

Impossible Saints, London: Virago, 1998.

In the Red Kitchen, London: Minerva, 1991 (1990).

'Michèle Roberts' in *Women Writers Talk: Interviews with Ten Women Writers*, 149–172. Oxford: Lennard Publishing, 1989.

A Piece of the Night, London: The Women's Press, 1978. 'Questions and Answers' in *On Gender and Writing*. ed. Michelene Wandor, London, Boston, Melbourne and Henley: Pandora Press, 1983, 62–8.

The Visitation, London: The Women's Press, 1986 (1983).

The Wild Girl, London: Minerva, 1991 (1984).

ALL OTHER PUBLISHED PRINTED WORKS

Abraham, Karl. 'A Short Study of the Development of the Libido, Viewed in the Light of Mental Disorders' in *Selected Papers*, London: Hogarth Press, 1927, 442–53.

Abraham, Nicolas, and Maria Torok. 'Introjection-Incorporation, *Mourning* or *Melancholia*', in *Psychoanalysis in France*, eds. Serge Lebovici and D. Widlocher, New York: International Universities Press, 1980, 3–16.

Arens, W. *The Man-Eating Myth: Anthropology and Anthropophagy*, Oxford University Press, 1979.

Ashworth, Sherry. *A Matter of Fat*, Manchester: Crocus (Commonword Ltd.), 1991.

Askenasy, Hans. *Cannibalism: from Sacrifice to Survival*, New York: Prometheus Books, 1994.

Atkinson, Clarissa, Constance H. Buchanan, and Margaret R. Miles, eds. *Immaculate and Powerful: The Female in Sacred Image and Social Reality*, Wellingborough: Crucible, 1987.

Auden, W. H. 'Introduction' to M. F. K. Fisher, *The Art of Eating*, London: Picador, 1983. (1963).

Auster, Paul. *The Art of Hunger and other Essays*, London: The Menard Press, 1982.

Bakhtin, Mikhail. 'Forms of Time and Chronotope in the Novel: VII, The Rabelaisian Chronotope' in *The Dialogic Imagination: Four Essays*. trans. Caryl Emerson and Michael Holquist, ed. Michael Holquist, Austin: University of Texas Press, 1981, 167–206.

The Problems of Dostoevsky's Poetics, Manchester University Press, 1984.

Rabelais and his World, trans. Hélène Iswolsky, Bloomington: Indiana University Press, 1984 (1965).

Barnouw, Dagmar. 'Disorderly Company: from *The Golden Notebook* to *The Four-Gated City*' in *Doris Lessing: Critical Studies*, eds. Annis Pratt and L. S. Dembo, University of Wisconsin Press, 1974, 74–97.

Barthes, Roland. 'Wine and Milk' and 'Steak and Chips' in *Mythologies*, trans. Annette Lavers, London: Jonathan Cape, 1972. (1957), 58–64.

Bayley, John. 'Fighting for the Crown', *The New York Review* (23 April 1992): 9–11.

Beauvoir, Simone de. 'Must we Burn Sade?' in *The Marquis de Sade*, trans. Annette Michelson, London: John Calder, 1962.

The Second Sex, trans. H. M. Parshley, London: Four Square Books, 1960 (1949).

Bell, Robert E. *Dictionary of Classical Mythology: Symbols, Attributes, Associations*, Santa Barbara, CA, and Oxford: ABC-Clio, Oxford Clio, 1982.

Bender, Eileen T. 'The woman who came to dinner: dining and divining a feminist "aesthetic"', *Women's Studies*, 12, no. 3 (1986), 315–33.

Bennett, Gerald. *Eating Matters: Why we Eat what we Eat*, London: Heinemann, 1988.

Berger, John. *Ways of Seeing*, London: BBC and Penguin Books, 1972.

Bevan, David, ed. *Literary Gastronomy*, Amsterdam: Rodopi, 1988.

Biasin, Gian-Paolo. *The Flavors of Modernity: Food and the Novel*, Princeton University Press, 1993.

Bordo, Susan. 'Reading the Slender Body' in *Body/Politics: Women and the Discourses of Science*, eds. Mary Jacobus et al. London and New York, NY: Routledge, 1990, 83–112.

Unbearable Weight: Feminism, Western Culture, and the Body, Berkeley, CA, and London: University of California Press, 1993.

Bowlby, Rachel. *Shopping with Freud*, London: Routledge, 1993.

Brillat-Savarin, Jean Anthèlme. *The Physiology of Taste or Meditations on Transcendental Gastronomy*, introd. Arthur Machen, New York: Dover, 1960 (1825).

Bristow, Joseph, and Trev Lynn Broughton, eds. *The Infernal Desires of Angela Carter: Fiction, Femininity, Feminism*, London and New York, NY: Longman, 1997.

Brown, Georgina. 'From hand to mouth', interview with Michèle Roberts, *The Independent* (12 March 1993) 21.

Bruch, Hilde. *Eating Disorders: Obesity, Anorexia Nervosa and the Person Within*, London: Routledge & Kegan Paul, 1974.

The Golden Cage: the Enigma of Anorexia Nervosa, London: Open Books, 1978.

Brumberg, Joan Jacobs. *Fasting Girls: The Emergence of Anorexia Nervosa as a Modern Disease*, Cambridge, MA, and London: Harvard University Press, 1988.

Buckroyd, Julia. *Eating Your Heart Out: The Emotional Meaning of Eating Disorders*, London: Optima, 1989.

Calvino, Italo. *Under the Jaguar Sun*, trans. William Weaver, London: Jonathan Cape, 1992 (1986).

Capaldi, Elizabeth P., and Terry L. Powley, eds. *Taste, Experience and Feeding*, Washington DC: American Psychological Association, 1990.

Charney, Maurice. *Sexual Fiction*, London: Methuen, 1981.

Chernin, Kim. *The Hungry Self: Women, Eating and Identity*, London: Virago Press, 1986.

Womansize: The Tyranny of Slenderness, London: The Women's Press, 1983 (first published as *The Obsession: Reflections on the Tyranny of Slenderness*, New York, NY: Harper & Row, 1981).

Chodorow, Nancy. *The Reproduction of Mothering: Psychoanalysis and the Sociology of Gender*, Berkeley, CA, and London: University of California Press, 1978.

Cline, Sally. *Just Deserts: Women and Food*, London: André Deutsch, 1990.

Coward, Rosalind. *Female Desire: Women's Sexuality Today*, London: Paladin, 1984.

Curtin, Deane W., and Lisa M. Heldke, eds. *Cooking, Eating, Thinking: Transformative Philosophies of Food*, Bloomington and Indianapolis, IN: Indiana University Press, 1992.

Davidson, Arnold E., and Cathy N. Davidson, eds. *The Art of Margaret Atwood: Essays in Criticism*, Toronto: Anansi Press, 1981.

Demetrakopoulos, Stephanie. 'The Nursing Mother and Feminine Metaphysics: An Essay on Embodiment', *Soundings: an Interdisciplinary Journal*, 65, no. 4 (1982), 430–43.

Diamond, Nicky. 'Thin is the Feminist Issue', *Feminist Review*, 19, no. 58 (March 1995): 7–65.

Dipple, Elizabeth. 'Doris Lessing, ideologue' in *The Unresolvable Plot*, Oxford University Press, 1988, 238–60.

Douglas, Mary. 'Deciphering a Meal', *Daedalus*, 101, no. 1 (December 1972), 61–81.

In the Active Voice, London: Routledge & Kegan Paul, 1982.

Natural Symbols: Explorations in Cosmology, London: Pelican, 1973.

Purity and Danger: an Analysis of Concepts of Pollution and Taboo, London: Routledge & Kegan Paul, 1966.

During, Simon. *Foucault and Literature: towards a Genealogy of Writing*, London: Routledge, 1992.

Ehrenreich, Barbara and Deirdre English. *For her Own Good: One Hundred and Fifty Years of the Experts' Advice to Women*, London: Pluto Press, 1979.

Ellmann, Maud. *The Hunger Artists: Starving, Writing and Imprisonment*, London: Virago Press, 1993.

Epstein, Bunny. 'Women's Anger and Compulsive Eating' in *Fed up and Hungry: Women, Oppression and Food*. ed. Marylin Lawrence, London: The Women's Press, 1987, 27–45.

Erikson, Erik H. *Childhood and Society*, rev. edn. Harmondsworth: Penguin in association with Hogarth Press, 1965.

Farb, Peter, and George Armelagos. *Consuming Passions: the Anthropology of Eating*, Boston, MA: Houghton Mifflin, 1980.

Featherstone, Mike. 'The Body in Consumer Culture', in *The Body: Social Process and Cultural Theory*, eds. Mike Featherstone et al. London: Sage Publications, 1991, 170–96.

Featherstone, Mike, Mike Hepworth and Bryan S. Turner, eds., *The Body: Social Process and Cultural Theory*, London: Sage, 1991.

Fiedler, Leslie. *Freaks: Myths and Images of the Secret Self*, Harmondsworth: Penguin Books, 1981 (1978).

Fletcher, John, and Andrew Benjamin, eds. *Abjection, Melancholia and Love: the Work of Julia Kristeva*, London and New York, NY: Routledge, 1990.

'Food: the Vital Stuff', *Granta*, 52 (December 1995) (complete issue on food and eating).

Foucault, Michel. *Discipline and Punish: the Birth of the Prison*, trans. Alan Sheridan, Harmondsworth: Penguin Books, 1979.

The History of Sexuality, vol. 1: *An Introduction*, trans. Robert Hurley, London: Penguin Books, 1979.

Madness and Civilisation: a History of Insanity in the Age of Reason, trans. Richard Howard, London: Tavistock Publications, 1965.

'The Order of Discourse: Text, Discourse, Ideology' in *Untying the Text: a Post-Structuralist Reader*, ed. Robert Young, trans. Ian McLeod, London: Routledge, 1981, 47–78. (Inaugural Lecture at Collège de France, 2 December 1970.)

Frank, Arthur W. 'For a Sociology of the Body: an Analytical Review' in *The Body: Social Process and Cultural Theory*. eds. Mike Featherstone et al. London: Sage, 1991, 36–102.

Freud, Sigmund. 'Beyond the Pleasure Principle' in *Standard Edition of the Complete Psychological Works of Sigmund Freud*, eds. James Strachey, Anna

Freud, Alix Strachey and Alan Tyson, London: Hogarth Press and The Institute of Psycho-Analysis, vol. XVIII, 1955 (1920), 7–64.

'Civilisation and its Discontents' in *Standard Edition* vol. XXI, London: Hogarth, 1961 (1929/30), 59–145.

'The Ego and the Id' in *Standard Edition* vol. XIX, London: Hogarth, 1961 (1923), 12–60.

'Female Sexuality' in *Standard Edition* vol. XXI, London: Hogarth, 1961 (1931), 223–43.

'Moses and Monotheism' in *Standard Edition* vol. XXIII, London: Hogarth, 1964 (1939), 6–137.

'Mourning and Melancholia' in *Standard Edition* vol. XIV, London: Hogarth, 1957 (1915), 239–58.

'Negation' in *Standard Edition* vol. XIX, London: Hogarth, 1961 (1925), 235–9.

'New Introductory Lectures on Psychoanalysis' in *Standard Edition* vol. XXII, London: Hogarth, 1964 (1932/3), 5–182.

'On the Universal Tendency to Debasement in the Sphere of Love' in *Standard Edition* vol. XI, London: Hogarth, 1957 (1912), 177–90.

'Three Essays on the Theory of Sexuality' in *Standard Edition* vol. VII, eds. London: Hogarth, 1953 (1905), 125–243.

'Totem and Taboo' in *Standard Edition* vol. XIII, London: Hogarth, 1953 (1912–13), 1–161.

'The Uncanny' in *Standard Edition* vol. XVII, London: Hogarth, 1955 (1919), 219–52.

Friedan, Betty. *The Feminine Mystique*, London: Victor Gollancz, 1963.

Frye, Northrop. 'Varieties of Literary Utopia' in *Utopias and Utopian Thought*, ed. Frank E. Manuel. Boston: Houghton Mifflin, 1966, 25–49.

Fullbrook, Kate. 'Doris Lessing: The Limits of Liberty' in *Free Women: Ethics and Aesthetics in Twentieth Century Women's Fiction*, London: Harvester Wheatsheaf, 1990, 141–169.

Fursland, Annie. 'Eve was Framed: Food and Sex and Women's Shame' in *Fed up and Hungry: Women, Oppression and Food*, ed. Marylin Lawrence. London: The Women's Press, 1987, 15–26.

Gamman, Lorraine, and Merja Makinen. *Female Fetishism: a New Look*, London: Lawrence & Wishart, 1994.

Gattey, Charles Neilson. *Excess in Food, Drink and Sex*, London: Harrap, 1986.

George, Diana Hume. 'Sister Survivors', *The Women's Review of Books*, 9, no. 12 (September 1992), 9–11.

Giddens, Anthony. *The Consequences of Modernity*, Cambridge and Oxford: Polity Press in association with Basil Blackwell, 1990.

Modernity and Self-Identity: Self and Society in the Late Modern Age, Cambridge and Oxford: Polity Press in association with Basil Blackwell, 1991.

Gilbert, Sandra. 'Hunger Pains', *University Publishing*, 8 (September 1979), 1, 11–12.

Goody, Jack. *Cooking, Cuisine and Class: a Study in Comparative Sociology*, Cambridge University Press, 1982.

Gross, Elizabeth. 'The Body of Signification' in *Abjection, Melancholia and Love*, eds. John Fletcher, and Andrew Benjamin, London and New York: Routledge, 1990, 80–103.

Haffenden, John. *Novelists in Interview*, London: Methuen, 1985.

Hanks, Patrick, ed. *Collins English Dictionary*, London and Glasgow: Collins, 1979.

Hatterer, Lawrence. *The Pleasure Addicts*, New York, NY, and London: Thomas Yoseloff, 1980.

Herik, Judith van. 'Simone Weil's Religious Imagery: How Looking Becomes Eating' in *Immaculate and Powerful: The Female in Sacred Image and Social Reality*, eds. Clarissa W. Atkinson et al. Wellingborough: Crucible, 1987.

Hillier, Jennifer. 'Feasting at the Grotesque Symposium', *Meanjin*, 49, no. 2 (1990), 252–62.

Hinz, Evelyn J., ed. 'Diet and Discourse: Eating, Drinking and Literature', *Mosaic, a Journal for the Interdisciplinary Study of Literature*, 24, no. 3–4 (June 1991), (complete issue on food).

Howells, Coral Ann. *Margaret Atwood*, Modern Novelists Series, Basingstoke: Macmillan, 1996.

Ingersoll, Earl G., ed. *Margaret Atwood: Conversations*, London: Virago, 1992.
  Putting the Questions Differently: Interviews with Doris Lessing, 1964–1994, London: Flamingo, 1996.

Jackson, Rosemary. *Fantasy: the Literature of Subversion*, London and New York: Methuen, 1981.

Jacobus, Mary, Evelyn Fox Keller, and Sally Shuttleworth, eds. *Body/Politics: Women and the Discourses of Science*, New York, NY, and London: Routledge, 1990.

Jones, Ernest. *The Life and Work of Sigmund Freud*, eds. Lionel Trilling and Steven Marcus, introd. Lionel Trilling, Harmondsworth: Penguin Books (with Hogarth Press), 1964.

Jordan, Elaine. 'The Dangerous Edge' in *Flesh and the Mirror*, ed. Lorna Sage, London: Virago, 1994, 189–215.

Kass, Leon R. *The Hungry Soul: Eating and the Perfecting of our Nature*, New York: The Free Press, 1994.

Keane, Molly. *Good Behaviour*, London: Sphere Books Ltd., 1982.

Kemp, Peter. *H. G. Wells and the Culminating Ape: Biological Themes and Imaginative Obsessions*, London: Macmillan, 1982.

Kenyon, Olga. 'Alice Thomas Ellis' in *Women Writers Talk: Interviews with Ten Women Writers*. Oxford: Lennard Publishing, 1989, 51–67.

Kilgour, Maggie. *From Communion to Cannibalism: an Anatomy of Metaphors of Incorporation*, Princeton University Press, 1990.

King, Jeannette. *Doris Lessing*, Modern Fiction Series, London: Edward Arnold, 1989.

Klein, Melanie. *Love, Guilt and Reparation and other Works, 1921–1945*, London: Virago Press, 1988. (1975).
  'On the Theory of Anxiety and Guilt' and 'Some Theoretical Conclusions Regarding the Emotional Life of the Infant' in *Envy and Gratitude and other*

Works, 1946–1963, International Psycho-Analytic Library, 1, London: Hogarth Press and The Institute of Psycho-Analysis, 1975 (1952), 61–93.

Klein, Melanie, Paula Heimann, Susan Isaacs, and Joan Riviere. *Developments in Psycho-Analysis*, ed. Joan Riviere, preface Ernest Jones, London: Karnac Books and The Institute of Psycho-Analysis, 1989 (1952).

Klein, Melanie, Paula Heimann, and R. E. Money-Kyrle, eds. *New Directions in Psycho-Analysis: the Significance of Infant Conflict in the Pattern of Adult Behaviour*, preface Ernest Jones, London: Karnac Books, 1977.

Kristeva, Julia. *Powers of Horror: an Essay on Abjection*, trans. Leon S. Roudiez, New York, NY: Columbia University Press, 1982.

Lacan, Jacques. 'The Mirror Stage as Formative of the Function of the I' in *Ecrits: a Selection*, trans. Alan Sheridan, London: Tavistock, 1980, 1–7.

Laplanche, J. and J. B. Pontalis. *The Language of Psychoanalysis*, trans. Donald Nicholson-Smith, London: Karnac Books and the Institute of Psycho-Analysis, 1988.

Lawson, Nigella. 'The Women who Think this Perfect Body is the Wrong Shape', *Evening Standard* (23 January 1992), 21.

Leonardi, Susan J. 'Recipes for Reading: Summer Pasta, Lobster à la Riseholme, and Key Lime Pie', *PMLA*, 104 (May 1989), 340–7.

Levenstein, Harvey. *Paradox of Plenty: a Social History of Eating in Modern America*, Oxford University Press, 1993.

Lévi-Strauss, Claude. *The Origin of Table Manners: Introduction to a Science of Mythology*, vol. III, trans. John Weightman and Doreen Weightman, London: Jonathan Cape, 1978 (1968).

The Raw and the Cooked: Introduction to a Science of Mythology, vol. I, trans. John Weightman and Doreen Weightman, London: Jonathan Cape, 1970 (1964).

Structural Anthropology, trans. Claire Jacobson and Brooke Srundfest Schoepf, London: Allen Lane/Penguin, 1969 (1963).

Lewallen, Avis. 'Wayward Girls but Wicked Women?: Female Sexuality in Angela Carter's *The Bloody Chamber*' in *Perspectives on Pornography: Sexuality in Film and Literature*, eds. Gary Day and Clive Bloom. Basingstoke: Macmillan Press, 1988, 144–158.

Lupton, Deborah. *Food, the Body and the Self*, London: Sage Publications, 1996.

MacLeod, Sheila. *The Art of Starvation*, London: Virago Press, 1981.

Malson, Lucien and Jean Itard. *Wolf Children and The Wild Boy of Aveyron*, ed. Lucien Malson, trans. Edmund Fawcett, Peter Ayrton and Joan White. London: NLB, 1972 (*Les Enfant sauvages*, 1964).

Marin, Louis. *Food for Thought*, trans. Mette Hjort, Baltimore and London: Johns Hopkins University Press, 1989.

Marriner, Brian. *Cannibalism, the Last Taboo*, London: Arrow, 1992.

Maslen, Elizabeth. *Doris Lessing*, Writers and their Work series, Plymouth: Northcote House/British Council, 1994.

Mennell, Stephen. *All Manners of Food: Eating and Taste in England and France from the Middle Ages to the Present*, Oxford: Basil Blackwell, 1985.

Mitchell, Juliet, ed. *The Selected Melanie Klein*, London: Penguin Books, 1991.

Morrison, Toni. *Beloved*, London: Picador, 1988.

  Sula, London: Triad Grafton, 1982.

Murcot, Anne, ed. *The Sociology of Food and Eating*, Aldershot: Gower Publishing, 1983.

O'Day, Marc. '"Mutability is Having a Field Day": The Sixties Aura of Angela Carter's Bristol Trilogy' in *Flesh and the Mirror: Essays on the Art of Angela Carter*, ed. Lorna Sage. London: Virago, 1994, 24–59.

O'Neill, Cherry Boone. *Starving for Attention*, New York, NY: Continuum, 1982.

Orbach, Susie. *Fat is a Feminist Issue*, New York, NY, and London: Paddington Press, 1978.

  Hunger Strike: the Anorexic's Struggle as a Metaphor for our Age, London and Boston, MA: Faber & Faber, 1986.

Parker, Patricia. *Literary Fat Ladies: Rhetoric, Gender, Property*, London and New York, NY: Methuen, 1987.

Pratt, Annis, and L. S. Dembo, eds. *Doris Lessing: Critical Studies*, University of Wisconsin Press, 1974.

Punter, David. 'Angela Carter: Supersessions of the Masculine', *Critique*, 25, no. 4 (June 1984), 209–22.

  The Literature of Terror: a History of Gothic Fictions from 1765 to the Present Day, London: Longman, 1980.

Radice, Betty. *Who's Who in the Ancient World*, London: Penguin, 1973.

Read, Piers Paul. *Alive! the Story of the Andes Survivors*, London: Pan Books, 1975.

Reyes, Alina. *The Butcher*, London: Minerva, 1992 (*Le Boucher*, Editions du Seuil, 1988).

Riviere, Joan. 'Introduction' in Melanie Klein et al., *Developments in Psycho-Analysis*, ed. Joan Riviere, preface Ernest Jones, London: Karnac Books and The Institute of Psycho-Analysis, 1989 (1952).

Rose, Jacqueline. *The Haunting of Sylvia Plath*, London: Virago Press, 1991.

Roth, Philip. *Portnoy's Complaint*, London: Jonathan Cape, 1969.

Ruderman, Judith. 'An Invitation to a Dinner Party: Margaret Drabble on Women and Food' in *Margaret Drabble: Golden Realms*, eds. Dorey Schmidt, and Jan Seale, Living Author Series, 4, Edinburg, Texas: Pan American University, 1982, 104–16.

Russo, Mary. *The Female Grotesque: Risk, Excess and Modernity*, London and New York, NY: Routledge, 1994.

Sage, Lorna. *Angela Carter*, Plymouth: Northcote House in association with The British Council, 1994.

  'Angela Carter interviewed by Lorna Sage' in *New Writing*, eds. Malcolm Bradbury and Judy Cooke, London: Minerva in association with The British Council, 1992, 185–193.

  'Death of the Author', *Granta*, 41 (1992), 235–54 (Angela Carter obituary).

  Doris Lessing, Contemporary Writers series, London: Methuen, 1983.

  Women in the House of Fiction: Post-War Women Novelists, London: Macmillan, 1992.

Sage, Lorna, ed. *Flesh and the Mirror: Essays on the Art of Angela Carter*, London: Virago, 1994.

Sanday, Peggy Reeves. *Divine Hunger: Cannibalism as a Cultural System*, Cambridge University Press, 1986.

Saxton, Ruth. 'The Female Body Veiled: From Crocus to Clitoris' in *Woolf and Lessing: Breaking the Mold*, eds. Ruth Saxton and Jean Tobin, Basingstoke: Macmillan, 1994, 95–122.

Sceats, Sarah and Gail Cunningham, eds. *Image and Power: Women in Fiction in the Twentieth Century*, Harlow: Longman, 1996.

Schmidt, Paul. 'What do oysters mean?', *Antaeus*, no. 68 (March 1992), 105–11.

Schofield, Mary Anne, ed. 'Spinster's Fare: Rites of Passage in Anita Brookner's Fiction' in *Cooking by the Book: Food in Literature and Culture*, ed. Mary Anne Schofield. Bowling Green State University Popular Press, 1989, 61–77.

Schur, Edwin M. *Labeling Women Deviant: Gender, Stigma and Social Control*, New York, NY: Random House, 1984.

Schwartz, Hillel. *Never Satisfied: a Cultural History of Diets, Fantasies and Fat*, New York, NY, and London: Collier Macmillan Publishers, 1986.

Sharpe, Ella Freeman. 'Psycho-Physical Problems Revealed in Language: an Examination of Metaphor' in *Collected Papers on Psycho-Analysis*, ed. Marjorie Brierley, preface Ernest Jones, London: Hogarth Press Ltd and The Institute of Psycho-Analysis, 1950 (1940).

Sheridan, Alan. *Michel Foucault: the Will to Truth*, London and New York, NY: Tavistock Publications, 1980.

Sherman, Delia. 'Grand illusionist', *The Women's Review of Books*, 9, nos. 10–11 (July 1992), 33.

Shilling, Chris. *The Body and Social Theory*, London: Sage Publications, 1993.

Shute, Jenefer. *Life-Size*, London: Mandarin, 1993.

Simpson, Helen. 'Sugar and Spice', *Femmes de Siècle (Stories from the '90s: Women Writing at the End of Two Centuries)*, ed. Joan Smith. London: Chatto and Windus, 1992, 26–32.

Smith, Gavin. 'Food for Thought', *Film Comment*, 26, no. 3 (May 1990), 54–61.

Sprague, Claire. *Rereading Doris Lessing: Narrative Patterns of Doubling and Repetition*, Chapel Hill, NC, and London: University of North Carolina Press, 1987.

Steinem, Gloria. 'The Politics of Muscle' in *Moving Beyond Words*, London: Bloomsbury, 1995, 93–8.

Stimpson, Catharine R. 'Doris Lessing and the Parables of Growth' in *The Voyage In: Fictions of Female Development*, eds. Elizabeth Abel, Marianne Hirsch and Elizabeth Langland. Hanover, NH, and London: University Press of New England, 1983, 186–205.

Tannahill, Reay. *Flesh and Blood: a History of the Cannibal Complex*, New York, NY: Dorset Press, 1975.

Food in History, London: Penguin Books, 1988 (1973).

Taylor, Jenny, ed. *Notebooks/Memoirs/Archives: Reading and Rereading Doris Lessing*, London: Routledge & Kegan Paul, 1982.

Trebilcot, Joyce, ed. *Mothering: Essays in Feminist Theory*, Totowa, New Jersey, NJ: Rowman and Allanheld, 1984.

Turner, Bryan S. 'Recent Developments in the Theory of the Body' and 'The Discourse of Diet' in *The Body: Social Process and Cultural Theory*, eds. Mike Featherstone et al. London: Sage, 1991, 1–35 and 157–69.

Turner, Jenny. 'Consumed by Anorexia', *The Guardian* (6 August 1992), 25.

Visser, Margaret. *The Rituals of Dinner: the Origins, Evolution, Eccentricities, and Meaning of Table Manners*, London: Penguin, 1993 (1991).

Vlahos, Olivia. *Body: the Ultimate Symbol*, New York, NY: J. B. Lippincott, 1979.

Ward Jouve, Nicole. 'Mother is a Figure of Speech . . . ' in *Flesh and the Mirror*. ed. Lorna Sage. London: Virago, 1994, 136–70.

Warner, Marina. 'Angela Carter: Bottle Blonde, Double Drag' in *Flesh and the Mirror*. ed. Lorna Sage, London: Virago, 1994, 243–56.

Winnicott, D. W. *The Child, the Family and the Outside World*, Harmondsworth: Penguin Books, 1964.

Woolf, Virginia. *A Room of one's Own*, London: Hogarth Press, 1929.

OTHER MEDIA

Angela Carter's Curious Room, dir. Kim Evans. *Omnibus*, BBC Television, 15 September 1992.

The Company of Wolves, dir. Neil Jordan, ITC/Palace, 1984. Television adaptation of Angela Carter short stories.

The Cook, the Thief, his Wife and her Lover, writer/dir. Peter Greenaway. Palace/Allarts Cook/Erato Films, 1989.

Delicatessen, writer/dir. Jean-Pierre Jeunet and Marc Caro. Electric/Constellation/UGC/Hachette Première, 1990.

Jordan, Elaine, 'Fireworks: Angela Carter and the Futures of Writing', University of York, 30 September–2 October 1994.

Porter, Roy and U. A. Fanthorpe, 'Body and Mind', Parallel Lines series, Voice Box, Royal Festival Hall, 11 February 1992. Lecture and poetry reading.

Tampopo, writer/dir. Juzo Itami. Itami Productions/New Century Producers, 1986.

Index

DATE DUE